IN THE CLOUDS OF
THE NIGHT

Donal Winters

978-1-917728-02-7

Copyright © Donal Winters 2025

All rights reserved.

All intellectual property rights including copyright, design right and publishing rights rest with the author. No part of this book may be reproduced or transmitted in any way including any written, electronic, recording, or photocopying without written permission of the author. The information contained within and views expressed in this memoir are those of the author and those who freely contributed their recollections to the author.

Published in Ireland by Orla Kelly Publishing Cork.

Printed in Ireland by Print Bureau.

Orla Kelly Publishing,
27 Kilbrody,
Mount Oval,
Rochestown,
Cork,
Ireland.

Dedication

This book is dedicated to the memory of my grand-aunt Kate Beirne, born July 1877.

Kate died in July 1954 at the age of 74.

Contents

Dedication iii
In The Clouds Of The Night – Main Characters viii
Prologue xiii

PART 1: SEPARATION 1
Chapter 1 3
Chapter 2 9
Chapter 3 15
Chapter 4 22
Chapter 5 31
Chapter 6 37
Chapter 7 48
Chapter 8 57

PART 2: HUNGER **69**
Chapter 9 71
Chapter 10 79
Chapter 11 88
Chapter 12 96
Chapter 13 104
Chapter 14 111
Chapter 15 115
Chapter 16 122
Chapter 17 130
Chapter 18 138
Chapter 19 149
Chapter 20 158
Chapter 21 163

PART 3: HOME 173
Chapter 22 175
Chapter 23 182
Chapter 24 189
Chapter 25 198
Chapter 26 208
Chapter 27 215
Chapter 28 225
Chapter 29 234
Chapter 30 239

PART 4: THE REUNION 243
Chapter 31 245
Chapter 32 252
Chapter 33 261
Chapter 34 270
Chapter 35 275

EPILOGUE 283
ACKNOWLEDGEMENTS 290

Figures Contents

Memorial photo of Kate Beirne iii
Family Tree for Mary Anne (Ciss) Beirne x
Family Tree for Thomas Pakenham xi
Ciss and TP's wedding photo (July 1930) 34
Ciss at the family farmhouse in Leitrim with Joan and Kathleen, her brother Albert and her cousin Babs. (Baby not identified) 39
Ciss with Joan and Kathleen and her brother Ned in the cornfield on the farm in Leitrim 40
Ciss at her home in Blackrock with Joan, Kathleen and her cousin Annie Kate 42
TP and Ciss in happier times 47
Jack in the arms of Harriet meeting his siblings shortly after the three older entered Childhaven 97
A photo of the four children taken by their father in Carlingford while on holiday break from Childhaven. (Summer 1944) 139
Ciss, TP visiting Pakenham Hall with his mother and children, Joan, Kathleen and Ted (1935) 209
TP on his 80th birthday with Joan, Jack, Ted and Kathleen 267
Portrait of Ciss by her great-grandson, artist Karl Hagan (grandson of Ted Pakenham) 282

IN THE CLOUDS OF THE NIGHT – MAIN CHARACTERS

The key players

Thomas Pakenham (TP)

Mary Anne Beirne (Ciss)

Their children – Joan, Kathleen, Ted & Jack

The Beirne/O'Beirnes

Edward Beirne & Kate Winters

Their children – Hugh, John Joe, **Ciss**, Pat, Ned, Michael, Bernie, Thomas, Terence, Albert

Agnes Fennel – Pat's wife

Nancy Brown – Bernie's wife

May Molloy – Ned's wife

John and Olive – two of Ned & May's children

The Winters/Conboys

John Winters & Annie Conboy – Kate's Brother and Donal's grandparents

Their children – Mike Joe (Donal's father), Mollie (Jack & Donal's godmother), Babs

Annie Kate – Ciss's cousin & Kathleen's godmother

Brigie Conboy – Donal's grand-aunt

The Pakenhams

Edward Pakenham & Annie Bleakley

Their children – John, Maria, Edward, Eva, Annie, Robert, Etta, Georgina, Florrie, **Thomas**, George

Georgina – John's daughter

Charlie & Mary Pakenham – TP's distant cousin

Harriet Magill – Annie's cousin

Mark Ison – Joan's husband

Watson Hazzard – Kathleen's husband

Noreen McLarnon – Ted's wife

Ethel Howard – Jack's wife

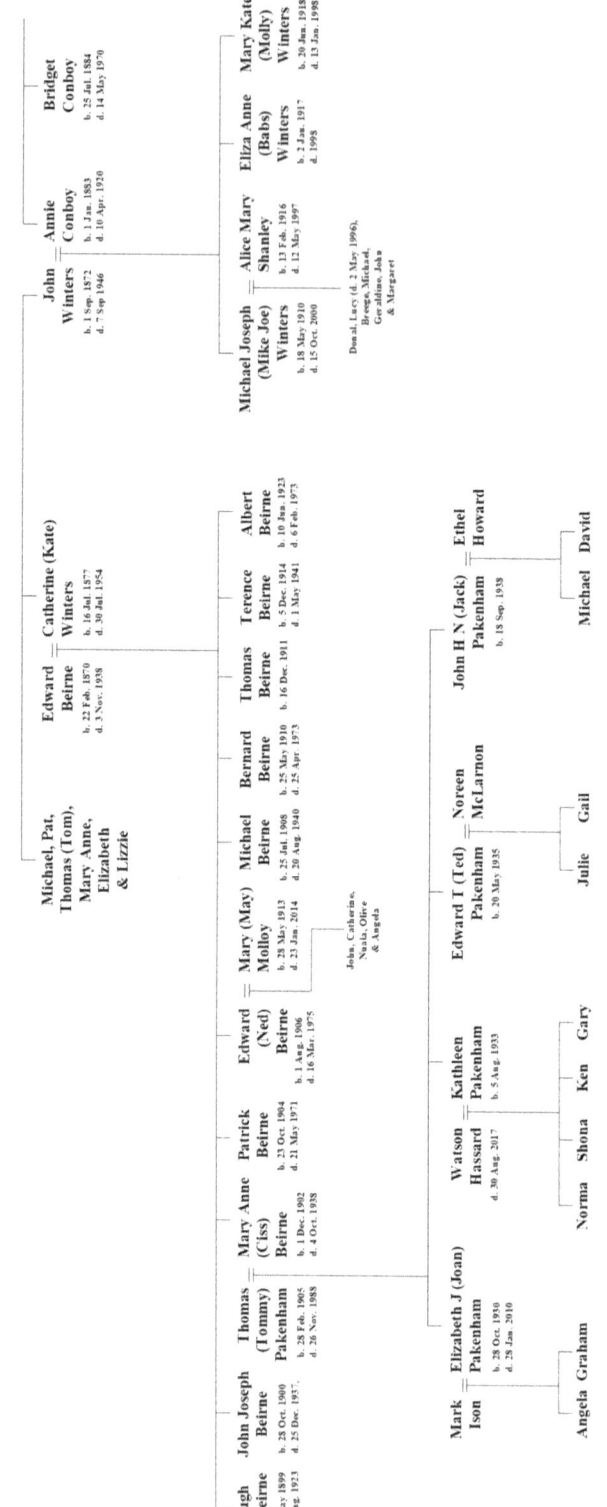

FAMILY TREE
OF
THOMAS PAKENHAM

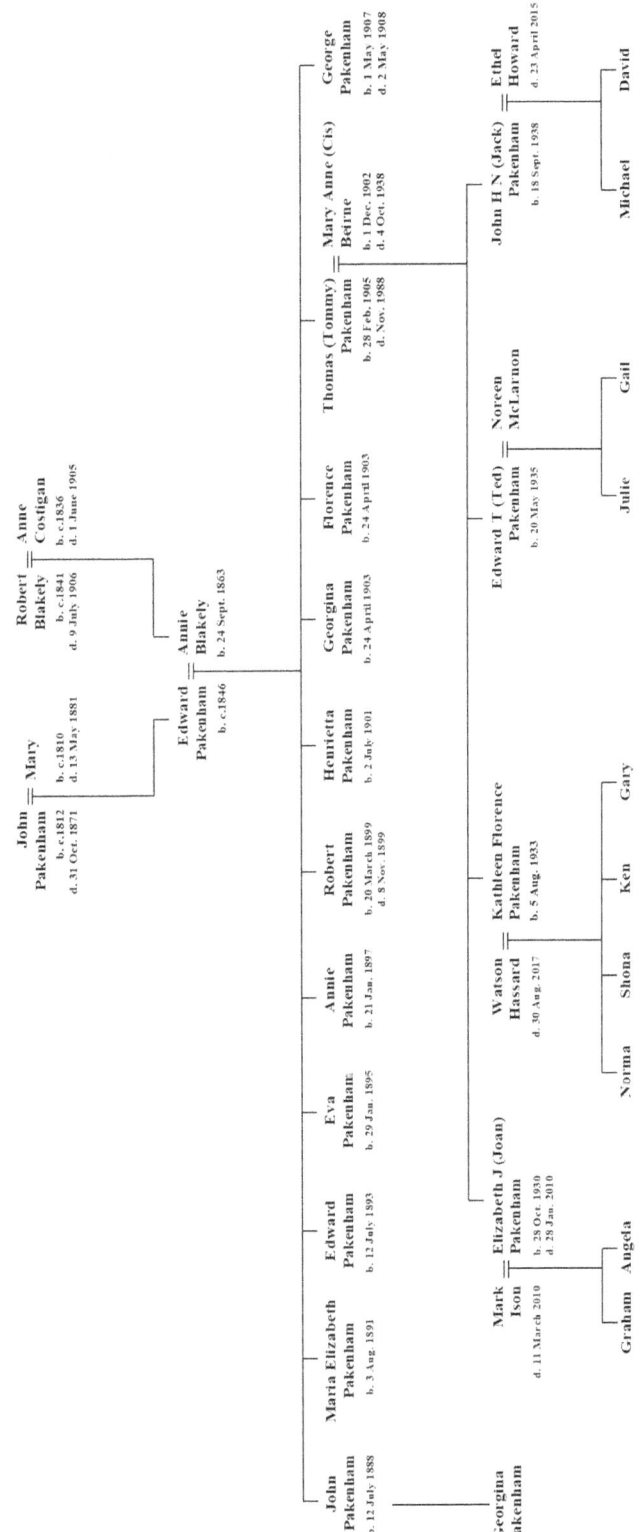

PROLOGUE

If you are not too long, I will wait here for you all my life
~ from *The Importance of Being Earnest by* **Oscar Wilde**

On Christmas Eve 1947, in a tall terrace house in North Belfast, four children gathered around the Victorian cast iron mantlepiece in the sitting room to hang up their stockings. A roaring fire blazed in the grate. A Christmas tree twinkled in the corner of the room. Carols played on the radio. A slight, solemn man sat in an armchair surveying his children through his small round spectacles. At seventeen, Joan was the eldest. A serious, quiet girl, she carried a weight of responsibility for her younger siblings on her shoulders. Fourteen-year-old Kathleen, feisty and pragmatic, organised the positioning of the stockings. Twelve-year-old Ted, calm and placid, quietly took in the marvel of the occasion. The youngest, nine-year-old Jack, high on excitement, hurtled around the room, refusing to take instructions from his big sister Joan, or his father.

It was cold outside, but the great snowstorms that had transformed the entire island of Ireland from emerald to white in the early months of the year had not returned. The children would have liked that; a white Christmas providing the proverbial icing on the fruit cake that sat on the kitchen table wrapped in parchment paper and tied with string, awaiting the cut of the sharpened bread knife the following day.

If a passer-by had happened to glance through the sitting room window of the house on Cliftonpark Avenue, on their way home themselves perhaps, last minute gifts tucked under their arms, they might have smiled at the scene they briefly surveyed. A family, like scores of other families across the city, performing their own cherished rituals on this most precious of nights. If they had paused to look closer, they may have presumed that the children's mother was busy in the kitchen preparing the turkey, or putting a younger child to bed perhaps, or warming milk on the range for pre-bedtime drinks.

But there was no mother and the children had no rituals. They would have known about Father Christmas and stockings and plum pudding from stories and picture books. As the eldest two, Joan and Kathleen might have harboured deep buried memoires about such things from a life long ago, a life that although they could not quite fathom it, once belonged to them. Ted had known those things too, briefly, but he was too young to make a memory of them. But Jack had never had them.

It was the first time the four siblings had spent Christmas with their father in their very own home for nine years; the first time they had lived together as a family since the dark early March morning in 1939 when he bundled them into a waiting car, smuggled them out of their Dublin home and across the border to a new life in the North.

This is their story.

PART 1
SEPARATION

Since you have left the house
Its emptiness has hurt
All thought
~ From *Valediction* by Seamus Heaney

CHAPTER 1

"Packie Beirne is in Dublin. He's married. Bernie, another, is there too. He's running a pub, also married. Ciss, do you remember her? The only girl they had. She was in Dublin too. Married a protestant. She died and left four children after her. The husband decamped in the clouds of the night with the children and wasn't heard of since. It's supposed he's up North rearing them up good Protestants."

I was 60 years old when I read those words, lines from a letter written by my grand-aunt Brigie back in January 1944. Bridget Conboy was my father's aunt, a sister of his mother, Annie. She died in 1970 when I was a boy of eleven, and I remember her as a stern old lady, tall and thin, dressed head to toe in black; like something from another era altogether. The letter was written to her brother James, a teacher in Galway. There had been a rift between the two, the details of which we do not know, and they lost touch for several years. Then, out of the blue, James wrote to his sister in December 1943. Brigie's swift reply, penned at her home in the townland of Currycramp in County Leitrim, just across the bog from where I grew up, filled James in on almost a decade of news and gossip. The letter, which was perfectly preserved, had been given to me by James's granddaughter Mandy, a second cousin, who was helping with some research into my family tree. Many of the names Brigie mentioned were familiar to me, like my aunt and godmother Mollie Winters, my own father, Mike Joe Winters, and Ned Beirne, my father's cousin. Ned and his wife May were important figures in my life. Their five children, although older than me, were close to my eldest siblings. I'd heard about Ned's brothers over the years: Pat and Bernie in Dublin, Michael, who had served with the British Army during World War Two, John Joe and Anthony who had both stayed in Cashel, and Terence too. Then there was Thomas who had settled in England, and Albert, the youngest, a successful businessman who had lived in a wealthy suburb of Dublin. But I had never heard of a sister, never known of a Ciss, never caught so much as a whisper about a Protestant brother-in-law who had absconded to the North in the dead of night with four of Ned's nieces or nephews. Those four children, I realised, would be my own second cousins, just as Ned's children were. And I didn't even know their names. Why, I wondered, had my father never mentioned them or their mother, his first cousin, Ciss? He would have talked frequently over the years about her brothers, yet to my memory, her name had never passed his lips. Having lost my own sister Lucy in the prime of her life, and witnessed the impact of her death on my parents and the entire family circle, I understood the particularly piercing grief that comes from the loss of a child and a sibling. I could not image any member of my family forgetting Lucy, not even for one day. Almost thirty years on, her memory still lives amongst us, her name still frequently spoken. So why had Ciss been seemingly forgotten, her children too? Mandy could not shed any light on this mystery having never heard of Ciss herself, but surely if these Protestant children did exist, if Ned had indeed had a sister, someone in my extended family circle would know.

* * *

I was born in February 1959 in Cashel, a small townland in the parish of Bornacoola near the town of Mohill, the youngest of seven children. My father, Michael Joseph Winters, or Mike Joe as he was affectionately known, and my mother, Alice Mary Shanley, both came from the same parish. My mother grew up near Dromod, on the banks of the River Shannon, the eldest of eleven children born to Martin and Margaret Shanley. But the roots of this story are planted in Cashel and Mohill, and with my father's family circle, the Winters, the Conboys, and the Beirnes. My father was born in Cashel in 1910, the first child of John Winters and Annie Conboy. John, my grandfather, had six siblings, including Kate, the mother of Ciss. Annie, my grandmother, had nine siblings, including Brigie, the author of that letter. When my father was seven, his first sister Eliza Jane, known to all as Babs, arrived, and a year later, Mary Kate, known as Mollie, was born. Sadly, Annie developed 'white leg', a blood clot in the leg, following Mollie's birth, and died in 1920 leaving Grandfather John with three young children to rear by himself. In the midst of his grief, he agreed it would be best if little Mollie was raised by aunt Brigie, who lived just across the bog and had no children of her own. But a few days after he had delivered the child to Brigie, he changed his mind. Certain that Annie would not want the children to be separated, and missing Mollie terribly, he crossed the bog again and brought his daughter home. And so, at just ten years of age, my father became his own father's right-hand man, leaving school to help with work on the farm, and in the home too, caring for his two little sisters. It was tough, but young Mike Joe took his new responsibilities in his stride. He educated himself in his own time, sometimes reciting poetry he learned at school while milking the cows and reading books at every opportunity.

Aunt Mollie moved to Dublin as a young woman, taking up a position at CIE: Córas Iompair Éireann, the Irish Railway Company. Her cousin Pat Beirne, son of Kate, also worked at the company, and it was he who helped secure her the position. Mollie was a career woman, somewhat unusual in her time. She never married, bought her own house in Dublin, and travelled extensively. Babs remained in Leitrim, settling in the townland of Tulcon, not far from Cashel, with her husband Tommy Reynolds and their six children. My father and Babs remained close throughout their lives. They shared a love of reading, and for as long as his legs would let him, my father would walk across the bog once a week to visit Babs and exchange books.

My parents married in January 1947 and set up home close to my father's family farm. My childhood was a happy one. As a young boy, life centred around the farm, school, Auntie Babs and Uncle Tommy's house across the bog, and Ned and May Beirne's farm up the road. Aside from being cousins and neighbours, Ned and my father were close friends, and he and May and their children were very present in our lives. Ned was a big man, quiet, modest, and kind, who devoted himself to farming and his family. But there was something about his demeanour that I could never quite pinpoint, a distance of sorts. I had no idea then of the grief and pain he was carrying on those big broad shoulders. May was warm and generous, always welcoming, always smiling. My sister Lucy and I would pass by their house on our walk to and from school, often calling in for a slice of May's griddle bread, baked on an open fire and topped with sugar and thick slabs of handmade butter. Most of her own children had left home by then, and she was always happy to have an extra mouth or two to feed.

Growing up, our own house was a busy one, vibrating with noise and oozing with the aromas of something or other baking in the oven or bubbling on the range. With the age spread between us, my eldest sister Margaret being eleven years my senior, there was always someone coming or going, friends of one child or another visiting, or a family member of some description popping by. Family was enormously important to my parents; not just us children, but the wider family circle. Between them they had what seemed to us like a million aunts, uncles, cousins, second cousins … even fourth cousins. As children we struggled to keep up, but they apparently knew every one of them by name, as well as their children's names, the dates of their birthdays, and where they lived. This encyclopaedic knowledge of family details made the apparent absence of a Ciss Beirne, or whatever her married name might have been, and her four young children even more extraordinary, especially if she was indeed Ned's sister.

* * *

I began with my own siblings, telephoning each one in turn. Had any of them ever heard of Ned's sister Ciss, or caught wind of any family gossip about her Protestant husband whisking their children up North, in, as Aunt Brigie had said, "the clouds of the night"? They had become used to my phone calls about family in the preceding weeks, asking about this person or that, requesting old photographs, teasing out memories. It had started in early 2019 when I began to research my family tree with Mary, my wife. I became immediately absorbed in the process, and, aware of just how large our family circle was, understood the enormity of the task ahead, expecting to uncover some surprises along the way, the odd family secret perhaps, and even a little bit of scandal. But an entire family that I'd never heard mentioned before, well, that was entirely unexpected. None of my siblings could help. None, not even the eldest two Margaret and John, who were the closest in age to Ned and May's children, could recall hearing the name Ciss, or had even the haziest of memories of Brigie's story. Phone Ned's daughter, Olive, one of my siblings suggested.

"Olive," I said, "now this might sound like a madcap story, but did you ever hear tell of your dad having a sister who died, then her Protestant husband smuggled their children up North, never to be seen nor heard of again?"

"Well, now," said Olive, "it's a story alright, but a true one. Or mostly, at any rate."

CHAPTER 2

The first quarter of the 20th century was a difficult time in Irish history. The aftermath of the Great Famine still reverberated across the country. Rural communities that had been decimated by death and emigration struggled to recover as a growing sense of unrest and the desire for independence took root, in most of the country anyway. The Irish Home Rule bill, or Government of Ireland Act, initially presented in 1886, was finally passed by the United Kingdom Government in 1914, but almost immediately suspended due to the outbreak of World War 1. While war raged in much of Europe, the island of Ireland was caught in its own bloody conflict. The Easter Rising of 1916 led to the Declaration of Independence from the United Kingdom in 1919, which in turn led to the War of Independence, the establishment of Northern Ireland, and ultimately the Irish Civil War. Peace was finally restored in May 1923, but the conflict resulted in a divided country with a contentious land border between the twenty-six counties in the independent South, and the six counties of the North which remained part of the United Kingdom. The demographics of the two Irelands reflected a predominantly Catholic South and a largely Protestant North, and whilst in most areas of the island people of the two religions co-existed in a neighbourly if not always harmonious fashion, tensions were never far from the surface, and an allegiance to one's birth faith was uncompromising.

Born into this period of upheaval were the Beirne children of Cashel in County Leitrim. Their father Edward Beirne was a farmer, and their mother Kate was a sister of my grandfather, John Winters.

Kate had been born a twin in July 1877, but her sister Elizabeth died from whooping cough nine months after their birth, and three years later, another sister, six-year-old Mary Anne, also passed away. Kate and Edward's firstborn, Hugh, arrived in the spring of 1899, and in the twenty-four years following his birth, Kate would deliver nine more babies, only one of whom was a daughter. Mary Anne, named for her mother's deceased sister, or Ciss as she was known, was born on the first of December 1902, the third child to Kate and Edward. As well as Hugh, her other brothers were John Joe, Pat, Ned, Michael, Bernie, Thomas, Terence, and finally, eight and a half years after Terence's birth, came Albert, born on 10th June 1923. Hugh, the eldest, was twenty-four when his last baby brother arrived. Sadly, the brothers would never get to know each other, as ten weeks after Albert's birth, Hugh died from tonsilitis, the first in a succession of tragedies to befall the Beirne family in the coming years.

Edward and Kate had both grown up on small farms in Cashel, hemmed in by bogland on two sides. They married on 18th July 1898 in St. Joseph's Church, Clonturk, and as was customary, Kate moved into the Beirne family farm with her new husband, his widowed father, also called Edward, and his older unmarried brother, Hugh. Their small immediate community consisted of twelve dwellings, all of which were recorded in the 1901 census as having a thatched roof, three rooms and three windows to the front. In the early 1900s, 70% of Ireland's population lived in rural areas. But despite the dense populace of the countryside, housing was sparse, and extended families crammed together in small cottages ill equipped for multi-generational living was not unusual. These houses were often in extremely poor condition, dark and damp with leaking roofs and small windows.

At the time of the 1901 census, there were six people living in the small Beirne cottage: Edward senior, his eldest son Hugh, Edward and Kate, two-year-old Hugh, and baby John Joe. As more children came along the crowded house became untenable, and at some point before the 1911 census, an additional room was added. By this time, Edward senior had died, but brother Hugh was still living with Edward and Kate and their now seven children. Baby number eight was already on the way, and two years later number nine would arrive. As with many dwellings throughout the country in the post-famine, pre-war era, the Beirne farm cannot have been the best environment in which to raise a family, never mind a family of nine. The holding was small and struggled to generate enough money to feed the ever-expanding household, not to mention attend to repairs or further renovations. With so many people packed tightly together, it was no surprise perhaps when sickness came calling. At some point of her teenage years, Ciss contracted polio, leaving her with a permanent limp. She most likely spent some months recovering in a Dublin sanitorium, but she survived the disease, and all the children made it through to adulthood, by no means a given in those difficult years. It would be 1923 before death first came calling for the Beirnes of Cashel, tapping young Hugh on the shoulder.

While brothers Hugh senior and Edward worked on the land, Kate ran the house, raised the children and helped on the farm. A grafter, every second of her day was accounted for, so much so that she rarely had time to visit her own Winters family dwelling just a few hundred yards down the road. She cut the potato splits, picked and boiled the smallest potatoes for the pigs, and grew comfrey in the garden that she would make into a potion cure for horses with muscle aches and sell to neighbouring farms. She also kept bees for honey, baked soda bread every day, and did her best to keep her children safe from illness in the damp old house, boiling milk and garlic for their bedtime drink to help ward off infections. Kate loved her children fiercely, that much we know from family recollections and stories handed down. And she was devoted to the sixteen grandchildren who would be born during her lifetime; the ones at close quarters, the ones who were growing up in Dublin, the ones across the Irish Sea in Liverpool, and the ones whose whereabouts she did not know.

Pat was the first of the Beirne children to leave Cashel, moving to the bright lights of Dublin City in his early twenties. He took a job at the state railway company, CIE, where he would spend the rest of his working life, and met and married a Dublin girl named Agnes Fennel. He also changed his surname to O'Beirne. It was common practice at that time for people who moved to the city from rural areas to attach an 'O' to their surname, perceiving the addition to be more fashionable or genteel. It was also, in some instances, a way for some to pronounce their Irish heritage, and Pat was a proud Irishman. Following their marriage in September 1929, Pat and Agnes lived in a rented terrace house on Clontarf Road right beside the promenade at Clontarf, a pretty seaside suburb on the north side of Dublin. And for a period of time, another person lived with them in the house, Pat's big sister, Ciss.

There are parts of this story that we will never fully know the truth of; i's that refuse to be dotted and t's that obstinately remain uncrossed, gaps in the timeline and missing details that no amount of research or head scratching will resolve. But in many of those cases, we can surmise the most likely scenario or predict the chronology. It is probable that Pat left for Dublin in either 1924 or 1925, at the age of twenty, or twenty-one. The civil war ended in May 1923, so it's unlikely he would have moved to the capital before then, and Edward and Kate would have wanted to see a post-war settling down in the city before they lost their son to it. It's unlikely that Ciss went with him to begin with. Even if there had been talk of it, Pat would have been sent ahead to sort out lodgings and employment, to research opportunities. Perhaps Ciss visited him, and fell in love with Dublin. Or perhaps her brother sent for her. With just twenty months between them, the two were no doubt close, and once he was settled in the city and living in his own smart house overlooking Dublin Bay, a million miles away from the small family farm in the South Leitrim bogland, he may have persuaded his sister to try out city living for herself. Whatever motivated Ciss to leave Cashel for Dublin, when she did go, it would have been with high hopes of a better life. Aside from marriage and farming or service work, there were limited opportunities for women in rural Ireland at the time, and the fact that Ciss had a limp from her brush with polio may have curtailed her prospects further. It would have marked her, in the eyes of some at any rate. It is likely that she joined Pat in Dublin in late 1924 or in 1925 when she was twenty-two or twenty-three. She may have initially trained as a clerical assistant or a bookkeeper, or she might have found a job as soon as she arrived in the city. But we do know that at some point she became a clerk. And, just as Pat had done, she adopted the surname O'Beirne.

While we cannot be precise about the movements of Ciss O'Beirne in the mid to late 1920s, we do know that a young man named Thomas Pakenham was living in Dublin at the same time. And we know from family sources that Ciss and Thomas met at work. They struck up a friendship which led to an intimate relationship, and then, in the late spring of 1930, Ciss discovered she was pregnant. The pregnancy presented her with two enormous problems. The first, of course, was that she was carrying an illegitimate child, something that was tantamount to criminal in Ireland at that time. The second, and equally problematic issue, was that Thomas Pakenham was a Protestant.

CHAPTER 3

As Kate Beirne was welcoming her first-born, Hugh, into the world, on 15th May 1899, thirty-odd miles southeast of Cashel, in Castlepollard, County Westmeath, Annie Pakenham was nursing her sixth child, Robert. Born eight weeks before Hugh on 20th March, Robert was a baby brother for eleven-year-old John, eight-year-old Maria, six-year-old Edward, four-year-old Eva, and two-year-old Annie. Sadly Robert would only live for seven short months, suffering a fatal episode of enteritis, the first of three child bereavements that Annie would endure. She would deliver five more children: Henrietta in 1901, twin girls Georgina and Florence in 1903, Thomas, who arrived on 28th February 1905, and finally George, on 1st May 1907. George became the second of Annie's children to die, succumbing to bronchitis a year and a day after his birth. Her eldest son John was the third, losing in life in 1925 at the age of thirty-seven, after contracting TB.

On paper, Annie Pakenham and Kate Beirne would appear to have a lot in common. Kate gave birth to ten children over a twenty-four-year period and was forty-six years old when her youngest, Albert, was born. Annie bore eleven children, her pregnancies spanning nineteen years, and was forty-four when her final baby, George, arrived. Both would experience the agonising grief of losing a child, and more than once. The two women lived in rural communities, their respective husbands, both named Edward, working on the land. Edward Beirne, as we know, was a farmer in Cashel, while Edward Pakenham was employed as a gamekeeper in the somewhat grander surroundings of Tullnally Estate. And Kate and Annie were both deeply religious. But that is where the similarities end, and although Kate's daughter Ciss would marry Annie's son Thomas, the two women would never meet. They would never share a pot of tea and a hot griddle cake at a kitchen table. They would never unite in grief over the children they had lost. And they would not attend the wedding of their son and daughter, nor the christenings of the four children the couple would bear. For Annie Pakenham, a staunch Church of Ireland Protestant who hailed from County Tyrone in the North, the union of her son with a young Catholic woman in Dublin would have been just as heavy a burden for her to bear as for the devoutly Catholic Kate Beirne. If the two women *had* met, if they had shared their stories and shed tears together, they may have found comfort in the things that bound them, for grief does not care for religious divide, or political discord, or social boundaries. But in the Ireland of the 1930s, that was never going to be an option. And if indeed they ever even thought of each other, it would most likely have been with resentment and suspicion.

Annie was born on 24th September 1863 in Oghill, County Tyrone, to Robert and Annie Blakely. Robert was a gardener, most likely at Loughry Manor in Cookstown, which at that time was owned by the Lindesay family. As a young woman, Annie went into service and at the time of her marriage to Edward Pakenham on 2nd December 1886, she was working in a house on Scotch Street, Armagh. Annie was just twenty-three when she and Edward wed, while at forty-one, her new husband was eighteen years her senior. We don't know where or how they met. Perhaps Annie accompanied her employer on a visit to Tullynally Castle and encountered the resident gamekeeper during one of the communal 'downstairs' meals. Or they may have met in Armagh while Edward was visiting for one reason or another; possibly at a church event as by all accounts they were both regular Church of

Ireland attendees. We do know that after they married, Annie left her home county of Tyrone and moved to Tullynally estate, where she lived in staff housing until she was ninety.

Tullynally Castle, where Edward and Annie Pakenham lived, where their eleven children were born, where two of them died, where Thomas, the tenth-born, became the youngest sibling at the age of three after his baby brother George passed away, was known, indeed still is known, by another name: Pakenham Hall. The castle and its multiple acres of gardens and woodland date back to 1665 when one Henry Pakenham, a captain in the Parliamentary Dragoons, was gifted the land by Oliver Cromwell in lieu of military payment. In 1740, Henry's grandson, Thomas, became the first Earl of Longford following his marriage to a local heiress, Elizabeth Cuffe. A Pakenham has remained in residence at Tullynally Castle/Pakenham Hall ever since, and although the current occupant, another Thomas, does not use his title, he is in theory the eighth Lord Longford.

So where does our Thomas Pakenham fit into the picture? The truth is, we don't entirely know. TP, as he became known in adulthood, and who we will mostly refer to him as, was not prone to discussing his childhood or recalling stories about his family. But on occasion, he would tell his children that they were in fact descendants of the landed gentry Pakenhams of Tullynally, and that he firmly believed there was a traceable connection. The story is vague and the details are murky, but according to TP, in the mid-1600s, three Pakenham brothers from Suffolk were gifted land in County Westmeath. They relocated to Ireland, enjoying their newfound landowner status, but there was a scandal of some sort, leaving one brother homeless and broke. Another brother took the disgraced man in and promised him a home for life on his estate, but insisted he work as a gamekeeper in return. The disgraced man may have been called Edward Pakenham, the magnanimous brother, Henry; the aforementioned Henry who built Tullynally Castle. And so, the story goes, just as there have always been Pakenhams in residence at Tullynally Castle, for almost three hundred years, there was a Pakenham gamekeeper too, and Pakenham cooks, and housekeepers and gardeners, all most likely related in either close or distant ways. TP believed his family were descendants of Edward, and that is why they lived on the grounds of Pakenham Hall, the castle theirs in name alone.

We know very little about TP's father Edward, who died in 1925, apart from the fact that he came from generations of Pakenhams who had lived and worked on the estate. But by all accounts, each subsequent Lord Longford and his family were good to the Pakenham gamekeepers and their families. Annie was certainly allowed to stay in one of the estate cottages long after Edward had died and her children had scattered. And while she was rearing those children, her cottage had provided them with comfortable accommodation, a veritable palace compared to the small farmhouse thirty miles up the road where Kate Beirne was raising hers.

The childhood years of Thomas Pakenham, living *at* but not *in* Pakenham Hall, might go some way to explaining a thing or two about some of the decisions he made as an adult man, as a father. But we'll get to that. As a boy, he grew up on the periphery of grandness, just three years younger than the sitting Earl and Countess of Longford's eldest son, Edward, and the same age as their youngest, Frank. He not only knew the two young boys who lived in the castle and shared his name, he played with them when they were home from their

London boarding schools, forming a particular friendship with Frank that would last throughout his life. Indeed, the two boys referred to each other as Cousin Tom and Cousin Frank, and would always sign off letters to each other accordingly. Young Thomas must have been curious as to why Frank's Pakenham name granted him a life that his Pakenham name did not. Perhaps the cousin reference was simply an act of boyish fondness, delighted that they both by a bizarre coincidence shared the same surname. Or possibly they were all too aware that there was nothing coincidental about it, digging into their shared family history to unveil the true connection. It can't have sat easily with TP. He must have imagined what it would be like to walk in Frank's shoes, perhaps resenting his friend a little. Or maybe any resentment he did have was reserved for his own family.

Young Thomas, however, did avail of something that none of his brothers or sisters enjoyed: an education. For some reason, he was the only one of the nine surviving siblings to attend a private college once he had completed his early schooling. The rest most likely left school altogether between the ages of twelve to fourteen, as was standard in Ireland at that time. John, the eldest, moved to England and joined the British Army. Edward worked with his father on the estate. Most of the girls went into service, some starting their working life at Pakenham Hall. But in 1917, at the age of twelve, Thomas went to Wilson's Hospital School, a prestigious Church of Ireland run boarding school in the Mullingar countryside. It seems unlikely that Edward and Annie could have afforded to send their youngest child to boarding school, even if by 1917 the rest of their children were working and some had left the family home. In later years, Thomas would tell his children that he received a scholarship to Wilson's. As he was a pupil there for six years until the age of eighteen, it must have been an impressive scholarship. It is entirely possible that is indeed what happened. A distant cousin, one Charlie Pakenham, was a teacher at the school, and he may have been able to pull some strings. But there is also the possibility that the Pakenham family from the big house helped out in some way. On a visit to the Cashel farm with Ciss, perhaps the first time TP had met his wife's mother and other brothers, he told Ned that the "man on the estate" had brought them up. The man in question would have been the 5th Earl of Longford, Thomas Pakenham, who died in 1915, two years before TP went to Wilson's. If that was indeed the case, perhaps it was an arrangement agreed before the Earl's death. Or perhaps the Countess, thinking about the opportunities that life had bestowed upon her own sons and observing the path that young Thomas was destined for (most likely to follow in his father and brother's footsteps and become a gamekeeper) decided to make an altruistic gesture. The couple might even have seen something in the boy that led them to believe he could benefit from an education, make something of himself. We will never know the truth of the matter, but what we do know is that TP was a valued and highly regarded pupil at Wilson's, a prefect in his senior years, who thoroughly enjoyed his time at the school. On settling in Dublin, he co-founded the official Wilson's Old Boys' Association with some former pupils from his year group, returning regularly throughout the 1920s and 30s to attend functions and events. But in 1939 his circumstances changed, and he lost contact with the school, a hiatus that lasted almost fifty years. He finally returned again in August 1986, after which he penned an article for the school magazine, *Wilsonian*, citing his debt to the school and paying particular tribute to one Mr James Gillespie.

> *"Mr G as we called him, was one of the finest Christians that I have ever met. I still thank God that I came under his influence.*

What did I get out of my six years at Wilson's? Above all a strong Christian faith which enabled me to stand the shock of moving from my 'ivory tower' into the harsh world outside."

CHAPTER 4

When eighteen-year-old Thomas Pakenham left Wilson's Hospital School in 1923, Ireland was still in the process of adjusting after partition and the education system in what was now the Free State was going through a transition. But TP wasn't affected by the incoming changes. In his privileged position at Wilson's, he would have been one of just a few thousand teenagers across Ireland, Protestant and Catholic alike, to sit their Senior Examinations at that time of great chaos. We know he was studious and bright and can assume he performed well. He most likely would have been more than capable of a university education, but even if he had wanted to further his studies, he would not have had the funds to do so. His bursary, or benefactor, provided the money required to cover his fees and expenses at Wilson's alone. Securing a further scholarship for Trinity College Dublin would have been quite a hill for young Thomas to climb, and at that particular time, just post-partition, travelling north to Belfast to attend Queen's University would not have been advisable, even for a Protestant. And so, on leaving Wilson's, TP moved directly to Dublin to train as a clerk. We don't know for certain, but it is possible that his apprenticeship may have been undertaken at the Harding Technical College on Lower Edward Street. We definitely do know however that he lived in the adjoining Dublin Working Boys Home. The home, or hostel as it was commonly referred to, was designed and built by one Albert E Murray in 1891 to provide "comfortable and healthy lodgings" for working boys of the Protestant faith, and the technical college was established a few years later by the wealthy Protestant philanthropist, Miss Anna Middleton. Run by a committee of prominent Protestant Dublin clergymen, the building also housed a gymnasium, and its residents created cricket, football and rugby teams. TP's lodgings at the hostel were likely secured via Wilson's, something he would no doubt have agreed to with enthusiasm. He would have enjoyed the sports facilities and the camaraderie, enabling a reasonably smooth transition to city life following the years at his "ivory tower" boarding school in Mullingar and his early childhood at Pakenham Hall. The facility was designed to accommodate boys and young men up to the age of nineteen, so TP should really only have spent a year there, moving on after completing his apprenticeship, whether it had been conducted at the technical college or elsewhere, to employment and private digs. However, he didn't just stay for one year, he stayed for seven, finally leaving in 1930 at the age of twenty-five when he married Ciss Beirne. Just as their marriage certificate tells us that Ciss had been residing with Pat and Agnes at the time of the wedding, so it reveals that TP was still living at Lower Edward Street.

An advertisement for the Dublin Working Boys Home published in the *Irish Times* in 1914 stated:

> *"The object of the home is to provide a safe and comfortable residence for orphans and other boys (being Protestants, and of good character) who are earning small wages in junior positions, in trades, business and offices, etc., and who have no suitable home in the city. The age of admission is 13 to 19 years, but under special circumstances the limit of age may be extended."*

We can only assume that those special circumstances were, for some reason, afforded to TP. Perhaps he helped with the accounts in exchange for extended board and lodgings. Or perhaps he facilitated the Harding Rugby Club. Or he possibly drew on his contacts from Wilsons, or even Tullynally, to secure his extended stay at the hostel. Whatever the reason, remaining at the hostel long past the regular leaving age would have suited TP perfectly: no lodgings to find, no meals to cook, no domestic responsibilities whatsoever, a lifestyle pattern already ingrained within him, and one that TP would follow his whole life long. His time at the hostel, coupled with his years at boarding school, gave him a fondness for routine and the fellowship that communal living can bring. And just as growing up in the grounds of a stately home may have impacted some of the decisions TP made as a father, so did his years at both Wilson's and the Harding Boy's Home.

Ciss Beirne meanwhile, did not experience the same luxury of education that Thomas Pakenham had enjoyed. She would have walked several miles a day down a windswept road that cut through the bog to the local school in Cloneagh; just as her brothers and many of her cousins did, just as her own two daughters would too, for a brief moment in time, just as I myself would do many decades later. But Ciss would have left school when she was twelve or thirteen, fourteen at the most. We don't know much about her early life. We don't know when she contracted polio, although it was most likely during her late teenage years as the disease was not prevalent in Ireland until 1916. Even then it was still rare. Indeed Ciss may have been one of the first to be infected by an early sweep of the disease. We don't know if on leaving school she helped her mother make potion from the comfrey, or cut those potato splits. We don't know if she fed the pigs, or helped rear the younger children, or lent a hand to other mothers in the townland. As previously mentioned, we don't even know when she moved to Dublin and became Ciss O'Beirne, or exactly when and where she began her working life. But just as her marriage certificate informs us where she and her new husband were living in July of 1930 prior to their wedding, it also reveals that they both worked as clerks.

We believe that Ciss and Tommy, as Ciss called him, met at work, a fact that makes sense as it's unlikely a young Catholic woman would have encountered a young Protestant man in any other environment in 1920s Dublin. And we are almost certain that the company they both worked for was the Dawson Street branch of the Edison & Swan United Electric Light Company in the heart of Dublin's city centre. TP was probably a senior clerk, Ciss a clerical assistant. It might not have been the first place of employment for either of them, but equally it may have been, TP securing a junior position on completing his apprenticeship and working his way up, Ciss responding to a well-timed job advert for the company on her arrival in Dublin.

At that particular point in time, we don't think TP had much contact with his family, or enjoyed a close relationship with them at any rate. It is unlikely that any of his siblings were living in or even visited Dublin. His eldest brother John was dead. Edward was established as a gamekeeper at Pakenham Hall. Henrietta had married a stationmaster from Poyntzpass near Newry just across the border, and the other sisters were all either married or working in service. We're also fairly certain that although his Church of Ireland faith would have been ingrained in him from his mother and the teachers and ethos at Wilson's, a faith he held firm to, TP wasn't a regular churchgoer during his Dublin years, so he wouldn't have found community through the church. He did have a solid network of friends and acquaintances however, most of whom were other Church of Ireland Protestants he had met at Wilson's. There was Bertie Sharman, a solicitor, another solicitor named Cox, a

Johnson, a Hick, and a Captain Clarke, all of whom would feature in a drama of epic proportions in 1939. It is not a stretch to surmise that these men would have been distinctly unimpressed with the revelation that their good friend Thomas was courting a Catholic woman, and beyond horrified when he married her.

Ciss meanwhile had very much maintained her family ties. She was, as we know, living in Clontarf with her brother Pat in 1930. Although they stayed in Cashel to work on the family farm, Ned and John Joe would make regular trips to Dublin to visit their siblings, and no doubt the younger brothers did too. Bernie moved to the city himself as soon as he was old enough, and Albert would too, in time. The family were devout Catholics and on settling in Dublin, Ciss would have continued to attend mass on a regular basis, as would her brothers. We have evidence to suggest that Pat and Bernie became members of the Knights of St Columbanus. This fraternal organisation was formed in County Antrim in 1915 by one Father James Kearney O'Neill, initially to promote and foster the Catholic faith at a time of great strife for members of the Catholic church in the north of the island. By 1923 the order had established itself in Dublin, acquiring Ely House on Ely Place as its headquarters, from where it still operates today. It is sometimes described as the Catholic version of Freemasonry due to its traditions of robe wearing, using covert passwords, adopting secret handshakes, and stealthily helping other members to secure job promotions or resolve complicated personal or family issues. By the end of the 1920s, the Knights had become an organised and skilful pressure group, exerting their influence in many areas of the new Free State, from politics and education to finance and commerce. They operated a strict invitation-only membership for Catholic men of a certain standing, and at some point, both Pat and Bernie O'Beirne were brought into the ranks. They may not yet have been members in 1929 when their sister began to step out with a Protestant, but they definitely were ten years later when a crisis of immense proportion befell their family. And in 1929, Knights or not, they would undoubtedly have been most displeased with Ciss's choice of suitor, for not only was he a Protestant, but he was a Pakenham. Regardless of the fact that Tommy was not landed gentry himself, the Pakenham name at that time had robust connotations with English elitism and British imperialism, and that would not have sat well with the Beirnes.

So Ciss, the devout Catholic, and TP, the Church of Ireland Protestant, met against the backdrop of a new Ireland; an Ireland where mixed faith relationships were vehemently opposed, where it was difficult to be a Catholic in one part of the island, and a Protestant in the other. Just a few decades earlier, while not commonplace, mixed relationships when they did occur were more acceptable, the church apparently less influential when it came to matters of the heart in the 1800s. But by the start of the twentieth century, and with the appointment of Pope Pius X in 1903, things began to change. By 1930, in post-partition Ireland a union in marriage between a Catholic and a Protestant was denounced by both religions; considered immoral by some, unlawful by others. Both Ciss and TP's families would have been horrified by their relationship, and when they were eventually informed of it, there would have been rows and tears and gnashing of teeth, and many a swear word shouted. The shame of it, the scandal.

But of course, that was only the half of it, the tip of the iceberg where scandal was concerned, because then Ciss fell pregnant. Her pregnancy may have happened a year, or some months, or even just weeks after they met, but she conceived in mid-late January 1930. And once she knew she was with child, the shock would have been immeasurable. There were so many issues to contend with, the facts that she was unmarried and the child's father was a Protestant being the obvious and immediate two. In 1930, Ireland was not an easy place for an unmarried pregnant woman to be. There was an almost universal absence of compassion, and an abundance of judgement. The woman was, almost without question, blamed for the situation she found herself in, the man sidelined, or disregarded, or even excused. He may have been encouraged to lie low for a while, or skip the country until the coast was clear, so to speak. But that was generally the extent of his inconvenience. It was commonly her reputation in jeopardy, her family's standing at stake, not his, regardless of how the pregnancy had happened: be it within a loving relationship, or a fleeting affair, or something darker.

In a paper written for University College Dublin in 2008 by the historian Professor Lindsey Earner-Byrne, titled *Reinforcing the family: The role of gender, morality and sexuality in Irish welfare policy, 1922–1944*, she writes:

> *"The issue of reputation was central to much of the social control exercised in Ireland. The fear of the loss of one's reputation was based largely on the understanding of the family as a unit: if one member disgraced themselves the rest of the family was tarnished".*

Ciss would have been all too aware that her reputation, and that of her family, was hanging in the balance: her hard working, upstanding, devout Catholic mother in Cashel, her earnest, resolute brothers the Knights in Dublin. She risked being shunned by them, by the rest of her family, by her friends and work colleagues, by the church, and by TP himself. If he abandoned her, she might be sent to one of the now notorious Magdalene Laundries where her newborn baby would be taken from her for adoption, regardless of her wishes, or dispatched home to Cashel in disgrace, her pregnancy hidden from neighbours, with the church stepping in to sort the matter in some way after the birth. If Ciss had been younger, the baby could potentially have been passed off as Kate's once it was born, a common solution for families who wanted to keep the child of an unmarried daughter within their own walls, even if it was often a wholly transparent ruse to the community at large. But Ciss was twenty-eight, and Kate fifty-three, both too old to pull off that particular deception. There was also the possibility that she could be banished entirely, put on a boat to England to be met by a priest or a nun, cut off from her family for good, a fate that befell many young pregnant unmarried women at that time. Ciss would have known or at least encountered women to whom all of the above scenarios had happened, whether she was aware of it or not. A co-worker, perhaps, quietly grieving the baby who was now in America. A child she went to school with whose own child was being brought up as her sibling. A friend still living in a laundry somewhere, or a girl from her parish who had just been handed a ticket for the boat.

Even if she kept the baby and TP agreed to marry her, it would still be brandished as an illegitimate. In the Ireland of 1930, a child conceived out of wedlock was legally considered illegitimate, even if the parents married before the baby was born. It would be the following year when that particular antiquated law was abolished, with the introduction of the 1931 Legitimacy Act permitting children to be legitimised by the subsequent marriage of their parents. (As an aside, it would take a further fifty-six years before, in 1987, The Status of Children Act would finally abolish the concept of illegitimacy from law.) Although the 1931 bill had already been through debate in Dáil Éireann before Ciss was due to give birth, she may not have realised that her unborn child would eventually be protected through marriage. But she would have known with absolute certainty that if she decided to keep the baby, then marriage to Tommy was her only viable option, Protestant or not. Poor Ciss would most likely have wrestled with her dilemma alone, the weight of it almost suffocating her. She had no sisters, her female cousins were still too young to understand, her mother was 90-odd miles away, and even if she had lived just around the corner, the shame would probably have stopped Ciss from going to Kate anyway. Fear for her job, and for Tommy's, would have held her back from confiding in work colleagues. She couldn't go to the church, and she couldn't talk to her brothers. One can only hope that there was someone, one friend at least, one trusted confidante with whom she could lighten her load.

So Ciss would have known what her options were, and she would have guessed at what the others with a stake in the game would want her to do, expect her to do, pressurise her to do. But ultimately what *she* wanted was to keep her baby. She would have been horribly aware of the enormity of the scandal she was about to land on the doorsteps of her brothers in Dublin and her parents in Cashel, of the onslaught of outrage that would ensue. An illegitimate pregnancy, the prospect of a Protestant brother-in-law and son-in-law, and an English surname. But I suspect that Ciss genuinely loved Tommy Pakenham, or at least she knew that she could love him. She certainly loved her unborn child, and the fact that she wanted to be its mother, whatever the consequences, overrode everything

CHAPTER 5

TP and Ciss married on Monday 14th July 1930 at St John the Baptist Catholic Church, Clontarf, just a five-minute walk along the promenade from Pat and Agnes's home. Bernie was one of their witnesses, an Elizabeth Fay the other. We don't know who Elizabeth was to Ciss, possibly a friend from work or a neighbour from Clontarf Road. But she wasn't a relative. Ciss did have some female cousins back home in Leitrim, and although in the years to come she would become particularly close to two of them, Annie Kate Maguire and my aunt Mollie, they were both still teenagers at the time of her wedding. Besides, most of Ciss's extended family circle in Cashel and Mohill were probably not even aware that there was a wedding taking place in Dublin. The event would have been hushed up and swept under the carpet. Kate and Edward didn't attend, nor did any of Ciss's Leitrim based brothers. We don't think anyone from Tommy's family was present either, or his Wilson's pals. It was most likely a brief ceremony, devoid of fuss, with just Bernie, Elizabeth, Pat and Agnes in attendance. But it wouldn't have been the pregnancy that dictated such modest, restrained proceedings, for that particular news was not shared with anyone, not even, we believe, Ciss's closest family members. Rather, the nuptials would have been executed with discretion because the bride was Catholic and the groom Protestant, not a union for either family to celebrate. And the fewer people there, the less likely it was that Ciss and TP's secret would be exposed and news of the pregnancy would leak. How difficult that must have been for Ciss; a wedding without her parents, without her beloved mother, without joy and celebration. A wedding shrouded in disapproval and shame, and fixated on concealment.

Once Ciss had told Tommy that she was pregnant, there would no doubt have been many anguished conversations between the pair. Who should they tell? Who could they trust? What were their options? We don't know if the young couple were deeply in love at the time or if they were still tentatively getting to know each other, but three things are clear. Firstly, Ciss wanted to keep her baby and was determined not to have the child removed from her for adoption. Secondly, Tommy requested her hand in marriage. Thirdly, and possibly most significantly, Tommy agreed that the baby would be reared in the Catholic faith. A union between Ciss and Tommy would have been extremely difficult, if not impossible, without this crucial agreement, and a marriage ceremony conducted inside any part of a Catholic church would simply not have happened. Not in Ireland at that time.

In 1907, a decree was issued by Pope Pius X announcing updated rules for the rearing of children within a mixed faith marriage. Known as *Ne Temere*, it pronounced that all children born into a mixed marriage must now be brought up in the Catholic faith. Previously to 1907, the commonly adopted practice was that boys in such a marriage would follow their father's faith, and girls their mother's. In addition, the new declaration demanded that the Catholic partner must vow to work towards converting their spouse to Catholicism, and that the marriage, whilst witnessed by a priest, must not take place in a church. The *Ne Temere* ruling would have been sacrosanct to the devout Beirne family, especially to Pat and Bernie. Tommy's pledge to honour the ruling would have been non-negotiable. It would have been made clear to him by Ciss, by her brothers, and by the priest who would marry them, that he must sign a declaration of consent, agreeing to the *Ne Temere* terms. His own family, who would have been just as aghast at the unfolding situation as the Beirnes, were most likely not consulted. They may not even have been informed about the impeding nuptials; the shock announcement reserved until after the wedding had taken place. Some of Tommy's friends may have known that he was being pressurised to sign his future children away to the Catholic church - the solicitors Sharman and Cox, and Messrs Johnson and Hick. If they did know, they would unquestionably have urged him not to do so. Perhaps if Tommy had been actively involved in the Church of Ireland denomination in which he had been raised, regularly attending his own church, things might have turned out differently. As it was, and to his credit, he stood by Ciss and agreed to the conditions. Their future children would be baptised as Catholics, including the baby that no one knew Ciss was already carrying.

Many young couples who embarked on a mixed faith marriage at that time would have made the boat journey to England to tie the knot, even if the non-Catholic party had agreed to *Ne Temere*. It was often difficult to find a priest willing to conduct the ceremony, agreement aside, or generate enough support from within their own families or friendship circles to even find two agreeable witnesses. Marrying in anonymity in an unfamiliar environment with strangers drafted in to bear witness was, more often than not, the easier option. But it would have been important to Ciss, and to her brothers, to marry in church, regardless of the circumstances. And that's where the Knights of St Columbanus could potentially have played a part. A word may have been whispered in an ear, a guarantee made, a donation given. And as Pat most likely knew the priest well, St John's being his local church, a deal of sorts may well have been made. This is all conjecture, but for whatever reason, the priest agreed to marry Protestant Thomas Pakenham to Catholic Mary Anne O'Beirne, who by that stage, unbeknown to him, was almost six months pregnant, inside his church. Of course the priest may have suspected the bride was pregnant. Pat and Bernie may have suspected. Elizabeth Fay may have suspected. But even if they did, and even if their suspicions were voiced, Ciss and Tommy remained tight-lipped. They did take that boat to Great Britain though, to Holyhead in Wales, but only to enjoy their honeymoon.

Ciss and TP's wedding photo (July 1930)

After their wedding, Ciss and Tommy moved into a rental terrace house on Whitton Road in the suburb of Terenure, South Dublin, the opposite side of the city to Clontarf. There were no trips back to Leitrim to introduce Tommy to Ciss's family, or to Westmeath so the Pakenhams could meet Tommy's new bride. No celebration dinners, no stories or photographs shared from the honeymoon. And there was no build-up of family excitement at the impending arrival of the first Beirne grandchild, because still no one knew that Ciss was pregnant. The couple must have gone to great lengths in the weeks and months following their wedding to keep the secret. Ciss must have left work, feigning illness, perhaps, or inventing a new position elsewhere. Tommy would have had to maintain the ruse, batting off well-meaning enquiries from his co-workers. They must have avoided all contact with friends and family members, moving so far away from Pat and Agnes probably helped in that regard, and Ciss would have refrained from attending mass. But it would surely have been impossible to keep her condition hidden from their new neighbours on Whitton Road, who may have been provided with a false wedding date, should they have raised a questioning eyebrow. Or perhaps Ciss and Tommy did manage to pull off the deception entirely. For when Elizabeth Joan Pakenham arrived on Tuesday 28th October 1930, born in a house on Kenilworth Park, just a ten-minute walk from Whitton Road, her birth remained unannounced. The Kenilworth Park house was a private nursing home, run by a midwife named Frances Hale. This Frances Hale is recorded as being present at the baby's birth on the birth certificate. She is also registered as little Joan's sole godparent at her baptism in St. Joseph's Church, Terenure, nine days later, on Thursday 6th November. Not a relative, nor a family friend, but an unknown midwife. This would have been a deliberate move by Ciss and TP, as to invite a family member to be their daughter's godparent would have meant exposing their secret.

Back in Cashel, Kate Beirne didn't know that her only daughter had just given birth to a baby girl. She didn't know that she and Edward had become grandparents. And she didn't know that in Dublin, a plan had been hatched to pass their new granddaughter off as Tommy's niece. But it seems this was Ciss and Tommy's plan all along. They would keep the pregnancy a secret. News of the baby's birth would not be shared. Then, after several weeks, or however long they could get away with, the couple would announce that they had taken in a niece of Tommy's, whose parents had tragically died. A reverse version of that same story was most probably relayed to the Pakenhams in Tullynally; that the baby was an orphan, the child of one of Ciss's brothers, or cousins. Of course they may not all have bought the story, quietly recognising it as a practical solution to a very obvious problem. And when little Joan was eventually brought to Cashel to meet her extended 'adoptive' family, it may have been obvious to all that she was in fact one of theirs.

Joan herself never heard this particular story. She was told something different entirely. Decades later she would correspond with a man she met on holiday, exchanging several letters with him over the period of a year or so. Joan's children still have those letters. They are honest and raw and revealing and tender, heart-breaking too in parts, and they have played a pivotal role in piecing many parts of this story together. They have also raised several questions, and revealed some glaring anomalies. In one of the earliest letters, Joan begins to tentatively reveal the story of her life.

> *"It is difficult to know where to start,"* she writes, *"so I suppose the beginning would be the best. Mum and Dad were married two years when I arrived on the scene…"*

CHAPTER 6

Elizabeth Joan Pakenham was naturally not aware of the scandal and secrecy surrounding her birth, and at the end of the day, none of it mattered to her. All that little Joan needed was love and security, and she had that in abundance. Her parents were married and, in spite of their precarious start together, happily so, if old black and white family photos taken in the garden of their home and on the beach at Blackrock on Dublin's south coast are anything to go by. Her father had a decent job, they lived in a comfortable home, and her mother doted on her. Even if in later years Joan did question the accuracy of her birth timeline, or even if her father at some point revealed the truth, it wouldn't have mattered. By then Joan had endured so much worse in her life, and an illegitimate start, or at least a perceived one in the eyes of the Catholic church, would have been the least of her concerns.

Not long after Joan's birth, Ciss fell pregnant again. We must assume that this pregnancy *was* celebrated, that the news was happily shared with family and friends, that the arrival of this baby was eagerly awaited by everyone in the family. From the Berine's perspective, Ciss was still married to a protestant, there was no getting away from that. But the couple seemed settled, and little adopted Joan was thriving, and in spite of her protestant heritage, she was being raised as a Catholic; as indeed would this new baby, as TP had signed the *Ne Temere* agreement. The truth of Joan's parentage may have already been exposed by this stage, challenged by someone perhaps, or reluctantly revealed by Ciss and TP themselves. Or the adoption story could still have been lingering as the new baby's birth date approached. But from both an anticipation and preparation perspective, this pregnancy must have been an altogether different experience for Ciss. It ended in tragedy, however, when, on 18th September 1931, her second baby daughter was stillborn. The shock and sadness would have reverberated throughout the entire Pakenham and Beirne family circles, and no doubt broken poor Ciss and TP's hearts. We do not know what name the baby was given, her birth lost in the cogs of the family's history, unknown even to her big sister Joan and her future siblings. But the date of her birth date would become especially significant seven years later.

By 1932, TP, Ciss and Joan had left Whitton Road and moved into a smart Victorian terrace house on Lower Prince Edward Terrace in Dublin's upmarket suburb of Blackrock. With three storeys, a basement, stone steps sweeping up to the front door and a mature back garden lined with apple and cherry trees, the house was the perfect home in which to raise a growing family, and on 5th August 1933, Joan was finally joined by a baby sister. Kathleen Florence was born in St. Monica's Nursing Home, a private hospital on Lower Mount Street in Dublin city centre, most likely run by nuns. Then, in 1935, the sisters welcomed a baby brother, Edward Thomas, born on 20th May. Bearing the names of his father and two grandfathers, Ted as he would become known, or Teddy as he was fondly referred to in his infancy by TP, was born at a small private nursing home in Longford Place, Dún Laoghaire, a few miles south of Blackrock. Unlike with Joan's birth, Ciss was not alone when she brought her second and third children into the world. With Kathleen and Ted, both pregnancies were announced, both babies were celebrated, and family help was at hand during and after the births.

Ciss at the family farmhouse in Leitrim with Joan and Kathleen, her brother Albert and her cousin Babs. (Baby not identified)

For a while, life for the Pakenhams settled into a normal family routine. TP continued to work at Edison & Swan, receiving promotion to the position of accountant, as recorded on Ted's birth certificate. Kathleen and Ted were baptised into the Catholic church, just as TP had agreed to, Ciss's brother Thomas and her cousin Annie Kate McGuire standing as Kathleen's godparents, and the couple's marriage witnesses Bernie O'Beirne and Elizabeth Fay performing godparent commitments to Ted. It seems that after Kathleen's birth at least, Ciss's extended family were more involved in the Pakenham family's life. Ciss and the children spent many happy holidays at the Leitrim farm, joined there by TP when work commitments would allow. If there was ever an open, honest conversation about Joan, we do not know. I wonder still if Kate ever sat her daughter down and asked her the truth about the little girl's parentage, told her she knew she was a Beirne, and that it was fine, and that there were worse things that could happen. One thing is certain however, Kate Beirne knew and loved her grandchildren, and Ned and his brothers who still lived on the farm, knew and loved their nieces and nephew. They no doubt relished every second the little children spent with them on the farm, spreading joy and sunlight into the grind of their daily lives. There is a photo of Joan and Kathleen with their mother and Ned, sitting among the sheafs of oats in the cornfield at the farm. It may well have been taken by TP himself. Kathleen is a toddler, Joan around four years old. She is sitting comfortably against her uncle Ned, while Ciss holds Kathleen's hand. They are all happy, all content in their familiarity. They are family.

Ciss with Joan and Kathleen and her brother Ned in the cornfield on the farm in Leitrim.

It was not Kate, however, who travelled to Dublin when her daughter's second and third babies were born. Annie Kate Maguire, daughter of Kate's younger sister Lizzie, one of the two cousins with whom Ciss became close in the years before her death, took on that role. Annie Kate travelled to Dublin from Mohill following Kathleen and Ted's births to help Ciss in the house. She would have been just fifteen when Kathleen was born and named as her godmother, and eighteen when Ted came along. A faded photo from this time shows Ciss with Annie Kate and two other women. They are standing on the steps of the Blackrock house. Ciss is smiling, her eyes squinting in the sunlight, her arm companionably draped around the shoulder of one of the girls. She is happy, the stress and fear and fallout surrounding her eldest daughter's conception and birth forgotten, the grief of losing her stillborn second child eased by the safe arrival of her third.

And then life took a turn. Edison & Swan closed and TP lost his job. He was out of work for six months or so, and as a consequence the family had to leave their beloved Blackrock home for a smaller more modest house. And so, an end of terrace new-build on Errigal Road, in a new council housing estate on Dublin's southside, became the third Pakenham family home. It is likely that Pat helped his sister and her husband secure the house, as he was friendly with some high-ranking officials in the Corporation. TP did eventually get another job. We believe at Donnelly Meats, although it was lower paid and came with a demotion from his previous accountancy position to that of a bookkeeper. Once again Pat may have had a hand in this turn of events, as one of the managers at Donnelly's was a close friend of his. Regardless, it would have been a welcome development, and Joan remembered the time they spent at Errigal Road as a happy one. She started at a local primary school where Irish was one of her subjects, and began to attend mass, receiving her First Holy Communion at the age of seven. As with all small children who go through this important sacrament, Joan never forgot her special day, recalling it in one of her letters.

"I well remember having to put out my tongue to receive the wafer from the priest. I also remember being worried because I thought my

veil was going to fall off! Certainly for a girl the most important thing about confirmation was the clothes. I was cross with dad because he wouldn't let me wear my veil when getting some snaps taken!"

This lovely vignette gifts us a snapshot of a normal happy family on a normal happy day. And the fact that TP was included in the image, actively participating in his eldest daughter's First Holy Communion despite not being a Catholic himself, signifies how comfortable he must have been with the situation, at that time anyway. Joan spoke of him so fondly in her letters, painting an image of an active, loving father:

"Dad used to make time to play with us after tea every night. And oh the fun we had. When I think of it now, we must have exhausted the poor man after his hard day at work."

Ciss at her home in Blackrock with Joan, Kathleen and her cousin Annie Kate

Her memories of Ciss are hazier, as are Kathleen's who remembers little of those early years, being just five years old when their world fell apart. Ted, at three, was much too small to hold a memory of his mother at all. His sisters would tell him though, that he was their mother's favourite, that she doted on him, and was very protective of his toddler ailments. He suffered from colic and would often break out in hives, a result, it was suggested, of eating too many of the sausages TP brought home from work. Their memories may be sparse, but collectively the children knew that they were loved, that their home was a happy one with ample food to eat and milk to drink and warm, clean clothes to wear. They had each other, they had neighbours and extended family, and they had friends to play with. And then, in the late summer of 1938, when Joan was almost nine and Kathleen had just turned five and Ted was a toddler of three, the children were told that a little baby brother or sister would soon be joining them.

John Hubert Norman arrived on his stillborn sister's birthdate, Sunday 18th September, the only one of the four Pakenham children to be born at home. We don't know who attended the birth. We don't know if the pregnancy was problematic or if the birth was complex, or if the trouble started afterwards; but trouble did descend, and ferociously so. Soon after the baby boy was born, Ciss developed an infection. Mrs Keogh, who lived next door, didn't like the look of her neighbour and sent for a doctor. Ciss was initially treated at home, but rapidly deteriorated and was transferred to Cork Street Hospital for further intervention. It quickly became clear however that no amount of intervention would work. Ciss was going to die, and she wanted her baby to be baptised before she left this earth. A hasty ceremony was arranged, with Ciss's dear cousin Mollie, who by then was living in Dublin and had become a regular visitor to the Pakenham house, appointed as godmother, and Mrs Keogh's teenage son Liam drafted in as godfather. Just seventeen years old at the time, Liam was fond of the three youngsters who lived next door, keeping an eye on them when Ciss needed a break. He never got to know his baby godson, but he would remember him for the rest of his life, and talk about what had happened in 1938 to his own children and grandchildren. As for Mollie, twenty-one years later she became a godmother once more, this time to me. But almost six decades would pass before she set eyes on her first godson again.

The news was delivered to all who needed to know that Ciss was dying, and one by one her family visited her bedside to say their goodbyes. By all accounts she was dignified and courageous, imparting instructions and comforting her loved ones in their ascending grief.

"Tell me something happy," she said when her dear cousin Annie Kate arrived, distressed and bewildered by the events that were unravelling. So Annie Kate took Ciss's hand and told her she was engaged to be married to Jack Conboy, the local boy from Mohill she had been seeing for some time. They would marry the following February and remain living in Leitrim.

"I like that name," Ciss reportedly told her. "Let's give it to the baby." And so, although it states otherwise on his birth certificate and his baptism record and all his official papers, from that day on, John Hubert Norman has been known to all as Jack, apart from his father, who fondly called him Jackie.

When Kate Beirne came to the hospital, she was already worn down by grief. The previous Christmas Day, her beloved second son, John Joe, had died at home after contracting TB. Following Hugh's death, John Joe became the natural successor to the farm. With both his father and his uncle Hugh now in their late sixties, he was already pretty much running it when, in the spring of 1937, he travelled to Dublin for the annual agricultural show. On his return, as he walked home from the narrow-gauge station in nearby Derren, he waved at a neighbour, Mrs Mallon, who was out hanging laundry in her garden. Mrs Mallon waved back, and then, hearing John Joe cough, scuttled back inside her house. She knew that cough, she knew what it meant, and before long it was common news in the area that John Joe Beirne had TB. It was a long slow death for the young man, and when it finally came, as the bells tolled for midnight mass on one of the holiest of days, the family was plunged into grief. Kate was devastated, and ten months later was still in deep mourning as she faced the loss of another child, her third-born and only daughter. Ciss's heart cracked open when she saw her mother approach her hospital bed.

"Here comes my poor mother," she cried, understanding that the grief Kate was facing for the third time now was the worst kind of pain a mother could endure. She herself would not see her children grow into adults. She would not witness the landmark moments of their lives, be present at their weddings, hold her own grandchildren in her arms. Her new baby son would never know her. Ted, her darling boy, would not remember her. Kathleen, that wonderous little girl who amazed her with her strength of spirit at such a tender age, would most likely forget too. Only Joan, dear, precious Joan, her firstborn gentle child, might hold her in her mind. The agony of leaving her family would have been worse that the agony of dying. Perhaps Ciss's only solace was the knowledge that she would be reunited in death with her baby who had not lived, and that at least her other four children would survive her, which is the way it should be.

Ciss must have agonised too about how her family would manage on a practical and, crucially, religious level after her death. She had fought so hard to build the life she had been living with her Protestant husband and her Catholic children, and that life worked. It worked because *she* made it work. But what would happen now? She would have known with absolute certainty that her family, her brothers in particular, would want the children to remain in the Catholic faith, and that was her own dying wish too. She may also have suspected that certain family members, her mother even, might pressurise Tommy into releasing the younger two, or the baby at least, into their care; but that was not what she wanted. Ciss would have had heard multiple stories of such things happening in her own family circle and beyond, children separated from their remaining parent and siblings following the death of a parent, sent to other parts of Ireland, or England, or even, in many instances, America. However her uncle John, my grandfather, had gone against the grain and kept his family together when his wife Annie had died. Her cousin Mike Joe, my father, had been ten at the time, Babs the same age as Ted was now, Mollie, baby Jack's new godmother, just two. Mollie had initially been placed with Aunt Brigie, who was married but had no children, an act that was undoubtedly made with the very best of intentions, but then John had quickly brought his little daughter home. Ciss may have had her uncle John in mind. She may have decided that if he could do it, so could Tommy. Whatever was going through her mind, on her deathbed she made her husband promise to keep the children together, and he swore to her that he would. At least that's the story he would tell his children in the years to come.

Ciss Pakenham died in hospital on Tuesday 4th October 1938 from peripheral septicaemia. For the Pakenham family, the 18th of September had delivered death with the little stillborn girl, had delivered life with baby Jack, and had triggered death again, this time for Ciss. She was just thirty-five years old when she died sixteen days after Jack's birth. For the family she left behind, both the Pakenhams and the Beirnes, life would never be the same again. And although their hearts were broken and the regularity of their everyday existence had shattered into pieces, in so very many ways, the worst was yet to come.

TP and Ciss in happier times

CHAPTER 7

The events that followed Ciss's death have been chronicled by various sources. We have Joan's letters and we have Kathleen's recollections, and although both may be sparse and fragmented and are the reflections of traumatised little girls, they each provide important morsels of detail. There are memoires, stories and suppositions too that were handed down to the next generation, resting now with the children of Kate's siblings. And we have the words of TP himself, a handwritten testimony penned in October 1939, a year after the passing of his wife. There will be truths in all of their retellings, and, inevitably, false memories too. But between one story and another, we can paint a clear enough picture of the tragedy that unravelled.

Ciss was buried in Mount Jerome Cemetery on the south side of Dublin, a small wooden cross marking her resting place, with the quiet promise perhaps of a more befitting memorial to come. Once it became clear that their mother was going to die, the children were sent to the farm in Leitrim. They needed attention and routine and people around them, and the baby had to be mothered by someone, so it made sense that as their grandmother, Kate would, provisionally at least, assume that role. She would have seen it as her duty, and welcomed the distraction from her grief. It is likely that the four children accompanied their grandmother on her return journey to Cashel following her sorrowful visit to kiss her dying daughter. Imagine the sadness of that pilgrimage from Cashel to Dublin, Kate taking a pony and trap to Dromod to catch the train to the city, then a bus from Heuston Station to the hospital, a small bag of the most basic essentials tucked in beside her, praying all the while for a miracle she knew would not arrive. She was still mourning the son she had lost just ten months previously, and now she was losing her only beloved daughter. Then think of the grief-laden journey back to Cashel, this time with a tiny baby, a toddler, and two confused and frightened little girls in tow. Perhaps one of her sons accompanied her, or one of her nieces, Annie Kate or Mollie. Edward would most likely not have accompanied his wife to Dublin, the autumn harvest, almost destroyed by catastrophic floods the previous month, demanding his presence on the farm, regardless of the unfolding heartbreak. When Kate left the hospital, she knew she would never see Ciss again, knew she would most probably not even return to Dublin for her funeral, knew too that she must control her grief for the sake of the children. There would no doubt have been painful discussions with her son-in-law, perhaps even with Ciss herself, about what to do with the little ones as they waited for the inevitable, and ill-prepared as they were, the Beirne family farm was the most natural solution. The house was not equipped for a baby, never mind three young children. There had been TB within its walls so recently, and repairs that had gone untended to due to grief and lack of funds and the need to focus on the farm. But it was home for the Beirnes, and so Kate would do her utmost to make it home for her poor little grandchildren too. She would have busied herself preparing bedding for the three eldest children, sourcing a cot and bottles for the baby. She would have spoken with the school master about Joan and Kathleen attending class, and gathered some books and toys and clothing too, as just a basic supply of home comforts would have been packed for the journey to Leitrim from Dublin. And all the while awaiting the news that her daughter had gone to the Lord.

The community around her would have rallied. Her surviving sons who still lived with her on the farm would have helped, neighbours too, and nearby family members such as my own grandfather and father and Auntie Babs. Hugh and John Joe who had gone before Ciss were not married, did not have children, and the anguish Kate must have felt when she looked at the confused and innocent faces of her little grandchildren, knowing what lay ahead for them as the dark days of winter approached, must have further shattered her already broken heart.

Back in Dublin, a distraught TP was sitting by his beloved wife's bedside as she made her way out of this world. Then there would be papers to sort, people to inform, a funeral to organise. He would have agreed that in spite of everything, the children were better off on the farm, away from the immediacy of the unfolding horror. The funeral itself was most likely a small, quiet, subdued occasion. Aside from TP and Pat and Agnes and Bernie and his wife Nancy, there would probably have been very few mourners. Mollie and Annie Kate, no doubt, and the Keoghs from next door, and possibly Elizabeth Fay. A handful of other neighbours and maybe one or two colleagues from TP's work. Perhaps Ned and Terrence and Albert travelled to Dublin from Cashel, Edward too on this occasion, damming the fields that kept him from his dying daughter's bedside. They would not prevent him from laying her to rest. But Kate would have stayed on the farm, hugging her grandchildren close.

Immediately after Ciss's passing, TP went to the farm himself to break the news. He took his two girls into a bedroom, sat them on the bed, and gently explained that their mother had gone to heaven. Kathleen was just five years old then, but the moment remained imbedded in her memory. She can't recall much about what happened before, or what came afterwards, or the exact words that were uttered, but she remembers being told that her mother was dead. Joan, on the other hand, retained no recollection of that particular event. Her brain blocked it out completely, refusing to hold the memory. She did remember a wake however, and would write about that event years later, but it wasn't for her mother.

TP returned to Dublin and to work, agreeing that the children should remain in Cashel until he arranged for a housekeeper to move into Errigal Road. They stayed at the farm for around three months, spending that first dreadful Christmas without their mother there. And another tragedy would befall the family before then. On 3rd November, almost a month to the day after their mother died, their grandfather Edward dropped dead. With two sons and his only daughter gone, his heart could take no more. It was his wake that Joan recalled in one of her letters, the innocence of her eight-year-old-self radiating from the page. She didn't express grief or shock about what had happened, or provide any context as to why they were at the farm at that particular time, rather her memory was the age-old thrill of a young child allowed to stay up past their bedtime to observe an adult party:

> *"You may have heard of a wake. When there is a death in the house all the neighbours come from miles around to offer their sympathy, but also to enjoy themselves. There is music and dancing and drinking. Well grandad died when we were there and being the eldest, I was allowed to stay up a while for the wake."*

For Kate, Edward's death was the third catastrophic bereavement she had suffered in less than twelve months, leaving her to carry the burden of her daughter's loss as a widow. She would have donned black mourning attire the previous December when John Joe died, and still been adhering to the custom of wearing black clothing for a full year following a loved one's death when Ciss passed away. By the time Edward died, those garments would have been glued to Kate's soul, and she would never wear anything other than black for the rest of her days. Before 4th October 1938, Kate had been facing the coming Christmas without the son she had lost the previous one, the looming anniversary an agonising enough prospect. But then she lost her daughter, and then her husband, their family of eleven reduced to a family of eight between the bells of one Christmas eve and the chimes of the next. We can only surmise it was having to care for her grandchildren that got her through it, although the farmhouse would have been devoid of seasonal joy and Christmas traditions. Any traditions that year would have centred around grief. No Christmas cards would have been sent or received, no decorations hung, it's unlikely there was even a tree. But no doubt Ned, to whom the farm had now officially passed, and Terence who still lived at home and helped his older brother, and Albert, still just a teenager and home from boarding school in Longford, would have rallied to ensure there was at least something to mark the occasion for the sake of the little ones. None of the children would remember that Christmas, which is, perhaps, a blessing. Indeed, it would be many years before they could recall a happy Christmastime again.

Putting all the upheaval, confusion, and sadness aside, the months that the four Pakenham children spent in Cashel in late 1938, were most likely happy ones. Both Joan and Kathleen retained some memories of playing on the farm, riding the pony and trap along narrow country roads, being chased by cows in the fields. They even went to school for a short time, that same school in Cloneagh that their mother had gone to years before, trudging down the windswept bog road, just as she had. Ted, being three at the time recalls nothing of this period, but no doubt he would have had the run of the place, keeping his grandmother on her toes. Jack, just a babe in arms, was loved and tended to. Most importantly, they were together. Then, in early January 1939, TP made the trip to Leitrim to bring his children home. Though he hadn't yet found a housekeeper, his sister Florrie had agreed to move into Errigal Road for a short time to look after the family until he found someone suitable. A Lady's Maid, Florrie either requested and was granted temporary leave from her permanent position, or was in between employers. She must have considered it important that her nieces and nephews resume a regular routine in their own home, with their father.

It is worth pondering at this point if a conversation had begun within TP's circle regarding religion. Assuming Florrie inherited her own mother's steadfast Protestant beliefs, she would not have been happy with the arrangement made when Tommy and Ciss married and had children. It would have pained her deeply that the children were baptised Catholic, that Joan attended mass, that she was being taught the Irish language at school. It would have pained her mother Annie too, and her sisters, and her brother. When Ciss was alive, they would have had no say in the matter, but her death changed things. Not that Florrie or any of her family would have wished Ciss dead, or wished her ill at all, or relished in the agony that TP and the children were now subjected to. They would have acknowledged the tragedy of the situation. But now that Ciss was gone, they may have considered it inappropriate that the children continue in their mother's Catholic faith, and suggested that their father's Protestant one was now much more suitable. And this same sentiment would almost definitely have been shared by TP's associates Mr Sharman, Mr Cox, Mr Johnson, Mr Hick, and Captain Clarke. Tolerating their Protestant friend raising Catholic children whilst married to a Catholic wife was one thing, but as a widower, well that was something else entirely. TP himself must have been nurturing similar thoughts. In later life he always maintained that he did his best to fulfil Ciss's dying wish that the family should stay together, but he would never make any mention of a commitment to keep them in the Catholic faith. If such a conversation ever did take place, if such a promise were indeed made, it died with his wife.

Whatever conversations were going on in the background, Joan, Kathleen and Ted returned to Errigal Road in January 1939, but baby Jack remained in Cashel with his grandmother. Perhaps it was Kate herself who persuaded TP to leave the baby at the farm, for another while at least. Practically speaking it made sense, as he needed constant tending to and Florrie wasn't used to babies. It would give the other children time to settle into a life without their mother, and allow TP breathing space to readjust himself. And, selfishly or not, Kate needed Jack. That little baby was most likely the only thing keeping her standing, the only thing stopping the unfathomable beast of grief that had darkened her door from consuming her entirely. Or it may have been Florrie who imposed a proviso: *I'll take on you and the eldest three, Tommy, but not the baby, and only for a month.* Either way, Kate was granted the reprieve she so desperately wanted, and in the Beirne family farm at Cashel and the O'Beirne homes in Dublin, an idea was forming that Jack should remain with her permanently, or at least until he was reared. Perhaps suspicions were already being aroused that TP would try to withdraw the children from Catholicism, and if that were the case, they would resist. They would engage whatever manner of persuasion within the law that it was possible for them to do. But if they failed, if Joan and Kathleen and Ted were prevented from continuing in their Catholic faith, then the baby would not return to Dublin.

At the start of February, Florrie departed, returning to her own life and work, and, most likely with the help of his friends and Florrie's nod of approval, TP appointed a housekeeper, one Miss Hughes. Miss Hughes was a Protestant, a detail recorded in TP's testimony, and one that was not appreciated by the O'Beirnes, nor it would seem by TP's work colleagues and neighbours. He had already quietly pulled back on the children's weekly Catholic rituals as he could not implement them himself, but according to his testimony, it was when he employed Miss Hughes that *"things began to happen"*. Co-workers shunned him, claiming he was being unfair on the children. Some neighbours tried to interfere, proposing they take the children to mass themselves, which he rejected. He also turned down Mollie Winter's offer to take the girls, or Joan at least, to mass. The O'Beirne brothers reminded TP of the *Ne Temere* agreement he had signed before his marriage to Ciss. A Protestant housekeeper could not maintain a Catholic upbringing. A Protestant housekeeper could not instruct the children in the use of the rosary, or recite with them their nightly prayers. And a Protestant housekeeper could not bring them to mass. If TP would not facilitate the religious birth right of their nieces and nephews, then Pat and Bernie would have to see to it themselves.

Joan recalled this time too in one of her letters, though whether it is her own memory or a retelling from her father sometime down the line is unclear.

> *"When we came back from the farm we had been well instructed in the use of the Rosary and Hail Mary's, and then the trouble started. Dad had no intention of letting us continue in the Roman Catholic faith."*

A storm was brewing, with dark clouds gathering over the Pakenham residence on Errigal Road, the Beirne farm in Cashel, the homes of Pat and Bernie O'Beirne in Dublin, and the dwellings of Thomas Pakenham's friends and family. And at the centre of the storm were four little children who could do nothing to stop the fervour of the quickening winds.

CHAPTER 8

One evening shortly after the appointment of Miss Hughes, Pat O'Beirne knocked on the door of Errigal Road. Though uninvited, his appearance was most likely not unexpected, given the recent developments. What would have taken TP by surprise, however, was that Pat was not alone. And it wasn't Bernie who accompanied him, nor Agnes his wife, but one Kevin Bunyan, a fellow Knight of St. Columbanus who was a member of some importance. According to TP, this gentleman was "*at the root of all the trouble*". The purpose of their visit was to arrange for Joan and Kathleen to attend mass, Ted still being too young. Playing for time, and with an escalating nervousness about baby Jack in Leitrim, TP placated his guests in some way, possibly agreeing to a plan, possibly giving them an assurance that he would think about it. In his testimony he writes:

> "*I knew full well that if I showed my hand whilst the baby was still in the care of the mother-in-law, I would certainly lose him and never see him again. I decided to play for time and endeavour to do the impossible - run with the hare and hunt with the hounds.*"

The following evening he received another caller, this time it was his sister-in-law Nancy, Bernie's wife. Nancy and Bernie had married the previous year and TP wouldn't have known her as well as he knew Agnes, so perhaps sending her was a distraction strategy agreed by the family, or perhaps she acted alone. Either way, according to TP, Nancy told him that everyone in the family knew Kate was not prepared to give Jack up, and that if TP attempted to take him back to Dublin, *"there will be murder."* If Nancy's plan was to convince TP that his baby son would be better off in Leitrim, it backfired, badly. If, on the other hand, she was secretly on TP's side, her visit a warning of sorts, an unspoken suggestion that it was time for him to act, it worked.

A few days later, on Sunday 19th February, TP, Miss Hughes, Mr Johnston, and Mr Hick set off on the ninety-mile journey to Cashel in Mr Johnston's car. They paused for lunch in Longford, some twenty miles south of Cashel, ensuring they were adequately fed and watered to make the three-hour return trip to Errigal Road without a stop once their mission had been accomplished. Arriving at the farm at two thirty in the afternoon, they were greeted by one of Ciss's brothers and a cousin. They were not expected, although, as with Pat's visit to TP just a few days previously, their appearance was most probably not entirely unanticipated. The brother in question was most likely Terence, as on that particular afternoon Ned was visiting his grandfather John Winters at the Winter's family farm a short distance down the road, and Albert would have been in Longford at his boarding school. The cousin that TP refers to could have been Patrick or Terence Maguire, sons of Kate's sister Lizzie, brothers of Annie Kate. Whichever family members they were, according to TP the brother-in-law announced that the baby wasn't able to travel on that day as he was unwell with a cold, then dispatched the cousin off to garner reinforcements. Those reinforcements were Ned and another cousin or two, possibly my own father included. But they were too late, as just fifteen minutes after their arrival, TP and his entourage were back on the road, an extra passenger on board.

Imagine for a second the scene that unfolded inside the Beirne house on that bleak February afternoon in 1939: raised voices, accusations, recriminations, physical force, howls of anguish from Kate and the upset cries of a five-month-old baby snatched from his cradle. Except we don't just have to imagine it – we have TP's vivid recollection, from his perspective at any rate. In his own words, this is what transpired:

> "As soon as I mentioned to my mother-in-law that we were going to take the baby back with us there was an immediate uproar. I was told 'he will not leave this house except by force'. This was repeated several times as if it had been pre-arranged. 'Who has a better right to look after him than me – you can have him when he is reared.' The brother-in-law then took up a threatening attitude and seeing that it was useless trying to discuss the matter further, I told Miss Hughes to take the baby out. The mother-in-law immediately grabbed the baby, I pulled her hands away, the brother-in-law tried to stop H. Johnston and H. Hick from getting out, but eventually after some pushing, shoving and screaming we got to the front door, to discover it locked and the key gone. Running to the back door, I opened it and took the baby from Miss Hughes as she was on the verge of collapse. In the meantime the brother-in-law ran to close the back door but was prevented by H. Johnston. Pushed out by H. Hick I made my way to the car, leaving H. Hick to help Miss Hughes. At 2.45pm., 15 minutes after our entry, we were on the return journey, by a very different route, with the baby but without clothes or food for him."

Kate's recollection of the event was not the same, nor was that of her son who was present. They would remember an invasion of Protestants, shouting and shoving their way into their house, the man their daughter and sister had married, with two strange men and a woman. They would recall the baby being lifted by the woman without Kate's consent, TP forcibly preventing her from taking her grandson back. They would tell of their pleas to leave the baby be, that they would raise him better than TP could without a wife, that leaving the only home he had known would unsettle little Jack, that TP had enough on his hands back in Dublin, that he and the other children were welcome to visit anytime they liked. And the son would talk of his mother's collapse on the path as the car sped away from the farm, down the Cashel Road and on to Dublin, clutching to her heart, perhaps, the baby's blanket, or his feeding bottle, or his only toy. The neighbours for miles around heard poor Kate Beirne wail that day.

TP arrived back in Dublin with his son successfully repatriated, but no plan in place for what would happen next. The basic practicalities would have been covered: Miss Hughes in residence to help, equipment and clothing from little Ted's babyhood still stored at the house. But the realisation that news of the episode would soon reach the Dublin brothers, and in turn his colleagues, his neighbours, and perhaps worst of all the Knights of St Columbanus, sent him into a spiralling panic. Pre-empting the trouble that would inevitably follow, he either hastily thought of a solution himself, or was presented with a proposal by one or other, or even all of his Protestant associates. He must go North. It was the only conceivable option. And so, again either of his own volition or spurred on by others, he wrote to a distant cousin who lived north of the border in Lurgan, outlining both his predicament and his plan, and asked him to come to Dublin for a meeting.

Four days after the incident at the farm, TP received a phone call at work from Pat requesting a meeting at Errigal Road that evening to discuss *"the gangster-like proceedings which had taken place."* He asked that Messrs Johnston and Hick both be in attendance too, though in the event, only Mr Hick showed up. Pat arrived with his own entourage: his brother Bernie, Kevin Bunyan, and Alderman Martin O'Sullivan of the Dublin Corporation, all of them Knights. A heated discussion naturally ensued, with Alderman O'Sullivan intervening to restore order. Referring again to TP's testimony, the Alderman asked for an assurance that the children's faith would not be forsaken.

> *"'Look here, Tommy, will you give me an assurance that the children will be brought up in the Catholic faith.' Playing for time, I replied that the wife and I had worked things out very satisfactorily and I would continue to do so. This was apparently accepted, and a general discussion followed, touching many things in connection with the kiddies."*

We can presume that Pat and Bernie left Errigal Road that night breathing a sigh of relief. They may not have believed that the battle with their brother-in-law was over. They may have remained furious with him for snatching the baby from his grandmother's arms. Or they might, perhaps, have considered that in spite of their mother's pain, the baby was where he truly belonged – with his father and brother and sisters; so long, of course, as TP collaborated with their wishes. And after that visit they most likely thought they were winning him around to their way of thinking. Perhaps a little financial boost would help keep him on board. Two days later, on Friday 24th February, TP's boss came to his desk with a letter, and the unexpected news of a 5-shilling raise. *"Something to keep you smiling,"* he said patting TP's shoulder. The letter was from Pat, suggesting a further meeting to firm up what they had discussed two nights previously.

"Dear Tommy – you referred to the difficulties in connection with Joan going to Mass on Sundays and it has occurred to me that your difficulties will now be increased owing to the fact that the baby is now at home. I am therefore suggesting to you that you have Joan ready about 9.50a.m. and Mollie will call and bring her to Mass, also Kathleen when the weather is fine.

Arising out of Sunday last and matters in connection with the children, I should like to have a chat with yourself and put matters on a proper basis if possible. I am working overtime, for some time, but if it would be convenient for you to come down to Bernie's tonight at about 9.30 for half-an-hour, I shall be obliged – or say when and where suits you. I want as little delay as possible due to the position in which Messrs Hick and Johnston have placed themselves, and the pressure which undoubtedly must be exerted on you from other sources.

Very sincerely yours, Pat."

You and I, and many another person of sane and rational mind, might read that letter with optimism. We might view it as an olive branch, a genuine attempt to show understanding, compassion even, to resolve the complexity of the situation they all found themselves in with dignity and compromise. At that moment in time, however, TP was not of sane mind. How could he have been given the events of the past five months? He viewed the letter as a threat, the sudden wage increase as a sweetener, arranged no doubt by Pat. Wasn't he the boss's friend after all? Perhaps that was the reason for Pat's long-term overtime - to pay for TP's raise. He smelled the interference of the Knights and knew he needed to act quickly, to put the wheels of the plan that had been brewing in his head into immediate motion. He left his desk and found an outside phone box, making two calls: one to the office of his friends and legal advisors Mr Hick and Mr Sharman, and the other to Captain Clark. The four men met in Captain Clark's office at 6 p.m. that evening where TP outlined his plan. He was to flee the country and he needed their help. They readily agreed, viewing their friend's abscondence to the North as preferable to his children being raised as Roman Catholics. There were promises of assistance, reassurances that the children would be well looked after and receive a decent Protestant education.

The following day, the distant cousin from Lurgan and his wife arrived at TP's house for the requested meeting. Hick and Sharman were probably present, some of the others too. The man in question was Charlie Pakenham, the teacher from Wilson's Hospital, now Headmaster at a small country school in County Armagh. TP would have had some other family connections in the North on his mother's side, but though he didn't know Charlie and his wife Mary well, he would not have known his mother's relatives at all. And as well as being distant cousins, there was that Wilson's connection too, a connection that TP, Hick, Sharman and the others all held very firm to. Charlie and Mary had five children of their own, yet when TP asked for their assistance, they apparently agreed without hesitation. Perhaps they concluded that what he was asking of them was worth the rescue of these poor motherless children, worth liberating them from a future immersed in the Catholic church.

The next day, Sunday 26th February, TP agreed that Pat could visit him at home, presumably in lieu of that suggested meeting at Bernie's bar on the Friday evening. Pat arrived with *"his bodyguard"*, who we assume was Mr Bunyan. He suggested, no doubt cordially, that the children should be sent to Cashel each summer for the duration of the school holiday. TP readily agreed. Pat also proposed that Tommy should rethink the situation with the baby, that when all was said and done, he would be better off in the country with his grandmother, for the foreseeable future at least. Once more, TP agreed. Pat left a happy man, apparently placated. If he didn't smell a rat then he absolutely should have, for the following Sunday morning when Mollie arrived to collect Joan for mass as per the arrangement, she would find an empty house.

TP had spent the week furtively packing his belongings at night *"when the kiddies were asleep"*. He enlisted a Protestant neighbour to drive his trunks to a destination in the city centre under the cover of darkness, presumably the offices or home of one of his Wilson's associates. As morning dawned on Saturday 4th March, a taxi drew up outside the house on Errigal Road. Waiting inside was Mary Pakenham. TP bundled his confused, sleepy children into the car, eight-year-old Joan holding baby Jack in her arms while her father locked the door to their family home for the very last time. They may have still been in their nightwear, coats hastily thrown over pyjamas, feet clumsily shoved into winter shoes or boots. He might have allowed them to grab their most cherished toy, or book, or blanket; or he may have insisted there wasn't time. If the elder two, scared and nervous and terribly confused, asked questions of their daddy, it is possible he told them something of what was happening with rushed and frantic words. Or he may have instructed them to whisht. It's unlikely, however, that in the state of mind we can only imagine he was in, he turned the escapade into an adventure. Minutes later the taxi arrived at the pre-arranged rendezvous location, the premises where TP's belongings had secretly been stashed. Charlie had already loaded the luggage into his own car, helped by Mr Hick and Mr Sharman. Keys to Errigal Road would have been handed over, for the solicitors had been tasked with selling TP's worldly goods, brisk handshakes exchanged, a final tap on the bonnet of the car as the doors closed, and the vehicle sped away through the city centre streets, out towards Swords, on up to Balbriggan and Drogheda and Dundalk. Approaching the border, they would have veered off the main route, twisting through tight country lanes to avoid any checkpoints, and passed through the invisible line that separated Ireland, unnoticed, unchallenged. Another hour or so and they'd be in Lurgan, the children perhaps asleep, crushed into each other, Ted on Joan's knee, Kathleen's head on her sister's shoulder, Jack held to the strange lady's chest. Or maybe fear and hunger kept them awake, the little ones whimpering, Joan silently holding their hands, stiff with trepidation. They would have had no idea of what lay ahead, of what their father's grand plan was. But then neither did he. As far as we can surmise, there was no plan beyond leaving Dublin, beyond escaping the perceived persecution of his dead wife's family, beyond converting his Southern Catholic children into Northern Protestants.

TP's testimony, which provides both a remarkable insight into the events of early 1939 and an indication of his state of mind at the time, was penned seven months after the family fled Dublin, and written to no one in particular. It is part explanation, part stubborn justification, part perhaps, an appeal for exoneration, if not forgiveness. We must, of course, take his account of what happened as factual, albeit from his perspective. History as we know does not follow a straight line. But there are anomalies, and there are untruths. TP did not own the house on Errigal Road, for example, it was a rented council house, and yet he talks of charging Mr Sharman with the task of selling it. This is a story that was repeated in the years to come to his children and no doubt many others, one that may first have been told when he contacted Charlie asking for help with transport and temporary lodgings. *I can pay you*, he may have said, *I have money coming*. Except he couldn't, and he didn't. There is also paranoia, induced by the religious pressure and escalating coercion crushing him from both sides: *the children must remain Catholic* mantra repeated by Ciss's family and the Knights of St Columbanus; cries of *the children must now become Protestants* from his own family and associates.

But just look at the situation in which he suddenly, shockingly found himself: a widower with four young children, one a tiny baby, all baptised into a religion he did not share nor care for but had tolerated due to his love for his wife. He was a professional working man who was not earning close to his capacity and may have struggled to maintain the services of a live-in housekeeper. We know nothing of Miss Hughes beyond her name, but it is entirely possible that she may have marked herself as a potential future wife for Thomas Pakenham, as might others in the mix. Such a union would certainly have solved the issue of paying her a wage and provided the children with a mother of sorts. But TP did not want a substitute for Ciss. Perhaps the clandestine wage increase arranged by Pat was indeed a sweetener of sorts, or perhaps it was simply an act of kindness, a genuine attempt to help TP. Perhaps too the offers of help to bring the girls to mass from Pat and Bernie and Mollie and neighbours were just that: support in a time of crisis. And perhaps the suggestion that Jack should remain at the farm with his grandmother was indeed the best solution. It was the country way of things, and would certainly have lessened the pressure. Ciss's family had loved her. They also loved her children, and they would have steadfastly believed that her dying wish was for them to remain in the Catholic faith after her death. They would have felt grief for TP alongside their own grief, sorrow for this man who had loved their sister and daughter, empathy for the position he now found himself in, and they would do what they could to help him. But carrying out what they believed to be Ciss's wishes, and ensuring TP remained faithful to the *Ne Temere* agreement he had signed on their marriage, were their priorities.

If TP had paused for breath, if he had been given space and time to readjust, life for the Pakenhams of Errigal Road might have gradually fallen into a new way of being, found a rhythm that suited them all. Compromise could have been reached, family ties maintained, the children's Catholic status preserved. But in the midst of all the grief and confusion and mistrust and animosity, TP's own faith began to emerge. Encouraged by his Protestant associates, and possibly some of his own family members who were very much on the sidelines of the unfolding drama, dishing out opinions and directives without providing actual, practical help, his Protestantism rose up. His growing mistrust of the Catholic church and those who worshipped in it finally overwhelmed him. And so he did the only thing he believed he could do, he left the South, and headed up North.

PART 2
HUNGER

In my pockets I discover the crusts
I saved from Visiting Day
When everything was rosy
And children smiled
As food was piled upon the plate;
I remember well
Our looks of utter disbelief

~ From *Memories*, by Jack Pakenham

CHAPTER 9

Thomas Pakenham and his four young children arrived in the North of Ireland on the afternoon of Saturday 4th March 1939 to begin their new, non-Catholic life. Their old life, the one they had abandoned that very morning, was compressed into a couple of suitcases: some clothes, a few toiletries perhaps, and a handful of papers and photographs. They had no other possessions, no money, and no clear plan. Charlie and Mary must have agreed to provide the family with a bed for the night, a few nights probably, just until TP got things sorted; things being a job, appropriate accommodation, schooling for the oldest children and hands-on help with the youngest. With five children of their own, the house would have been full to the gills, so the bed may indeed have been just that: one single bed that Joan, Kathleen and Ted were squeezed into, with little Jack placed in a makeshift cradle and TP making do with an armchair.

There is a gap in our knowledge here that we just can't fill, a chasm that remains unbridged, a multitude of questions that no matter how many times we ask them, refuse to be answered. Based on the facts that we do have however, this is what we believe happened next. TP stayed in Lurgan for just a few days, realising that to secure work he would need to head further north to Belfast, a city he had never visited before. It would appear that Charlie and Mary agreed to keep the three eldest children, but not the baby. This arrangement was surely laced with caveats: a time constraint no doubt; behavioural conditions that the children must adhere to; and a financial contribution from TP, as three more mouths to feed, even such little ones, would hurt the family purse.

TP's mother had a cousin who lived in Belfast, a woman named Harriet Magill. It is possible that TP had never met her, but if he had, it was most likely fleetingly when he was a child himself. We think TP wrote to Harriet, and another temporary arrangement was hastily made. And so, leaving his eldest three children in Lurgan, he headed to Belfast with Jack, and handed the baby over to this distant relative and virtual stranger. Remember, Joan was just eight years old, Kathleen five, Ted still three. They had already lived what must have seemed like an entire lifetime in the space of five short months. They had lost their mother, suddenly and shockingly. They had been removed from their home, their own beds, the familiarity of their everydayness, and brought to the farm in Cashel. They were presented with a new baby brother with no mother to rear him and a grandmother riven with grief. They had witnessed their grandfather's death, or at least the immediate aftermath of his passing; more agony, more upheaval, more grief. They were brought back to Dublin without their new brother to find an aunt who they didn't know very well, if indeed at all, wearing their mother's apron. A few weeks later she too vanished, and another woman, a total stranger, arrived to take care of them. They may have wondered at all the comings and goings, the constant stream of visitors to the house: their uncles and aunts and neighbours and their father's collection of friends. They may have heard rows and raised voices and hushed whispers and fists hammering on tables. They may have felt fear and confusion on top of the grief that they didn't understand, the grief that no one had talked to them about. Then suddenly one day the baby returned to Errigal Road, and the siblings became four again. And just when it might have looked as though things would settle down, that a different form of normal would now unfold on the sidelines of their old familiar life, they were bundled into a car and driven across the border to a strange house filled with children who spoke differently to them. And then the baby disappeared again, and their father left them. Did he talk to them at all about what was happening, or what his plans were? Did he attempt to explain why they had to leave Dublin, why they had to abandon their home and belongings? Did he rage against their grandmother, spit in fury about their uncles, blame the Catholic church for the situation they were all now in, for this latest unavoidable separation? Or did he say nothing, just utter as convincing a reassurance as he could muster that he would return for them, that all would be well.

Charlie was the headmaster at Ardmore Primary in Derryadd on the outskirts of Lurgan, and Mary was the school's only other teacher. The couple had moved to Lurgan to take over the running of the small country school around 1926, swapping the green fields of Mullingar and their teacher accommodation at Wilson's Hospital for the shores of Lough Neagh and a comfortable headmaster's house. Their young son, Tommy, was two years old at the time of the move, and over the following six years he would be joined by four sisters. The school was a Protestant primary school, or at least not a Catholic one; a state-run establishment that whilst influenced by a general Protestant Christian ethos, was not directly run by the church. Joan and Kathleen were put into class, most likely on the Monday after their arrival in Lurgan, giving them no time at all to adjust to their new environment. Ted was still too young to attend school. We don't know what arrangement was made for his daytime care. Perhaps a neighbour, or a parent of one of the pupils, or a member of Charlie and Mary's local church congregation stepped in to mind him. Or perhaps he was brought to the school anyway, put in a corner and given a small board and some chalk to keep him quiet and occupied. While Kathleen had briefly attended Cloneagh School alongside her sister during their stay in Leitrim just a few months earlier, she would in fact only have been due to start school in Dublin in September 1939, so learning was still a new and fresh experience for her. But being the determined little girl that she was, she probably adapted to school fairly quickly. There would certainly have been no expectations of her, and her lessons may have provided a welcome distraction from the chaos that had so recently ensued. Joan however struggled from the start. There was a supposition that because she was eight and had already been schooled for two years, she would know her times tables by heart, be proficient in her spelling and have reached the standard reading age expected by the Northern Irish education system. But Joan could do none of these things. The teaching system and curriculum was different south of the border, with certain subjects being taught in Irish, something that Charlie and Mary would have been all too aware of. Joan found it difficult to grasp this new way of learning, impeded by grief and fear and an overwhelming, debilitating disorientation. On Friday 3rd March 1939 she had been sitting in class in her Dublin school, surrounded by friends and familiar faces, being taught by a teacher she knew well, one who would have understood the trauma her young pupil had recently experienced. Three days later she found herself in an unfamiliar classroom surrounded by unfamiliar faces talking in an unfamiliar accent. Her teachers were the "aunt and uncle" she had met for the first time just a week or so previously when they had arrived at Errigal Road for a meeting with her father. Their children, her new cousins of a sort, whose names she had barely had the time to learn, all attended the school. In theory, having five new cousins of a similar age should have eased Joan's anxiety, especially as four of them were girls; instant friends, natural protectors, allies who would show her the ropes and take her under their wings. Sadly, it didn't work out that way. Lurgan was not a happy time for Joan.

While his eldest children struggled to make sense of what had just happened and adapt to the latest sudden change in their life, twenty-five miles north, TP was adjusting to his own new lifestyle in Belfast. He moved into lodgings in South Parade, an affluent tree-lined street in the south-east of the city, leaving baby Jack with Harriet, who lived just around the corner in the equally attractive North Parade with her husband, Willy. The couple had three adult children, one son and two daughters, and although we can't be sure if they all still lived at home at that time, we do know the son joined the RAF during the war and was stationed in Japan for a period of time. It is probable that TP asked Harriet and Willy to mind Jack for a short time, just until he got settled and found a place for himself and the 'kiddies', as he called them, to live together as a family. He may even have stayed with the Magill family briefly himself, but the living situation with another adult and a small baby in the house might have proved too stressful for all involved. Perhaps Harriet and Willy asked TP to find lodgings, but agreed to keep Jack temporarily, or possibly TP decided to move out himself, unable to cope with the household routines of a family he barely knew. At least his boarding house was just a few minutes' walk away from the Magill residence, which meant he could see Jack as often as he liked.

In later years, Joan would write that TP was initially employed as a motor mechanic, although his other children can't recall their father ever having much of an interest in cars, never mind an inclination towards repairing them. Regardless of his initial employment, TP settled well into life in Belfast, primarily due to his fellow boarders, a group of student Methodist ministers who were serving out placements at the many Methodist churches in the south-east Belfast area. Having been brought up within the Church of Ireland tradition, Methodism was new to TP. But he took to it quickly, the basic principles of the denomination stirring something in him that would last throughout the rest of his life: abstinence, evangelism, a concern for the underprivileged, the improvement of social conditions, and a personal relationship with God. He had also inadvertently stumbled upon the thing that had been absent from his life since marrying Ciss and becoming a father: community. TP had known the comfort of community with other Protestant men at Wilson's, he had experienced the same thing at the Dublin Home for Boys, and now he had found it again in a boarding house in Belfast. And this unexpected twist of fate most probably saved him, in more ways than one. It is highly likely that by the time Thomas Pakenham left his three eldest children with a family they didn't know in Lurgan, and placed his baby son with a cousin of his mother's whom he didn't know himself, and took a job as a motor mechanic when he barely knew what a car engine looked like, and moved into lodgings with a clatter of strangers who turned out to be Methodist clergymen, he was in the throes of some form of breakdown, or at least teetering on the edge of one. With the luxury of hindsight and the passage of time, it is easy for us now to look back and question why TP did what he did. But in 1939, the man was not of rational mind. How could he have been? His wife had died suddenly and shockingly, shattering their happy family life. He was left on his own with four small children, and while he promised their dying mother to keep the family together, the reality was he simply didn't know how to do that. In his mind he had been driven out of Dublin, forced to leave his job, his home, and most of his possessions behind. With no hands-on support from his immediate family, aside from that brief period of assistance from Florrie, he was forced to rely on the generosity of family members he barely knew, pushing his agenda of rescuing the kiddies from their Catholic fate as motive. That agenda was in part crafted by his associates back in Dublin, but in his anguished and fearful state of mind, he believed it, and when he fled North, with no coherent plan in place for his children, it became a useful justification for his actions.

Since partition, the predominantly Protestant Northern Ireland had become an even more difficult place for Catholic people to live and work, with restricted employment opportunities in certain sectors, inadequate housing provision, and electoral gerrymandering – a prolonged discrimination that history now broadly acknowledges. Many Northern Protestants viewed the Free State with suspicion and derision, and even if they were not actively antagonistic towards their Catholic neighbours, there was often a lingering mistrust. For some, the opportunity to save a Catholic soul, as such, would have been viewed as their moral duty, especially if the souls in question belonged to four small Irish children. That's not to say that the family members and acquaintances who helped TP in the weeks and months following his flight to the North did so with any malevolent intent towards the Beirne family in the South, but they must have bought into his story, and why wouldn't they. It is entirely possible that some even helped him compose it.

So, as TP was restoring some balance to his life in the Methodist boarding house, enjoying no doubt the old familiar comfort of being tended to, with his meals cooked and no household chores to concern himself with, relishing in the company of his new associates, Charlie and Mary in Lurgan and Harriet and Willy just around the corner were looking after his children. Whatever the initial arrangements that had been hastily made with both parties were, they can only have been temporary. And as TP caught his breath, recalibrated, and considered what his next move might be, his children in Lurgan were deeply unhappy, especially Joan. They were dependent on their father's decisions, which so far had not served them well, and unfortunately there were worse and more perplexing ones to come.

CHAPTER 10

"We went to the school where my aunt and uncle taught. I had not started school until I was six and all subjects were taught using Irish. Now everything was different and the adjustment was difficult. I absolutely dreaded going to school, and I can remember so well sitting on the staircase trying to learn English spellings, and then next day in class I couldn't remember them, mainly because of fear. I hated getting caned and felt it was unjust."

Joan was thirty-two years old when she wrote those words, vividly remembering the feelings of dread, anxiety, and confusion that her eight-year-old-self had experienced during her time in Lurgan. She did her best to be a good girl, to keep up in class, to relearn everything in English, to look out for her little sister and brother, to please her aunt and uncle, to not eat too much food, to stay out of her cousin Tommy's way, to not annoy the girl cousins who could have been her friends, but weren't. But as the weeks rolled on, she felt increasingly disturbed, a heavy darkness clinging to her throughout the bright and lengthening days of spring and summer. Of all the children, it was Joan who would most clearly have remembered Ciss at that time; her voice, her mannerisms, the touch of her hand, the shoes she wore, the bread she baked, the rosaries she would recite with her each evening, the scent she wore. It was Joan who may have questioned how delivering a new life could have brought about her mother's death, who would have ached for her each morning as she tied her brother's shoelaces, and each night as she brushed her sister's hair. It was Joan who would have wondered why they had to flee their home, who would have missed her friends and her own bed and her own clothes, remembering the precious First Communion dress she had worn just the year before, stored in a box that sat on the top of her wardrobe. Sometimes, when she was sure that no one was looking, she would climb onto a stool and stand on her tiptoes to reach the box, lift it onto her bed, carefully unwrap the dress, and hold against her chest. She would have missed that dress and all that it represented, a time of joy and hope and family togetherness. It was Joan too who doubtless fretted if she would ever see her grandmother Kate again, and yearned for the baby brother she had not had time to love, whose whereabouts she might not even have known.

It was also Joan who would have worried about the future, about what their father's plans were. Would they return to Dublin and to Errigal Road once he had resolved whatever issue had made him leave? Were they to stay here forever with these people who would never truly feel like family, or would their father find a house for them in Belfast, a house where they could all be together, the baby too? Or did he have another plan entirely, and if so, would it be better than this one, the nightmare she was currently living. Daily punishments were the norm for Joan in Lurgan, caned regularly at school and berated in the house, ridiculed for her accent and teased for her apparent stupidity, persecuted too, perhaps, for her Southern Irish status. She did not make new friends, her girl cousins viewing her with suspicion rather than friendliness. Joan was frightened, confused and lonely, and very sad; weighed down with a sense of responsibility that no eight-year-old should ever have to carry. There was something else at play too, some darker reason for her distress.

While those months in Lurgan must have affected Kathleen and Ted too, neither carried the scars that Joan did. Age protected Ted from remembering his time there, as despite turning four in May, two months into their stay, he was still too young to make a conscious memory. As his big sister Kathleen would tell him in later years, it is probably just as well. How scared he must have been in the weeks following Ciss's death, how confused by so much change and strangeness. How he must have missed the touch of his mother's hand ruffling his hair, dressing him in the morning, bathing him at night. Ted was Ciss's darling boy. She doted on him, perhaps even favoured him a little. He had been a sickly baby, afflicted by colic and a poor digestive system that would trail though his childhood, and by recurrent hives, permitting only his mother to sooth his burning skin by blowing on it. "Mammy blows better" he would say when his father attempted the same technique. This was one of the very few intimate memories of those early years that TP would share with his children. A poor sleeper too, Ciss would indulge Ted's nightly cries, calming him until he finally settled, much to TP's chagrin. Joan would probably have been Ted's comforter when they were at the farm while their grandmother focused on the baby, and again at Lurgan he would have been her responsibility. By then five months had passed and the memory of his mother would have dulled. In another five, any lingering sense of her would most probably have evaporated entirely. But an air of apprehension would have remained, and the seeds of a defiant survival instinct began to take root.

Kathleen would have celebrated a birthday too in Lurgan, her sixth, in the August, but she can't remember it. If there was a fuss made for either herself or Ted, if there was cake to eat or gifts to unwrap, then the celebrations are lost to her. She retained a vague recollection of their time there, a hazy dream-like sense of confusion and separation and of her older sister's distress, an underlying atmosphere of rancour, and a dull awareness that they were not really wanted and were very much in the way. And obviously they *were* in the way, how could they not have been? These three strange children from across the border with their Dublin accents and their wide-eyed stares, clinging to each other, crying at night, taking up space in a house that was already full. After those first few nights, the family would have had to permanently give up a bed, or possibly two, to accommodate them. The Lurgan Pakenham children may have been instructed to share their toys and their clothes with the Dublin Pakenham children, to play with them in the garden whether they felt inclined to or not, to take the two girls under their wings at school. And Charlie and Mary had three more mouths to feed, three more little bodies to dress and supervise and discipline. One week they were a family of seven living comfortably in their nice headmaster's accommodation, following their well-oiled routines and familiar house rules, the next, after a frantic letter from TP and a mercy dash to Dublin, they were suddenly a family of ten. It is highly unlikely that the arrangement Charlie made in haste was supposed to last longer than a week or so, a month perhaps at most.

TP travelled down to Lurgan once every couple of weeks to visit the children and catch up with Charlie, convincing him, perhaps, that plans were afoot, or at least that he was working hard to find a resolution. You might imagine that any resolution under exploration consisted of finding a home to rent for his family. He was working, after all, albeit in a lower paid job than he would have liked. However, TP was settling nicely into his comfortable Belfast boarding house, enjoying both the company and counsel of his new Methodist acquaintances, and with Jack safely established at the Magill's just around the corner, he appeared to be in no rush to find accommodation for his family. To be fair to him, it wouldn't have been easy. Aside from a house, he would have had to organise schooling, and source a housekeeper to tend to the baby and Ted, and find furniture, and purchase clothes and bedding and the general accoutrements that one associates with family life. And he would have had no understanding of how to do just one of those things by himself, never mind all of them. It might be fair to say that few men at that time would have been able to manage such a situation by themselves, but it wasn't unheard of. And as TP had uprooted his children from a familiar home with neighbours to help and family on hand, albeit not his own family, it is also perhaps fair to say that he should have considered the consequences of doing so. We must remember too that the man was in an extremely distressed state during the period following his wife's untimely death, pressurised by both sides of the religious divide, and that both his exodus to the North, and the decision to leave his children with distant relatives, were knee-jerk reactions to the emotional stress he was experiencing. He most probably believed that he was taking the only plausible way out of an intolerable situation, without pausing to fully consider the impact his actions would have on his children.

At some point after the move North, TP declared that the sale of his house in Dublin and all his worldly possessions had been boycotted, presumably by Ciss's brothers and the Knights. As we know though, he never actually owned the house, but to give him the benefit of doubt, let's assume he was in fact referring to a deposit that he had hoped might be returned. Perhaps he had some savings that couldn't be accessed from the North, or perhaps some of his possessions were indeed eventually sold, but for much less than he was anticipating. It is difficult to swallow the notion, however, that Pat and Bernie O'Beirne, who had fought so hard to keep their nieces and nephews within the family and on a Catholic path, who had tried to convince their brother-in-law to leave the baby with their mother, his grandmother, who had offered help and initiated a wage increase for Tommy, would have prevented the sale of any possessions out of malice. In fact, we believe that Pat negotiated with his contacts at the Corporation to allow new tenants to move into Errigal Road, but keep the lease in TPs name, no doubt in the hope that he would come to his senses and return to Dublin. And by the same reasoning, they would have kept most of the family's belongings intact too, ready for the time when their nephews and nieces were back living in their Dublin home. After all, their priority would have been the wellbeing of the children. There would of course have come a time when the possessions were removed; sold or stored or disposed of. We have no idea what became of them. But we do know that the lease of Errigal Road remained in Thomas Pakenham's name until 1952.

TP loved his children, of that there is no question, he simply didn't know how to be a father without a wife. However, as the weeks rolled into months, the contentment he felt living at his digs in South Parade was tempered by a growing concern that something wasn't right in Lurgan. He had noticed Joan's increasingly visible anxiety on his visits. Her wringing hands, her jumpy, nervous temperament, her pale complexion and dark, sunken eyes. Initially he may have passed her behaviour off as a normal reaction to the change in her environment and circumstances, believing that she would settle down in time. But as time did pass, she seemed to diminish even further in stature and spirit, something deeply troubling radiating from her. Her little sister picked up on it too. One of those hazy recollections that Kathleen retained was Joan's ever-present fear.

"Whatever happened to Joan there" she has said, "she was very distressed". Though Joan didn't articulate this anguish to her father on his visits, nor reveal the source of it, TP finally realised just how unhappy his eldest daughter was. Years later he would recount the story of how on one particular visit when Joan entered a room that he was in with Charlie, and perhaps some other members of the family, the look of panic on her face convinced him that something was very wrong.

We will never know for certain the full truth of what happened in Lurgan, but the impact of it stayed with her throughout her life. In one of her letters she wrote the words:

> "Something else besides schoolwork may have contributed to my state, but the mind has wonderful ways of helping one to forget unpleasant things."

Her young mind may have protected her from whatever horrors she had suffered to a degree, but not entirely. And an event that took place some years in the future gives us some insight, perhaps, into what may have occurred. When Joan was nineteen, she worked in the office of Kelly's Coal Merchant in Belfast. One day a young man came into the building asking for her. Spotting him, Joan became visibly distressed and ran to the staff bathroom. Her colleagues told the man to leave and phoned TP at his place of work, asking him to come and take her home which he did. The man in question was in his mid-twenties, and had a Lurgan accent.

Even if TP didn't know the full extent of what was going on with Joan, he did, to his credit, realise that his daughter was at breaking point and that something had to be done. But what? The arrangement at Lurgan was no longer tenable, though most probably not just because of Joan's deteriorating mental state. In all likelihood, TP had not fulfilled his end of the bargain with Charlie and Mary, either foisting his children upon them beyond the agreed timeline, or not contributing sufficient financial compensation, or both. One might think that this would have been the time for TP to find suitable accommodation for the family in Belfast, somewhere small and modest, but a home at least for the five of them. Or perhaps he could have paused for a moment to consider the Beirne family back in Leitrim and the brothers-in-law in Dublin. Would reaching out to them have been the worst thing in the world? There would be an abundance of apologies to make and complicated compromises to thrash out, but wouldn't it be worth it to keep the family together under one roof, just as Ciss had requested? Again, what about his own family, his immediate family, not those on the periphery. Could he not have bitten whichever bullet was preventing him from asking for their hands-on assistance, or challenged whatever rationale was preventing them from offering it? There is obviously the possibility that TP considered one, or even all of these options. He may well have looked for a suitable house to rent, even made enquiries about employing a housekeeper, but realised that such a solution was out of his financial scope. Perhaps he did reach out to some of his siblings or his mother, only to receive a sharp rebuke. He might even have fleetingly considered returning to Dublin, tail between his legs, but the associated humiliation was too much to bear. Or if such a thought did indeed cross his mind, and he shared it with his protestant brethren, he may have been dissuaded from such foolishness, assured that Belfast was the safest place to be. Regardless of what options TP did or did not consider, ultimately, he did none of these things. An alternative solution was presented to him by his fellow boarders in South Parade, the trainee ministers. *There's a Methodist run orphanage in Millisle*, one of them said. *It's on the coast road, not far from Bangor, overlooking the sea.*

CHAPTER 11

Childhaven was an orphanage complex at Millisle on the County Down coast run by the Belfast Central Mission, a Methodist church and charity based at the Grosvenor Hall in Belfast city centre. The main house, some additional buildings, and a few acres of surrounding land had all been donated to Belfast Central Mission in 1928 by a businessman and philanthropist called Hugh Turtle. Turtle was the managing director of McLaughlin & Harvey, the construction company that had rebuilt the Grosvenor Hall the previous year. He owned the house, then a private country residence called Templepatrick House, but having been impressed with the way in which Belfast Central Mission were operating some other children's homes and holiday facilities for underprivileged people in various parts of Northern Ireland, decided to gift his property and land to the charity. After some renovations and additions to the existing buildings, Childhaven opened in 1930, the complex providing an orphanage, a holiday home, a gymnasium, and accommodation for the matron and caretaker. The setting was idyllic. Large attractive buildings set in landscaped gardens, surrounded by green farmland, and overlooking the Irish Sea. The tiny village of Millisle was just a couple of miles down the road on the outer curve of the Ards Peninsula. Donaghadee with its attractive harbour sat a few miles in the other direction, heading towards the bustling seaside holiday town of Bangor and its direct train link to Belfast.

Prior to 1930, Belfast Central Mission had operated several other children's homes and holiday facilities in Northern Ireland, including, ironically, an orphanage on the outskirts of Lurgan. But Craigmore, as the Lurgan home was called, was open only to boys. At any rate, it closed in 1937, when the requirement for such a facility would have been the very last thing TP might have anticipated his own children would ever need. When it closed, the majority of its 40-odd residents were transferred to their new home, the orphanage at Childhaven. And in homage to Craigmore, the holiday home at Childhaven became Craigmore House.

We can't know for sure how the move from Lurgan to Millisle for Joan, Kathleen and Ted came about, but let's assume that when the idea of putting his three eldest children into an orphanage was first suggested to TP, he would have instinctively railed against it. His children were not orphans after all, and growing up himself in the grand surrounds of Tullynally Castle, the notion of an orphanage must have deeply troubled him. But with no other option on the table, gradually his mind was changed. Through his friends at the boarding house, TP was becoming increasingly involved with the Methodist church. They had introduced him to the Grosvenor Hall and the work of the Belfast Central Mission, encouraging him to attend mission meetings and church services. He found himself developing new relationships, not just with these men of God and members of the church congregations, but with God himself. His inherent Christian beliefs were reignited and Methodism became his religious home, the peg on which he would hang his spiritual hat for the remainder of his life. And so, when the mention of Childhaven was quietly put to him a second time, and then perhaps a third, by people he respected, people who had listened to his story without judgement and offered him both counsel and assistance, he in turn listened to them. He may have even taken a trip to Millisle to see the facility for himself. And if he did, he would most likely have been quickly reassured. A grand dwelling in the countryside overlooking the water. Space for his kiddies to run around and breathe in fresh sea air. Other children to play with, some true orphans, some like them just partial ones. And a school just down the road. It was perfect. And more to the point, if any of the Dublin O'Beirnes or the Beirnes of Leitrim came north in search of the children, they would never think to look in an orphanage run by a Methodist mission. It is possible too that when he first heard about Childhaven, he decided there and then that this orphanage was the solution to his problem and set about putting a plan in motion to move the children there as soon as possible. Either way, strings were no doubt pulled by someone, as to place three new children in the home at the click of a finger can't have been entirely straightforward. There may have been a slight wait once the deal was done, so to speak, or there may have been another mercy dash to remove them from Lurgan, but in September 1939, six months after they were whisked away from their Dublin home and left with a family they didn't know, Joan, Kathleen and Ted were relocated and abandoned once again; this time in an orphanage.

There is no doubt that Childhaven and institutions like it were created with the very best of intentions, with a Christian spirit and a genuine desire to do good work. The Belfast Central Mission has always been, and remains to this day, an upstanding organisation that exists to help those in need, regardless of background, race, or religion. And Childhaven was indeed a sanctuary for a great many children who had no family and no other means of being cared for. But as with all such institutions, it had issues: limitations at best, negligence at worst. And for the Pakenham children, well, they couldn't have arrived at a more challenging time for the home; the onset of war. However, in spite of the trauma they had been through in the months before moving to Childhaven, the first couple of years that Joan, Kathleen and Ted spent at the orphanage were relatively settled ones. To say they were happy would be a stretch, but they were content. Once they became familiar with the home and its rules, with the staff and the other children, they eased into the routines of their new life. There were no more unpleasant or frightening surprises, at least for a while. Naturally, they each had distinctly individual experiences at the orphanage and in later life would assess their time there very differently, just as all children growing up in a regular home environment with siblings do. Some of the memories they retained are collective, some are intensely personal. Some are as vivid as the day they were made, and some will remain locked away forever.

The building that housed the orphans was a large double fronted house, built at the turn of the 20th century. There were four dormitory style bedrooms, two for girls and two for boys, none of which seemed to be occupied by distinct age groups. It seems that children younger than four were not accommodated at Childhaven and most of the occupants left by the age of fourteen, although there is evidence that in certain instances some young people stayed until they were eighteen. When they arrived, Joan and Kathleen were not placed in the same room, a bewildering decision given the trauma the two little girls had been through in the previous year. Ted, who at just four years and four months must have been one of the youngest residents at the time, was put into the smaller of the boy's dorms, alongside boys much older than he was. His very first conscious memory is sitting on the lawn at the front of the house, the sun shining in his eyes, the sound of other children playing around him. He doesn't know when that particular moment occurred, or if it is an amalgamation of similar fragmented memories, but he believes it was in the early weeks or months at Millisle, certainly during the time when life at Childhaven was still, as he describes it, "comfortable." Kathleen and Joan both remembered the early months at the orphanage as relatively comfortable ones too. A pragmatic child with a fiery spirit, Kathleen developed a thick skin and a survival instinct from too young an age, mechanisms that helped her adapt to and survive her tumultuous circumstances. She didn't love the orphanage, she was still confused by the turn in their circumstances, but she recognised that her big sister was happier, and that made her feel steadier too. Joan was simply relieved to be free from the horrors of Lurgan, initially at any rate. It may not have been what she yearned for, to live as a family again, and she still couldn't understand why they were separated from their father and baby brother, but she felt able to breathe again. Even school was better.

School was Millisle National School, a twenty or thirty-minute walk from Childhaven, depending on what way the coastal wind was blowing. The small school taught children from the village, the surrounding farms and countryside, and the orphanage, and during the war it would also welcome a number of young Jewish refugees. Joan and Kathleen were enrolled upon their move to Childhaven, joining the other children from the orphanage in their daily crocodile style walk to and from the school, whatever the weather. It had two classrooms, one for children under eight, taught by Mrs Mawhinney, and the second for pupils eight years and upwards, taught by the headmaster, Mr Palmer. Baldy Palmer, as he was cheekily referred to by several generations of pupils, was extremely strict. He had a particular penchant for maths, with limited patience for pupils who didn't respond well to the subject, and according to all of the Pakenham children was excessively free with the cane, displaying a routine, casual cruelty. But they also acknowledge that he was an excellent teacher. Although she was almost nine years old and by rights should have gone straight into the senior class, Mr Palmer permitted Joan to enter the junior class when she first arrived at the school. A conversation must have been had about her difficulties at Lurgan, the challenges she had encountered during the previous year, and the fact that some of her early schooling had been in Irish. Whether that conversation was between Mr Palmer and TP, or with the matron at Childhaven, we do not know, but it seems the matron, Miss Ludlow, kept a close eye on Joan in the early days. She reportedly told TP that if he had left his daughter in Lurgan much longer she would have suffered a complete mental breakdown. The decision to place Joan in the younger class paid off, as she recalls in one of her letters.

> *"This time I was not put into a class of children my own age, but started at the bottom in a lower class and worked my way up. Then some months later I was moved up. A big sheet on the wall showed everyone's position in the class, using stars. The sense of achievement I experienced when I got to the top! I think I was about 10 before I caught up with the others of the same age and that was by skipping one full year. Then, when I was 13, I was put into a special class with three boys to study for a scholarship. I had really triumphed over my late start."*

Kathleen was relatively happy at school too. It was a haven of sorts away from the orphanage, a place where she had, perhaps, more of a sense of belonging. She made friends at school and got to see glimpses of "normal" life outside of the orphanage environment. And ironically, what she saw wasn't always entirely appealing.

"We thought we were hard done by living in an orphanage," she recalls, "but my friend Jean McCauley who sat beside me had it worse. She lived on a farm and was up every morning at six o'clock to milk the cows before coming to school. She was forever falling asleep, and I was forever nudging her to waken her up before Baldy Palmer noticed. Dear love her."

That generosity of spirit, the ability to recognise that there was always someone worse off than herself, even if it wasn't entirely the case, carried Kathleen through her childhood. After all, poor Jean McCauley may have had to rise from her bed every morning at an unearthly hour to milk the cows, but on the flip side, she lived in a family unit with her mother and father and siblings, and she never went hungry. Kathleen's magnanimous attitude perhaps helped her to block out some of the most harrowing things that happened to her over the years. To this day she remains more concerned about how Joan, Ted and Jack fared through those traumatic years, than how she herself was affected.

Ted is a little bit like Kathleen in that respect. Rational, calm and level-headed, he has always been someone who puts his head down and pushes forward, determinedly dealing with whatever comes next; a survival instinct he began to mould at the tender age of three when his beloved mother died, and one that helped him to cope with a devastating tragedy in adulthood. He would have been too young to attend school when he arrived at Childhaven, as the national school starting age was five. We don't know how he spent his first year at the orphanage. He has no memory of not being at school while his sisters were, and they had no recollection of him being left alone at the house. Of course Matron and the other staff would have been there, and perhaps there was even another four-year-old child to play with, but it's unlikely that he would have had round the clock attention during school hours. When he did eventually start school, he too relished it, discovering that he loved to learn. He developed a particular aptitude for maths, and for drawing too. He was regularly caned by Baldy Palmer, for one reason or another, or no reason at all, but learning, gathering knowledge, and acquiring new skills became Ted's armour.

All things considered, life at Childhaven was bearable to begin with. There was no love and no nurturing, but the three children were at least provided with clean clothes and bedding, had space to run around in, and were given sufficient food to eat. The food may not have been particularly appetising, but it was edible, and there was enough of it. Plus they didn't feel they were depleting another family's provisions. They gradually became accustomed to the routines of this new life and looked forward to the fortnightly visits from their father who cycled the forty-odd-mile round trip from Belfast every other Saturday to see his three eldest children.

And then the war that had been rumbling in the background since their arrival at Childhaven took a turn, and everything changed again.

CHAPTER 12

As Joan, Kathleen and Ted were acclimatising to life in the orphanage, up in Belfast, baby Jack was facing another change in his care and routine. On his first birthday in September 1939 he was still living with the Magills in North Parade. We believe he remained there for several months after that, perhaps even another full year. There is a photograph taken on the beach at Millilse in the early summer of 1940. It shows five adults and four young children lined up in the sunlight. The adults are the Magills; Harriet, her husband Willy, and their three adult children. Harriet is holding Jack in her arms, a toddler of around twenty months with wispy curls and an inquisitive expression. Her son is holding Ted who would have recently turned five. He is small for his age, but sturdy. Joan is nine, coming ten that autumn, and Kathleen will soon turn seven. The girls are wearing pale coloured simple summer dresses. They stand tightly beside each other, Kathleen squinting at the camera, Joan unsmiling, her head pensively titled. There are other photos from that day. Jack and Ted sat on the long leather front seat of a car, Jack's hand on the steering wheel, the sisters leaning over from the backseat. And another of TP with his children standing on a grassy verge, the sea in the background. He is holding Jack up to keep him from falling, the three eldest stand slightly in front. TP is the only one smiling at the camera.

Jack in the arms of Harriet meeting his siblings shortly after the three older children entered Childhaven.
Also in the photo are Willy, Harriet's husband, their daughter Dorothy, their son Bertie and his wife.

Although TP visited the children regularly, this must have been a very special occasion, a rare day trip in a motor car with the baby and his unofficial foster family joining them. It may have been the first time that Joan, Kathleen and Ted had seen their little brother since their move to Childhaven the previous September, possibly even the first full family reunion since their father had left them in Lurgan some sixteen months earlier and headed to Belfast with Jack. Joan, Kathleen and Ted would have been strangers to Jack, and he to them. Only Joan would have clearly remembered the rounding of their mother's stomach just two short years before as a baby grew inside it. Only she would have fully recalled the sudden shift in atmosphere within their Dublin home, as the joy at the arrival of a new life was replaced with a fear and a tension she could not interpret, and the horror of everything that followed. How confusing it must have been to see him again, now walking and talking and growing into a little boy; a boy who was cared for by another family of strangers. Her brother, but not her brother. There may have been a tour of the orphanage, the children showing the visitors their neatly made beds and the dining room with the long communal table and the garden where they played with other orphans and unfortunates. Perhaps they walked on the beach and were allowed, on this occasion, to dip their feet into the water. They might have had a picnic on the sand, or perhaps the party descended on Mrs Moffat's Tearooms in the village, where TP sometimes took the children for a treat on his solo Saturday visits. And then, when the afternoon drew to a close, the three children would have stood on the lawn waving their father and brother and the nice strangers off, before returning to their orphan lives. What a strange and disconcerting experience it must have been, seeing their little brother seemingly embraced in the luxury of a normal family life, a life they were not allowed to have. No doubt their father had explained the situation many times, so they would have understood that Jack was not living with him. But still, he lived in a proper house and was being cared for by family of a sort, people who seemed to adore him at any rate. And their father lived close by; close enough to see him every day if he so chose.

But up in Belfast, all was not quite as straightforward as it seemed in TP's setup. We don't know what happened next; whether there was a falling out between TP and the Magills, or if an amicable agreement was made, but sometime in late 1940 or early 1941, Jack was moved again. Perhaps the Magills had enough of raising someone else's child and challenged TP to care for his son himself. They may even have suggested, prompted by their visit to Millilse, that it was time for him to become a proper father to *all* of his children; that he should find somewhere suitable for them to live together and be a family again. Or maybe caring for Jack had simply become too much for them due to illness, or for financial reasons. Or possibly Harriet became a grandmother and had to devote her attention to her own grandchildren. We could theorise all day long and never hit on the truth of the matter, but whatever the reason, Jack was taken from his unofficial foster family in North Parade and placed with "official" foster parents, a Mr and Mrs Jenkins, who lived somewhere in the same vicinity, possibly in Well Street just off Shamrock Street. At least the story told was that the Jenkins' became Jack's official fosterers, but the arrangement may in fact have been an unofficial one, facilitated by the Belfast Central Mission, of which TP was now an active member. Again, we don't have many details about the Jenkins family, aside from the fact that they were a middle-aged couple with a daughter in her late teens called Edie, and a son who was old enough to enlist in the Royal Navy. Jack's first vague sense of a memory goes back to this time. He has a hazy recollection of the Jenkins boy, tall and broad, all dressed up in his naval uniform, presumably before heading off to war, throwing his naval cap in the air then placing it on Jack's little head. And there's another touch of a memory, the smell of cement from an air raid shelter being built close by. He knows that the family were good to him; kind and loving and affectionate, and he remembers feeling safe, in spite of the carnage happening in the outside world. We believe Jack lived with the Jenkins family for a year or two, probably closer to two, and then he was moved again. And this time we do know the reason why: the Jenkins asked if they could adopt him, and when they put their proposal to TP, he panicked. In his head he still believed he was fulfilling Ciss's dying wish of keeping the family together, even though the five of them were spread across three different locations. To be fair to TP, if he had been able to send Jack to Childhaven with the others, he most likely would have. But the orphanage didn't take babies, so he had no choice but to find a temporary solution for Jack until such time as Childhaven would accept him. He hoped, as with Ted, it would be before his school starting age, but he would need to be patient. The Magills had been a perfect solution, until suddenly they weren't. Then the Jenkins seemed to be a lucky find, until they threw an unexpected spanner in the works with their adoption request. Again, we can't be sure of the precise timings, nor do we know exactly how things panned out, but we can surmise that TP came up with another spur-of-the-moment plan. He removed Jack from the Jenkins' home, took him out of Belfast, and placed him in the temporary safety of another family member. This time the good Samaritan was his sister Etta who lived in Poyntzpass, a small village a few miles outside the border town of Newry, where she lived with her husband William Porterfield, the resident station master, and their five children. Aside from the very short time Florrie had spent at Errigal Road after Ciss's death, this was the first hands-on help TP had received from any of his immediate family. When Jack arrived in Poyntzpass towards the end of 1942, he would have just turned four, his conscious memories starting to properly form. For the first time in his little life he found himself living in a traditional family environment, with an aunt and uncle who were around the same age as his own father, and cousins who played with him as though they were his siblings. He struck up an instant friendship with Wesley, the youngest of the Porterfields, forming a bond that would last for years. Jack was a spirited little boy, full of adventure and pent-up energy that, in the freedom that the expansive fields around Poyntzpass Station presented, could finally be released. Suffice to say, the two boys got up to some mischief together. They would run along the railway tracks, an area that was strictly out of bounds, and play in the empty wagons. On one occasion Jack slipped climbing into one of the wagons, and was saved from injury, or worse, because the back of his trousers caught in a metal hook, leaving him dangling in mid-air. And then there was the day he and Wesley decided it would be a good idea to throw water onto the open fire in the station waiting room, just to see what would happen. Only the water wasn't water, it was petrol, and the two boys both ended up with singed eyebrows and some minor burns. Another lucky escape. Etta and William may have been at their wits end with these two unruly small boys to control, but for Jack, Poyntzpass was a sort of paradise. He was tremendously happy there.

Again we don't know the exact timings or circumstances of Jack's move to Childhaven, but we think it happened around March 1943 when he was four and a half years old. In all probability, his move to Poyntzpass was always intended to be short-term; just until he was closer to school age and a space became available at the orphanage. Yet as with Ted, it seems he was living at Childhaven for a few months before he was old enough to join Millisle National School. Maybe Etta had enough and insisted TP take Jack back, leaving her brother to look to his Methodist associates once again for help. Or perhaps TP felt it was time to have all four of his children in the same place and certain strings were pulled to bring the little boy to Millisle early. In his four short years of life so far, poor Jack had been mothered by four different women; his grandmother Kate, Harriet Magill, Mrs Jenkins, and his aunt Etta. Four attachments formed and abruptly ended. Four different pairs of hands changing and bathing and feeding him. Four different voices soothing his cries. The trauma of so many bonds made and severed in those crucial development years would leave a lifelong imprint on Jack's soul, and there was worse to come. Jack entered a very different Childhaven to the one his brother and sisters had encountered when they first arrived at the orphanage. The dormitories were overcrowded with many of the residents now older boys. The house was noisy and disorganised. Chaos ensued, with little attention to discipline or structure. Bedding was sparse, clothing was scant, and toys were locked away. Hygiene was questionable, all sense of comfort had disappeared, and worst of all, there wasn't enough food to eat.

In the Spring of 1941, Belfast was bombed by the German Luftwaffe in four sustained and devastating attacks. During what became known as the Docks Raid on 7th and 8th April, the Easter Raid on 15th and 16th April, the Fire Raid on 5th May, and the Final Raid on 6th May, the Belfast Blitz reduced the city to a shell. Almost 1,000 civilians died, with thousands more injured, and 50,000 homes, more than half of the city's housing capacity, were damaged. As a result, there were over 200,000 displaced people in Belfast, many of whom were children. The Belfast Central Mission, along with many other charities, churches, and philanthropic organisations, stepped in to do what they could to help. And with the very best of intentions, it sent a contingency of desperate children to Childhaven. Most of those children would have been traumatised by what they had seen and heard and lost during the Blitz. Some had become genuine orphans, some may have lost one parent, or a grandparent, or even a sibling.

Others would have watched as their home, or entire street, collapsed into a pile of rubble. Twenty-five miles down the coast, the children already resident in Childhaven had stood on the beach opposite the home, at the mouth of the underground tunnel that ran from the road to the shore and served as a make-shift air raid shelter, and watched as Belfast burned in the distance. Each of their young lives had already changed in one dramatic way or another, which is why they had ended up in Millisle in the first place. Some, like the Pakenham children, had encountered several traumatic turns. But they had become accustomed to life at the orphanage. The sight of the flames turning the night sky deep red, and the noise of the planes dropping their bombs, brought to them over the water's breeze, would have scared and unsettled the children. Joan and Kathleen may have fretted about their father, Ted still too young to do so. But they could not have foreseen how the bombs in the distance would impact them. They could not have guessed that their lives were about to upended yet again, this time by the arrival of the children from Belfast.

CHAPTER 13

Let us rewind slightly here and look again at TP's life in Belfast during these years, from the time he left his three eldest children in Lurgan in March 1939, to the day he brought their little brother to join them at the orphanage in the spring of 1943. We know he moved into digs in South Parade and became close to his fellow boarders, the Methodist ministers. We know that baby Jack was living just around the corner with Harriet Magill and her family. And we think he initially got a job as a car mechanic, despite having no experience in the trade. We are aware that he travelled to Derryadd every few weeks to visit Joan, Kathleen and Ted. We know too that he became aware of Joan's increasing distress, and realised that the plan hastily devised in Dublin to leave his children with Charlie Pakenham in Lurgan for as long as was necessary, was no longer viable. At least at that stage, the decision to place Jack with the Magill family was still working well. We believe he talked with and confided in his new clergymen friends, and subsequently became involved with Belfast Central Mission, resulting in the construction of his next plan. And it is probable that when that plan was executed, and his eldest three children were placed in an orphanage, Thomas Pakenham was not entirely of sound mind.

A month after TP left three of his children at Childhaven, and almost a year to the day after Ciss had died, he wrote that letter of testimony detailing his account of what happened in the weeks leading up to the family's flight north. It was a story he must have gone over in his head almost every day since leaving Dublin; one that he had no doubt relayed on multiple occasions, to the Pakenhams of Lurgan, to the Magills in Belfast, to his mother and brother and sisters in Westmeath, to his landlady in South Parade, to the Methodist ministers, and to the people who welcomed him into their fold at Belfast Central Mission. Even, quite possibly, to the matron and caretaker at Childhaven orphanage. It's also entirely possible that he was encouraged to write such a letter by some or all of the above-mentioned associates. Certain individuals may have collaborated with him in the writing of it, or coached him on what to say. The letter was typed, marked with some edits in his handwriting, an indication, perhaps, that the words were not entirely his own. We will never know for certain, but the letter itself was a well-rehearsed explanation, with dates and details, and the names of the relevant players involved; a statement, almost, of defence, written with a peculiar detachment.

> *"I have been asked so often why I left a good job, my home, furniture, etc in Dublin,"* he begins, *"that I have decided to write my story, giving only the merest of details…"*

Although it was written at a time when TP was still grieving the loss of his wife, and the loss of his children too, as though still alive, they were no longer living with him, the only real sense of emotion that comes through in the letter is anger; a smouldering rage at the wrongdoing he believed he had been subjected to by Kate Beirne and her sons. There is also an underlying paranoia throughout. He details the visits to Errigal Road by Pat and Bernie and their associates from the Knights, and his mercy dash to Cashel to retrieve Jack, and the pay rise at work, and the meetings with Johnston, Hick and co., and the plan that was hatched to smuggle them all out of Dublin. He certainly does not voice a shred of remorse or regret, nor any hint that he wishes things had turned out differently. In fact, in the concluding paragraph, he appears to suggest that everything he did, he did for God.

> *"I do not look for any credit for the way in which the situation was handled – this belongs to God, who guided and helped me through every detail. I hope and pray that my children and I will be able to thank Him by dedicating our lives to His service."*

And that is where the letter stops, with no reference to the fact that contrary to abiding by his deceased wife's wishes, he had not in fact kept their family together. He does not mention that the baby is now being cared for by his mother's cousin in Belfast. He does not reveal that the three eldest children have been placed in an orphanage. He does not mention that he himself is now mostly living the life of a bachelor man.

Aside from being an attempt to plead his case for absconding with the children, the letter, if he did write it himself with no outside influences, may in part have been driven by guilt, even if he didn't fully realise it. Guilt at leaving the place where his children's mother was buried, guilt at removing them from their entire Beirne family connection, and most of all, guilt at abandoning them, at placing them in care. But to acknowledge that guilt would have meant conceding that his actions had been hasty, misguided, and not at all in the children's best interests. And to admit to that would have left him humiliated, or compelled him perhaps to bundle the children into another accomplice's car and deliver them back to Dublin or to Cashel.

Whatever the truth behind the letter, it is clear that a year on from Ciss's death, TP's mind was still in turmoil, his decision making still driven by paranoia. For years he harboured an anxiety that the children might be found by a search party dispatched from Dublin or Leitrim. The three in the orphanage were probably safe enough as no one would think to look for them there, but in the early years he was particularly nervous about Jack. After all, it was the baby Kate specifically wanted to keep and rear herself. And so he changed Jack's name. For a period of time, John Hubert Norman Pakenham became Jack Bleakley, adopting the pet name given to him after birth, and his paternal grandmother's maiden name. Presumably TP would have had to file new papers of some description for the family when they fled North, and while we don't know how far he progressed this, we do know that when ration cards were issued to all UK citizens in 1940, Jack's bore the name Jack Bleakley.

With the eldest three safely tucked away in Millilse, and Jack secure just around the corner, TP ploughed on with this new life of his. He would see Jack a couple of times a week, and cycled to Millilse every other Saturday to visit the eldest children. He also got another job, one much more suited to his skills and qualifications, and with the company he had previously worked for in Dublin when he first met Ciss – Edison Swan. It appears he began working as a bookkeeper in the company's Belfast office on Royal Avenue within a year of settling in the city. Indeed, he would remain with the firm through various different guises and name changes, including Walsall Conduits and GEC, until he finally retired at the grand age of seventy. More content in his professional life, TP also forged a deeper connection with the Methodist church and the Belfast Central Mission, his devotion to God intensifying.

As the war gathered pace, TP became an official Air Raid Patrol Warden in the area of south-east Belfast where he and Jack both lived. Before the Blitz, there were only 200 public air raid shelters built across Belfast, not a significant amount for the UK's most densely populated city, and a principal port at that. Many people took matters into their own hands, erecting makeshift bunkers made from sheets of corrugated iron covered in mounds of earth in their gardens, streets, and parks. Several shelters, both official and unofficial, popped up in Ormeau Park, a large public park close to North and South Parade, and the streets that laced around it. This was TP's patch. He patrolled the area night after night through the horror of the Blitz bombings and for the remainder of the war years, receiving a medal for his service at the end of the conflict. It gave him a sense of purpose at that time. It would become evident over the years that purpose was something TP thrived on, and, as we will see, it drove him to do great work in various organisations and sections of society. Sadly however, his magnanimous spirit did not always extend to his own children. Perhaps without the guidance of his wife, and lacking a close relationship with his mother and sisters, he sometimes simply found it easier to be a friend to society than a hands-on father.

The Blitz and its aftermath present another puzzle, another peculiarity in TP's thinking. Thousands of children were evacuated from the city following the first bombing, and more with each subsequent attack. And yet Jack, it seems, remained in Belfast. In his role with the Air Raid Patrol, TP would have witnessed first-hand the devastation that the German bombings were wreaking on Belfast. Entire streets less than a mile away from North and South Parade were completely destroyed, resulting in multiple casualties and deaths. Surely this would have been the time to dispatch Jack to his sister Etta in Poyntzpass? Or even consider taking the toddler to the guaranteed safety of a farm in the Leitrim countryside. But it seems that Jack stayed in Belfast for another year at least. TP would also have been aware of the changes at Childhaven following the Blitz attacks. He would have known about the influx of refugees and orphans from Belfast, the number of residents at the orphanage doubling in size virtually overnight. On his Saturday visits his children must have complained. They must have told him about the overcrowded bedrooms, the bad behaviour of some of the new boys, the increasingly alarming lack of food. He must surely have noticed a change in their demeanour, their increasingly dishevelled appearance, a thinning of their frames. He must have witnessed a change in the house, sensed the chaos, seen the disorder. And yet, they too stayed where they were.

Once again, it is easy for us to look at TP with a critical eye from the comfort of hindsight and question his decision making, easy to look at the options we might have expected him to consider. Somewhere for him and the children to live together for a start, a house to rent outside of Belfast, in the surrounding countryside perhaps, or the seaside town of Bangor. Or dispatching all of the children to his sister Etta in Poyntzpass, at least temporarily. Or taking them back to Kate in Leitrim, cap in hand, with the express understanding that it was for the duration of the war only, and that once peace was restored, they would be making their lives in Belfast. He might have enlisted the help of one of his other sisters or his brother Edward, or considered his own mother; a short-term stay at her generously sized cottage on the grounds of Tullynally surely not out of the question. The Pakenhams of Pakenham Hall had always been good to TP's family, and especially kind to TP himself, and a letter to his boyhood friend Frank Pakenham, whose brother Edward was then the sitting Earl, asking for help would most probably have been well received. Perhaps he did look at some or even all of these options, but concluded that none were viable. It was wartime after all, and housing was scarce. Thousands of people who had fled Belfast were looking for temporary accommodation outside of the city, and it would have been foolhardy to take on a house in the capital that might be destroyed at any moment. Etta had her own family to consider, with no room or financial resources for four more to care for. His other siblings were either in the same position or didn't live in their own homes, and he couldn't call on the Pakenhams of Lurgan again. Pride and a lingering resentment would have prevented Kate from being a valid option, not even a last resort. As for his own mother, perhaps he imagined the children would be in danger there, that word might somehow seep through to Leitrim or Dublin and they would be snatched away by the brothers-in-law; that the peril they faced in a house in Belfast and an orphanage in Millisle was less of a risk. Whatever his reasoning, he believed he was doing his best for the children, a conviction he would steadfastly stand by for the rest of his life.

CHAPTER 14

As TP patrolled the streets of Belfast, the sirens wailing, the sound of German planes approaching in the distance, as Harriet Magill clutched young Jack to her chest in the crowded concrete air raid shelter, and as Joan, Kathleen and Ted stood on a County Down beach, their little gas masks dangling from their hands, watching the black night sky turn red from the flames of a burning Belfast, back in Cashel, Kate Beirne was suffering her own kind of hell.

When TP fled with the children, he left no forwarding address, or at least none that would have been shared with the Beirne family. The only people who knew where he was going were TP's Dublin associates, Mr Hick, Mr Johnston and Mr Sharman, and nothing short of violence would have enticed them to reveal their friend's whereabouts. Perhaps not even that. Of course to begin with the only address they would have had was Charlie Pakenham's, as TP's plans beyond Lurgan were still uncertain at the time of his departure. And if Pat and Bernie even considered launching a search party, it's unlikely they would have known where to start. They might have suspected their brother-in-law had headed North, as indeed implied in Aunt Brigie's letter, but to where exactly, and to whom? Charlie and Mary were not actively involved in the lives of Ciss and TP and would not have been visitors at their Dublin home; to any of the Dublin homes they had lived in during their marriage. In all probability Ciss had never met the couple, and Kate and her sons would have known nothing about them. There may well have been visits to the Dublin office of Hick and Sharman by Pat and Bernie, the brothers passionately insisting they be told where the family had gone, threats made, pressure applied from the Knights. Priests would have been consulted in Dublin and Leitrim too to see if they could offer any help, but all to no avail. The family had vanished, and as the children were in the care of their father, there was no legal recourse. And so Kate was left with nothing of her only daughter, who lay in a cemetery too far from home to visit, her grave still not graced with a headstone. The anguish she must have felt is unimaginable; a recent widow, two sons and her only daughter dead, and now four of her grandchildren missing. But she refused to give up hope and prayed every day for their safe return, the rituals of the daily rosary becoming her crutch.

As the months passed with no news of the children, the likelihood that they were somewhere in the North became ever more probable. And as 1939 rolled into 1940, Kate's thoughts would have turned to the war. While Ireland remained formally neutral throughout WW2, or The Emergency, as it was referred to, the country wasn't unaffected by the conflict. It was universally acknowledged that Eire was unofficially more sympathetic to the Allies than the Axis, and thousands of Irish citizens joined the British Armed forces, many losing their lives. The country didn't escape unscathed either, suffering several German bombing raids between August 1940 and July 1941, and whilst the resulting casualties and loss of life weren't on the same scale that Belfast would experience, the attacks were traumatising for ordinary Irish people. Kate would have worried about her family in Dublin, her family at home, and her family in England. And while she fretted too about the whereabouts of her missing grandchildren and whether or not they were safe, fate dealt her another blow. Sometime before Ciss died, Michael, Kate's sixth-born child, had grown tired of his job at O'Hara's hardware store in Dromod, and moved to London.

He wanted adventure and money, and figured the best way to do both was to work in a busy London pub. He quickly got a job managing a bar in Holborn, and then, to the horror and bewilderment of his mother and brothers, when the war started, he enlisted as a driver with the Royal Army Service Corps Regiment of the British Army. Though Michael tried to convince his family that the money was worth it, having a British solider in the family caused as much consternation as Ciss marrying a Protestant had. It was unimaginable. But Kate loved her son, and her concern for his wellbeing overrode her fury. On a visit home in July 1940 she begged him to stay. He could get his old job back at O'Hara's she pleaded, or go to Dublin and get something there. Money wasn't everything. He hugged her and told her not to worry, his duties were land based in Oxford, he'd be fine. Three weeks later, on 20th August, a bomb exploded on the base. The truck Michael was driving overturned and he was killed instantly, his body interred at Botley Cemetery in Oxfordshire.

And so Kate was plunged into mourning yet again, four of her children now dead while she still breathed. This was not the natural order of things. Alongside her grief, the distress at not knowing where her grandchildren were intensified. Imagine how she must have felt on hearing about the first Belfast bombing spree on the 8th of April 1941, wondering if the children were in the city at the time, if they had been hurt, or worse, praying for some news. Then the second raid hit on Easter Tuesday, a sacred time of year, and the rush of fear and worry would have almost suffocated her once again. And then another unthinkable tragedy occurred. On Thursday 1st of May, three days before the third air raid on Belfast, Terence (Anthony) died at home on the farm after contracting TB, just as his brother John Joe had done. Four children now, her husband, and four grandchildren lost to her in the space of three short years, and a fifth child already dead before that. There is another striking paragraph in great aunt Brigie's letter, one that comes after the assertion that Ciss's husband was up North, rearing their children as good Protestants. It catalogues some of the other losses Kate had endured:

> *"John Joe and Anthony died at home. Mike was blown up in England during one of the raids. Tom is in England too. Ned is married at home to a daughter of Paddy Molloy. Albert is still living. Eddie, the father, died suddenly a couple of years ago. Kate, Mrs Beirne, is there in Mohill, bent to the ground with trouble at her big family."*

How could Kate Beirne not have been bent to the ground with her troubles. That she did not end up in the grave where Edward and three of her sons were buried is a miracle. We can only assume it was the hope of seeing Joan, Kathleen, Ted and little Jack again that kept her alive, a hope that was never extinguished.

CHAPTER 15

When Jack moved into Childhaven, it became the sixth place he had lived in his short life – the farm, Errigal Road, South Parade, The Jenkins' home, Poyntzpass, and now the orphanage. Seven, if you count Lurgan, even if only for a very short while. Spirited and inquisitive with an abundance of nervous energy, the constant movement and lack of continuity must surely have affected him. Although he had been to Millilse a couple of times before his move to Childhaven, on that visit with the Magills in the summer of 1940, and again with his father just a few weeks beforehand, he didn't really know his siblings at all, nor they him. With no regular contact, Joan, Kathleen and Ted had all but forgotten their little brother. As the eldest, Joan may have thought about him from time to time and remembered him in her prayers, fretting a little about how he was doing, wishing perhaps that the four of them could be together. Or she might have thanked God that he wasn't at Childhaven, that he was enjoying the freedom of a life outside of the orphanage, war besides, a regular life with a regular family, even if that family wasn't theirs. Kathleen may have remembered him too a little; a vague recollection of the baby that vanished then reappeared, then vanished again. Ted had no memory of Jack at all. He was almost eight when his father arrived at Childhaven one Saturday afternoon on one of his regular visits with little Jack in tow. The five of them took the bus from the orphanage into Millilse for tea at Mrs Moffat's. Ted sat beside Jack on the short journey, his little brother nonchalantly punching at his arm and shoulder, as little brothers do.

"If that wee fella doesn't stop hitting me, I'm going to have to hit him back," Ted told his father impatiently. That was his first real memory of Jack, the realisation that this annoying "wee fella" who was a bit too ready with his fists was actually his brother not yet quite dawning. They were probably all informed that day that Jack would soon be coming to live at Childhaven too, TP no doubt making it sound like an exciting development, or at least a happy one. And in many respects, it was, as the four children would finally be living together again for the first time since the couple of months they had spent on the farm. TP was in one way fulfilling his promise to Ciss, just removing himself from the equation. But realistically, any claim that they'd be living *together* was a bit of a stretch. Living under the same roof was a more appropriate description.

By the time Jack became a resident at Childhaven, the orphanage had changed immeasurably from when his siblings had first arrived. The influx of orphans and evacuees from Belfast, coupled with an intake of young Jewish refugees, had altered everything. There weren't enough basics to go around, from beds and linen to uniforms and school supplies. And there wasn't enough food. There was also a distinct lack of discipline. Jack hated it from the start. He arrived with the bare basics, as would most of the children who moved into the orphanage. Like his siblings, Jack didn't have many possessions of his own, but at some point, someone had given him a small toy submarine. It may have been a birthday present from the Magills, or a treat in his stocking the previous Christmas. Or maybe it was a parting gift from his cousin Wesley when he left Poyntzpass. However he acquired it, he was attached to the little submarine, proud of it, and on his arrival, he made a point of showing it off. One of the older boys snatched it from him and snapped it in half, laughing in his little face. That was Jack's first memory of Childhaven, his introduction to orphanage life. He was initially put into Kathleen's dormitory, where he slept in a small makeshift bed beside hers. Why he was paired with Kathleen and not Joan we don't know, another baffling decision. Possibly there was simply more space in Kathleen's dorm, Joan's packed to the gills with girls from Belfast. Or perhaps the matron suspected that Katheen's sturdy, no-nonsense nature would be more useful to her little brother than Joan's anxious one. Perhaps she thought Kathleen could shield him from the bullies. And she probably did, for a while at any rate. But just as she couldn't save the submarine, she couldn't protect Jack for ever. Initially he was too young to attend school, just as Ted had been. And like Ted, he doesn't recall what happened to him during term time in the few months before school stopped for its summer break and all of the children stayed home together. There must have been someone who watched out for him, but he has a sense of being left to his own devices. Just before the new school term started in September 1943, when Jack would become a pupil, he was put into the larger of the two boys' rooms. Ted remained in the smaller one. So little Jack, not yet five years of age, was placed in a large dormitory room with lots of other boys, some of whom were very much older than he was.

Prior to the war, children generally left Childhaven at fourteen when they outgrew the small village school. But in the changed times the war had brought, some stayed well into their later teens, the odd few until they were eighteen or so, helping out in the house or doing odd jobs on the grounds in return for their keep. There was a family of brothers who arrived shortly after the Blitz, let's call them the Barr brothers. The eldest, we'll say his name was Davy, was one such resident. He was a nasty piece of work, a sadistic bully who took great joy in torturing and humiliating the other children, especially the girls and the younger boys. He would have been close to sixteen when Jack was first at Childhaven, and he ruled the roost with a sort of detached yet relentless cruelty. And naturally, as is the way with bullies, he had a dedicated following of boys whose job it was to make life hell for the other children. Also as is the way, some of the children coped with the bullies by ignoring them as Ted did, or standing up to them, like Kathleen. Jack and Joan did not fare so well. Unfortunately for Jack, he was put into the same dorm as Davy, who, as the oldest boy, had been placed in charge of the room; a position he shockingly abused.

Jack's second vivid memory of Childhaven was his fifth birthday on 18th September. There was no party, no cake, no gifts; birthdays were not celebrated at Childhaven. But as it was a Saturday, TP paid a visit and took the children out for a celebration treat at Mrs Moffat's. He brought a present with him for Jack, a small wooden scooter painted in bright, vivid colours. He had made it himself at a woodwork class he attended in Belfast and strapped it to his back for the long bicycle ride down to Millisle. He also gave Jack a birthday card with a big shiny number five embossed on the front. But he took the scooter back to Belfast with him, knowing perhaps that it would be taken from his son by one of the other children, or cruelly destroyed by someone, or locked in a cupboard by a member of staff, never to be used. It would be four years before Jack would see that little scooter again, and though he had held it in his memory for all of that time, he still wouldn't ride it. A handmade wooden scooter built for a five-year-old just didn't have the same appeal when he was nine. But he did at least get to keep the shiny birthday card, and presented it with pride to the other children. One of the older boys asked to see it and Jack, thrilled with the attention, readily handed it over. The boy attacked it with a geometry compass, punching hole after hole into the glossy paper.

"That'll teach you to be five," he sneered, throwing the ruined card onto the floor to cheers and laughter from the others.

It might not have been Davy himself who broke Jack's treasured submarine or destroyed his precious birthday card, but both acts would have been carried out to impress him. He led the others in daily acts of torment, the hours between dinner and lights-out being the worst. Physical fights where he would pit friends against each other, or make a weaker older boy fight a terrified younger one, were commonplace, and if someone refused to fight, he would set his bullyboys onto them. It was Davy's sport, or at least one of them. The Jewish boys were a particular target. Jack recalls the arrival of a new Jewish refugee who was painfully thin and visibly traumatised. Davy told Jack to beat the boy up, to teach him a lesson, though what that lesson was supposed to be, he had no idea. Jack was still very young then, maybe five or possibly six, small and slight and light on his feet. But he had already developed a way with his fists, an almost manic fighting style, fostered by the terrible combination of unaddressed pain, pent-up rage, and self-preservation. And so he hit the Jewish boy, and then he hit him again. The boy did not hit back. He couldn't. He simply didn't have the strength. Instead he began to cry and whisper something over and over in a language Jack did not understand. Obviously, Jack would have had no concept then of war or the holocaust, or what unspeakable horrors this boy might have experienced in his young life. He wouldn't have understood that the boy had arrived at Childhaven more terrified and distressed than any of them, but his young heart instinctively knew that what he was doing was wrong. And so he stopped. Davy's rage was instant and explosive, but despite his insistence, Jack refused to hit the little Jewish boy again. He knew he would pay for his insolence, a beating himself perhaps, or his head shoved down the toilet bowl, and he would probably be made to fight again the very next day. But for now Jack had scored a small victory against Davy Barr.

It wasn't just fist fights that Davy presided over. He and his cohorts would taunt and intimidate and humiliate at any opportunity. They would steal food from the already paltry portions on the smaller children's plates. They would destroy cherished personal possessions, like Jack's submarine and his birthday card. And it wasn't just the boys who carried out such heartless acts. Kathleen recalls a doll that she was given, again most likely for a birthday gift. It had a soft stuffed body with a porcelain head and she instantly fell in love with it. One of the girls in her dormitory grabbed the doll from her arms and threw it onto the hard concrete floor, smashing its painted face into smithereens. Joan suffered a similar loss, hers a pretty pink necklace, a Christmas gift from her father. An older girl ripped it from her neck causing the beads to scatter across the room and leaving her with an angry red mark. But Davy and his gang were the worst, sometimes stooping to the lowest levels of degradation and humiliation. They would dangle the younger and smaller boys by their ankles over a used toilet bowl, immerse their face in the filth, then flush the chain. They would throw an overcoat over someone's head and hold it tight until they came close to suffocation, the panic making them vomit with fear. They would force boys to drop their trousers in front of the girls, exposing their penises, and instruct the girls to laugh, beating up those who refused to comply. And they would even, on occasion, force some of the most vulnerable and anxious of children to eat their own excrement. The staff never intervened.

Not all of the children were subjected to Davy's harassment. He would pick on the ones he knew he could manipulate. Ted has no memory of being bullied, by Davy or any of the others. That's not to say nothing ever happened to him, but if it did, he has buried the incidents too deeply to remember them, and he would prefer it to stay that way. Feisty Kathleen stood up to the boys, and the girls, protecting others where she could, her little brother and older sister included. She would tell the matron and the other staff members when she witnessed something cruel, but there were never any consequences. It seems as though the staff had little control in those years, and a sluggish lack of compassion. Any discipline they applied came in the form of their own cruelty: a caning for not finishing a bowl of cold lumpy porridge, a slap for wetting the bed. Davy's antics were none of their concern. The staff were perhaps as frightened of Davy Barr and his gang as the other children were.

"It was Lord of the Flies before Lord of the Flies," says Jack.

And then there were other things, even worse things, unspeakable acts that this person we're calling Davy Barr quietly, secretly, carried out himself. Just how many children he targeted for this particular form of abuse, the worst form, we cannot begin to guess. Sadly, however, we do know who one of his victims was.

CHAPTER 16

While some of the children lived in a constant state of high alert, fearful of what Davy Barr and his gang might do next, and anxious about reprimands for some minor or imagined misdemeanour from the staff, for every single one of them, hunger became their default state of consciousness. The four Pakenham children all had very individual experiences of life in the orphanage, and while none of them were good, they would each be affected in different ways. As we've already touched upon, Kathleen and Ted have blocked much of their time in Millisle out of their minds and pulled down the shutters, preferring to march forward without looking back. Joan, it seems, did retain a significant amount, much of which she tried to eliminate. But her memories lingered underneath the surface for the rest of her life. Jack's memories are sharp and clear, hauntingly so. It is almost as though they happened yesterday, and not eighty-plus years ago. They still impact his life to this day and have significantly influenced his work. In later years the four siblings may have disagreed on a date, or a name, or had a slightly different recall on how a particular event or situation played out, or told each other *no, I don't remember that, I don't remember that at all*. But the one thing they all recalled, the one thing they all agreed on, the one memory that would never leave them, was the hunger. They were also constantly cold, especially during the winter months, the thin blankets that they had to share around once the intake of Blitz children arrived proving inadequate for their little bones. But the hunger was the worst; the daily, relentless, cruel agony of it.

Of course in the middle of the war years, rationing and food shortages meant that hunger was prevalent everywhere. But the children didn't understand that, and they didn't have mothers or grandmothers on hand to explain the situation, or stretch out the weekly rations, or cook nutritious, appetising meals regardless of what meagre provisions were at hand. Breakfast was porridge, just a spoonful or two made with water, with not a drop of milk or jam to sweeten it. The lumpy, coagulated oats were rarely cooked properly through, and often the porridge was cold before it hit the plate. But the children would eat it, mostly, their hunger overriding their disgust. Lunch was a gooseberry jam sandwich delivered to the school in a box, two rounds of bread before the war now reduced to one. The semi-stale bread was smeared with sticky sour green jam made using gooseberries that grew in the orphanage garden. The crop would be harvested, the jam made in bulk for a year-round supply. Dinner was generally a stew of some description, usually served with turnips from one of the local farms. This proved more of a challenge to the children than the porridge, as even the hungriest of little stomachs baulked at the lumps of fat and gristle floating in a pool of watery stock. If there had been any meat attached to the fat when it arrived in the kitchen, it didn't make it into the stew. The portions were tiny, just a small spoonful, the turnips easier to digest than the fat, so they ate what they could, which in reality was just enough to survive. Often the cane would come out at dinner time, ready to strike any child who refused to eat the fat. Sometimes even that dreaded punishment would be preferable to the horror of the fat itself. All four of the children grew up hating turnips. As adults, they needed the fat trimmed from their meat, every visible shred of it in Ted's case. Porridge is tolerable now with the luxury of milk and sugar, but not a drop of gooseberry jam has crossed their lips since the day they left Childhaven.

The staff at the orphanage must have been in a truly difficult position. Feeding the children before the war began was most likely challenging enough, but during it, with double the number of stomachs to fill and even less produce to do so with, well, it can't have been easy.

> "I don't suppose they intended to starve us," Joan wrote, "but we were always hungry. And poor dad when he visited us on Saturdays used to give us his lunch and do without himself."

Jack too wrote about the hunger he experienced, his recollections expressed through poetry, including the lines from his poem *Memories* that appear at the start of this section.

TP's fortnightly excursions to Childhaven were somewhat unusual at the time. He was the only relative to visit regularly, certainly the only parent to do so. The rest of the children, orphans or not, would gather by the fence overlooking the bus stop outside the orphanage entrance each Saturday morning in the hope that someone, anyone, would come to see them with a gift, or a food parcel, or a new pair of shoes. Some did receive occasional visitors, but most did not. TP's obvious commitment to his children, coupled with his connection to the Belfast Central Mission, gave him a certain status with the matron. In the early years of his visits, she would often lay out a little spread for him, tea and sandwiches that weren't filled with gooseberry jam. She sometimes took tea with him, but if she left TP to eat the refreshments alone, he would give the food to his children. And then there would be those trips to Mrs Moffat's, where they would lick the plates if they got away with it, not to savour any residual grains of sugar, but because they didn't want to waste a single crumb. TP knew the children were hungry. He would have seen it with his own eyes, and they told him repeatedly. Yet though he was happy to share the lunch that Matron provided on his visits, and would slip the children a humbug or two, he didn't bring them food parcels.

This special treatment of TP by Matron and the other staff didn't extend to the Pakenham children, but it still made them stand out. Resentment bubbled with some of the other children, and after a visit from their father, the bullying might notch up a rung or two. Joan would withdraw into herself, Kathleen would angrily retort, Ted might do his best to ignore them, retreating to the garden to kick a ball, and Jack's fists would curl, ready for action. TP wasn't the only visitor to receive special attention, however. On occasion there would be open days at the orphanage, an opportunity for clergymen, representatives from the Belfast Central Mission, and local benefactors to visit the children and see for themselves what a great place Childhaven was. On those occasions, the house was scrubbed from top to bottom, with the help of the children obviously, who were scrubbed up themselves. They were warned to be on their best behaviour; to be polite to their visitors, to smile and look happy and only speak when they were spoken to. There would be a spread put on, far more lavish than any of their normal meals, but not so abundant as to look extravagant. Jack spent these occasions wandering around the room, quietly putting any crusts or slices of leftover bread in his pocket, and he wouldn't have been the only child to do so. On one such visit, a kindly Methodist minister sat beside Jack, attempting to engage him in conversation. The table was low, too low for the man's long legs, his knees knocking against its base. Jack couldn't focus on what the man was saying, all too aware that this important visitor's trousers were going to be covered in the lumps of sticky gooseberries he had meticulously removed from the sandwiches being served and stuck there. He didn't have the stomach for those detested gooseberries that day. When the Minister saw the state of his trousers, he was furious and made his dissatisfaction quite clear to Matron. She assured him that Jack would receive the cane for his impudence, which he duly did.

Again, the situation can't have been easy for the staff. Before the war the house had been easy enough to manage, the children relatively straightforward to control. They may not have showered them with affection, but they probably cared for them as best they could. But when the numbers doubled almost overnight, with no extra staff enlisted to help, and no additional supplies provided, one can see how they must have struggled. As for the Belfast Central Mission, the governing committee would have absolutely believed they were doing the right thing in sending as many newly orphaned and evacuee children as they could to the home, and in offering to take in Jewish refugees too. After all, if they didn't provide these poor displaced children with a roof over their heads, what would become of them? It was, without a doubt, the Christian thing to do and meant with the very best of intentions. It just wasn't properly thought through, or adequately funded, or compassionately managed.

There was a knock-on impact at Millisle National School too. The increased number of children arriving at Childhaven coincided with the establishment of a Jewish refugee camp on a disused farm in Millisle, close to the orphanage. Jewish children from the settlement and the orphanage's new residents were all sent to the school, more than doubling its roll call in a matter of months. Unlike at Childhaven, some additional teachers were at least drafted in to cope with the influx. A temporary classroom was erected at the back of the school, and the local Masonic Hall was also used. The uninvited expansion of his quiet little country school must have created quite a headache for Mr Palmer, and he would often take out his frustrations on the children from the settlement and Childhaven. Orphans and Jews ignited his temper and tested his patience, and his cane would be more frequently and eventually only applied in their direction. The injustice of these random canings for no apparent or justified reason weighed heavily on the children, until finally one of them snapped. Joe Culbert, a half-orphan like the Pakenham children, whose mother was alive but unable to care for him, stood up from his chair one day just as Mr Palmer was about to cane another child from the orphanage, and yelled at him to stop.

"You don't treat the children from the village the way you treat us," he shouted, "and it isn't fair. We don't deserve to be caned just because we're orphans."

You can imagine the collective intake of breath from the classroom, the feeling of dread and fear that spread through the room. You can see Baldy Palmer's face flush red with rage, his grip tightening around the cane. But then a miraculous thing happened. Mr Palmer put down the cane and calmy returned to teaching his class. He didn't retire the punishment weapon for good, but from that day on he reduced its use, and no longer unfairly discriminated against the orphans and refugees. Joe Culbert became a bit of a hero that day, the story of his bold stance against Baldy Palmer retold for years to come by the children who benefited from his courage.

Joe and Ted were good friends, and rivals too, of a sort. A similar age, they shared a competitive determination for running, always trying to outdo each other in impromptu races around the orphanage grounds. Ted would usually win, but it was generally acknowledged that the two of them were the fastest sprinters in Childhaven. So on the day that someone found a shilling on the road on their way home from school, it was collectively agreed that Ted and Joe should be dispatched to the local grocery store to buy a loaf of bread. The shop was about a mile away from Childhaven, and as it was against the rules to leave the grounds unsupervised, they would need to be quick before someone on the staff noticed their absence. There were no better people for the job than the lightning bolts, Ted Pakenham and Joe Culbert. In reality, such was the level of chaos and disorganisation at the house that it's unlikely they would have been missed, for a while at least, but the children would have been worried about the repercussions. Two or three brave souls had escaped in the past, only to be caught and subjected to fairly brutal punishments. Still, the thought of a fresh loaf of bread was too enticing, and off the two boys set, running down the coast road as though their lives depended on it, ducking into the hedges if they heard a car approach. They bought the loaf and returned to the house, and every child in the house got at least one extra mouthful of bread that day, even Davy Barr. As none of the grownups in charge noticed a thing, it was decided to send the two boys on another food related expedition a few days later, this time to the orchard just across the fields that was brimming with perfectly ripe but frustratingly unattainable apples. The orchard belonged to Captain Rhodes who owned large country estate behind the orphanage, and it was strictly out of bounds to the Childhaven children. But juicy ripe apples were too good a prize to pass over, so Ted and Joe set off on another mission to acquire food for their fellow orphans. Once again, they were successful, returning with jerseys stuffed full of the forbidden fruit. That was a good day in Childhaven, a rare good day, so good in fact that a few days later the boys decided to make a return trip. Unbeknownst to the children however, Ted and Joe had been spotted on their first crusade by one of Captain Rhode's gardeners, and a tall fence was hastily erected around the perimeter of the orchard. Undeterred, the boys scaled the fence, only to be caught in the act by the furious gardener. He tried to grab hold of them, but they were too quick, legging it back to the house empty handed, but relieved. That relief was short lived, as when their trespassing expedition was reported to the matron, they were scolded and caned in front of the rest of the children, and sent to bed without dinner. TP was told in no uncertain terms what an unruly, naughty, and disrespectful son he had, and no doubt Joe's mother received the same information. In all probability not one of the adults associated with the incident, not the gardener nor Captain Rhodes, not the matron nor the other staff, not TP nor Joe's mother, paused for a second to consider the possibility that in actual fact the naughty impertinent boys and their equally disrespectful friends were simply very hungry.

CHAPTER 17

Aside from the incessant hunger and constant threat of persecution from Davy Barr and his cronies, boredom was another challenging issue for the children. There were no toys at the orphanage, or at least none that they were permitted to play with. Jack in particular recalls knowing that unwanted gifts or items no longer used were occasionally donated to the orphanage by local families or well-wishers; things like cricket stumps or skipping ropes or a doll's house. These donations would be gratefully accepted, and then locked away in cupboards or outhouses, out of reach from the children they were meant for. Occasionally they might be brought out of hiding on open days. The children made their own entertainment, climbing trees, playing British Bulldog and hopscotch, or challenging each other to races around the orphanage grounds, the races Ted would always win. And the boys did have a couple of footballs to kick around for impromptu football games. The grounds were fine in spring and summer time, and even in winter so long as it wasn't raining, but their merits were limiting. As Childhaven overlooked the sea, there was a natural playground full of wonder just across the road, accessible via the underground passage that ran directly from the orphanage to the beach, the passage they used as an air raid shelter during the Blitz. But they weren't allowed to go there. The beach was strictly out of bounds. It seems incredible, but these children with so little joy in their life were not permitted to build sandcastles on the beach, or dig their toes into the sand, or paddle in the water, even under supervision. The only time they were permitted to visit the beach was with a visitor, or for Sunday mission services on the nearby sand dunes during the summer months. Joan, Kathleen, Ted, and Jack all recall looking wistfully at this forbidden paradise from the windows of the orphanage or the lawn at the front of the house, wishing they could just run across the road. Joan was especially taken by the sight and sounds of the sea. It reminded her of life in Dublin, her early childhood years when she lived in the big house at Prince Edward Terrace with her mother and father and baby sister, where weekend walks to the beach at Blackrock were a regular occurrence. It was one memory she clung to when so many others were leaving her. That view, so close yet so unattainable, became a source of solace for Joan, and she would spend hours on her own standing on the lawn, listening to the sound of the waves and watching the drama of the ocean play out in front of her. Throughout her life she would always feel the call of the sea, no matter how far she may have physically been from it.

The denial of the beach was made harder to bear when the children saw other people playing on it, building those sandcastles, jumping over the waves, even flying a kite. It was especially hard to take when the other people were children, and even more so when they were children who were staying at Craigmore House, the holiday home on Childhaven's grounds. A large lodge-like building, the holiday home sat on the front lawn directly overlooking the sea. It was separated from the orphanage by a sizeable garden, almost a field really, and if it had its own entrance, you would never really have known the two homes were linked. But the two properties shared one entrance gate and one driveway, and both were run by Belfast Central Mission. Unlike the orphanage, Craigmore was used for holidays alone, namely short-term respite trips for children from disadvantaged areas of Belfast, and church groups. It accommodated around forty children at a time, and with its spacious rooms, expansive outdoor spaces and seaside setting, it really was a sort of paradise for the visiting youngsters. In the late 1940s and throughout the 1950s, the building would also host Christian conferences and youth mission weekends, but during the years that the Pakenhams lived in the orphanage next door, it was exclusively used by other children, especially during the summer months. And more often than not, the children from the orphanage did not get along with the visiting children at the holiday home. They would challenge each other to races, which again Ted always won, and games of Bulldog, and other sporting and physical contests. There would be fights, some with fists involving Jack, and some with words involving Kathleen. The holiday children were allowed to do things the orphanage children were not allowed to do, like play on the beach, while the orphanage children were made to walk. For two or three hours on a Saturday afternoon they would trudge along the coast road, crocodile style, or walk deep into the countryside up windy country lanes, returning to the orphanage exhausted, with aching legs and rumbling bellies. There didn't seem to be any purpose to these walks other than to exhaust the children and keep them out of trouble, away from the holidaying guests. Worst of all, the holiday children were also given better and more substantial food to eat, or at least that's how the orphanage children saw it. And no matter how difficult the home-lives of the visiting children might have been, at least they had a home to go back to. At least they had a family.

"There was always conflict between us," says Ted, "because they were free and we weren't."

On one occasion, a contingency of boys from the Belfast Central Mission's Boys' Brigade company visited the Childhaven complex, not to stay in the holiday home, but to camp on the grounds. The BB officer in charge organised a football match between his boys, and boys from the orphanage. The orphanage boys would occasionally form a team to play against local boys from Millisle or Donaghadee, and Jack in particular loved those games. He was the Childhaven goalie, quick, and nimble and acrobatic, he would dive for any ball coming his way, whether he had even an outside chance of a save or not. He didn't love playing against the BB boys on that particular day though, not because they were better, which they were, and not because they would probably win, which they did, but because their coach, the BB officer, was his very own father.

Through his association with Belfast Central Mission, TP had been introduced to the merits of the Boys' Brigade, a Christian youth movement for boys and young men. He was attracted to its ethos and structure, and became involved as an officer, devoting much of his free time to helping young boys in the inner-city Belfast community through the organisation. He took his troop on many camping expeditions, and would organise football matches and other challenges with neighbouring BB divisions across Belfast. TP probably felt very proud the day he brought his BB company to Childhaven, thrilled to introduce his BB boys to his actual boys, his sons. But his sons did not share in his delight. For them, watching their father interact with these Belfast boys in a way he had never interacted with them was a confusing, painful, and humiliating experience. He had never taken them camping. He had never organised a Childhaven football team. And which team, they wondered, did he actually want to win the game anyway: the boys from his precious BB, or the makeshift team his two sons were on? Worst of all, at the end of the weekend, he would return to Belfast with these BB boys, leaving them, his sons, behind. It was unfathomable. We must assume that TP did not pick up on his sons' discomfort, or his daughters' as they would have witnessed this occasion too. He cannot have realised the hurt he was causing, the confusion he was creating, the anguish he was leaving his children to deal when he and his BB boys packed up their tents and waved them goodbye. With his blinkers firmly in place, he must have wholeheartedly believed he was both helping his own children and doing good and worthy community work, guided by God.

Religion was another important aspect of daily life at Childhaven, unsurprising considering the orphanage was run by the Belfast Central Mission. The children said grace before each meal, regardless of how paltry and inadequate that meal may have been. There were morning and evening prayers, and at the evening prayer session they also sang hymns. The closest Methodist Church was in Donaghadee, which they attended twice on a Sunday, once in the morning for the weekly church service and again in the afternoon for Sunday School. The church dispatched a special bus to take them to and from the morning service, but in the afternoon, they had to walk the two-mile journey there and back, rain, hail or shine. Attending church and participating in prayers and hymn singing was non-negotiable, regardless of what religious background the children came from. Most would have been Protestants with a Methodist connection. There were the handful of Jewish children, who did not receive special dispensation and attended church alongside their fellow housemates. And then there were the Pakenham children, all baptised into the Catholic church, and one of whom had even received her First Holy Communion. It is highly unlikely that any of the other children knew this fact. Pakenham was not a Catholic name after all, and Ted and Jack would have borne no trace of a Dublin brogue. By the time Davy Barr arrived at the house in 1941, eight-year-old Kathleen's accent would have softened into a County Down lilt. Joan, however, might still have displayed some tell-tale Southern inflection, and this would not have gone down well with Davy. Even if he didn't suspect Joan was actually a Catholic, or at least had been one, he was the sort who would not have taken kindly to a Free Stater. It may have been one of the reasons he decided to make Joan one of his long-term targets. In turn, Joan's worry about sounding too Irish may have contributed to her quiet demeanour, a reluctance to talk much, especially in the house and even to her siblings, branding her a loner. She was ripe for Davy Barr's picking.

But Joan did find once source of solace during her time at Childhaven, aside from the pleasure she took at watching the ocean, and that was in religion. The rhythm and rituals of the daily prayers and hymn singing sat well with her, providing a distraction from the reality of what her life had become. When they were praying and singing and attending church, Davy Barr couldn't get to her, and as her relationship with God began to develop, she felt less alone. When Joan was thirteen, she along with some of the other teenagers in the house attended a special youth mission evening at the church conducted by a lay preacher from England called Mr Silverwood. Mr Silverwood's words solidified something that had been stirring for a while within Joan's soul, and at the end of the service when he invited the young people in the audience to join him in dedicating themselves to following Christ, Joan readily obliged. The little Catholic girl from Dublin who had dressed up for her First Communion five years previously had gone, a committed Methodist teenager from County Down now taking her place. The other children would go on their own religious journeys, two following Joan's path, one forging their own. But it's fair to say that in their youth, none of them were rescued by religion in the way that Joan was.

As well as the confiscated toys stuffed into cupboards and the forbidden beach just across the road, there was another facility that remained off limits to the children, or at least to most of them; the gymnasium. Around the time of Jack's arrival at the orphanage, Miss Ludlow left to marry a Methodist minister in Belfast. She was replaced as matron by a Mrs Young, whose husband joined her as Childhaven's caretaker and handyman. A retired soldier with firm beliefs in both discipline and physical exercise, Mr Young took ownership of the gymnasium that had been created in one of the outbuildings at the back of the house. Ted and Kathleen remember the gymnasium, but their recollection is of it being mostly out of bounds to them. Ted particularly would have loved regular access to the building, to be able to climb on the ropes and swing from the bars and spring over the vaults; but his memory tells him he was only in the building on a handful of occasions. Jack on the other hand recalls using it regularly. For him the gym was a place of solace, somewhere he could expend much of his pent-up energy and that simmering rage. He recalls Mr Young teaching him how to vault and tumble and do basic gymnastic work. But while he loved the physical activity, he did not love Mr Young, a fierce disciplinarian who seemed as intent on making the children cry as in teaching them gymnastics. Perhaps Ted and Kathleen did use the facility more than they can recall, and Mr Young's fierceness is just another aspect of life at Childhaven that they have blocked from their minds. Or perhaps Mr Young had his favourites. Perhaps he only allowed those he identified as having a natural talent, a flair for gymnastics, to use the facility. And Jack certainly had talent. He was small and agile and light on his feet, and took to all of the various disciplines like a duck to water. He even became adept at walking on his hands, but that was down to the encouragement of Joe Ray, one of his friends at the orphanage, and not Mr Young. It was important to Mr Young to only instruct the naturally gifted children in his gymnasium, because once a year his protégées would put on a display at the Belfast Central Mission's annual concert in the Grosvenor Hall, and he was determined to make a good impression. Some of the children sang at the event too, a special choir assembled for the occasion. Joan, Kathleen, and Ted were in the choir, Jack in the gymnastics squad. They remembered the occasion as an adventure, a day when they received a little bit of special attention, when their hair was combed and they were given freshly laundered clothes to wear. There would be a special bus to take them to the venue in the city, and they would get different food to eat. And after they performed, the audience would clap enthusiastically and gasp at how talented these poor orphaned children were, and congratulate Mr and Mrs Young on the wonderful job they were doing. TP would be in the audience, no doubt proud of his children, delighted to see them so happy. And they *were* happy on those occasions. But then their father would return to his boarding house and his life in Belfast, and they would return to Millilse on the bus. And the next day there would be meagre portions of barely edible food on their plates, and no toys to play with, and the gym would be closed, and the beach still out of bounds, and their father would be absent once again.

CHAPTER 18

As the years passed, and the war trundled on in the background with no further bombings but the constant threat of the Luftwaffe returning, TP's circumstances gradually changed. He was promoted at work and received a small pay increase, enough to buy the children new coats, and even take them on a little holiday. Though some dates and details remain unclear, it seems he took the eldest three to a boarding house in Bangor for a couple of days shortly after the Blitz attacks, when the sirens would still occasionally sound. Ted and Kathleen both recall the night they awoke to the wail of the alarm, fully expecting to be dragged from their beds to wherever the nearest air raid shelter was. But TP, his Air Raid Patrol antenna finely tuned, decided there was no real threat, and told the children to go back to sleep. Childhood memories of regular holidays at the same location can be prone to distortion, with several trips over several years all blending into one, but Ted and Kathleen vaguely recall at least three stays in Bangor. The third took place in the summer of 1943, and this time Jack, by now also living at Childhaven, joined them. Then, in the summer of 1944, TP took his children to Carlingford, a pretty seaside town on the Cooley Peninsula in County Louth, just across the border from Warrenpoint in the North. It was the first time they had set foot in the South of Ireland since that clandestine dash to leave the country five years previously. TP must have been feeling somewhat audacious returning to the South with all four children in tow. It could, potentially have been a risky move for him, although in reality there was little to no chance of bumping into any of the Beirne family in a holiday town like Carlingford. It was too far from Leitrim, too complicated a journey to reach, and the Dublin O'Beirnes had ample seaside locations to visit on the Dublin coastline. The journey from Millisle to Carlingford was not a straightforward one either. A bus from Millisle to Belfast, then a train to Newry, then, after a long wait at the station, a bus to Carlingford. It was dark by the time they arrived and five-year-old Jack was not impressed.

"What have you brought us to this dump for?" he grunted.

A photo of the four children taken by their father in Carlingford while on holiday break from Childhaven. (Summer 1944)

Considering the rather insalubrious environment they had left behind at Childhaven, he must have been truly fed up. But when they awoke the next morning, the sun was shining, and contrary to being a dump, the garden at their guest house actually appeared to be some form of paradise with its bloom of flowers, and plants, and vegetables, and plump, red tomatoes. It was the first time the five of them had slept under the same roof since the fleeting few nights they had all spent in Lurgan more than five years previously. Their landlady fed them well, with those tomatoes and other produce from the garden, and fresh eggs and creamy milk and meat that wasn't enveloped in fat. Ted was sick, his sensitive stomach not used to good, decent, healthy, home-cooked food. The others devoured it.

They returned to Carlingford the following year armed with the knowledge that the long and tiresome journey would be worth the prize that awaited them. Then, in the summer of 1946, TP decided to head in the other direction, this time north of Belfast to Carnlough, a small harbour town on the rugged Antrim Coast. There had been some notable changes in the two years since that first family holiday. Firstly, and most significantly, Joan had left Childhaven in the November of 1944, and was now attending a boarding school. By the age of thirteen she had caught up academically, rising to become one of the top performing pupils at Millisle National School. Along with three boys in her class, as noted in one of her letters, she was selected to study for a special scholarship that would allow her to continue her education once she turned fourteen. If successful, she would leave Millilse school in June 1945 at the end of the 1944/45 academic year, and apply for a place at a suitable senior school. There were two potential options in nearby Bangor that might have been considered. Both were private schools for young ladies with boarding facilities, and one in particular had a strong Methodist connection. Belfast also presented some possibilities, schools that would have been geographically closer to TP. However, before Joan had the opportunity to sit the scholarship exam, in the November of 1944, a month after her fourteenth birthday, she was informed by her father that she had been given a bursary from the Methodist Orphanage Society to attend Wesley College, another

Methodist linked school. Only Wesley College was in Dublin, and, to her surprise, she was to start immediately.

The second significant change was that the war had ended. Whilst the global conflict was officially declared over in September 1945 following victory in Japan, victory in Europe, V-E Day, had been jubilantly celebrated in Britain on the 8th of May 1945. Throughout Northern Ireland church bells rang and people danced in the streets, but on the North Down coast, inside the orphanage at Childhaven, there were no celebrations. The children knew that the war in Europe had ended because they were told so in school. But there was nothing of any note to mark the momentous occasion inside the big house. No freshly made lemonade, no celebration cake, certainly no party. There wasn't even, it would seem, an official announcement. And while the rest of the country began to put itself back together and move forward into a new, post-war future, nothing changed in terms of how the children in Childhaven lived day to day. Rationing continued for several years after the war, so food was still in short supply, and the residents who had arrived at the orphanage during the worst of the war years did not immediately return to their own homes or families, even if they still had homes or families to return to. TP felt uplifted and optimistic after the war. His finances were continuing to improve, his standing within the local community was rising, and he wore his Defence Medal awarded to Air Raid Patrol wardens with pride. He also moved from his South Parade digs to a boarding house at Cliftonpark Avenue in the north of the city, one that was once again inhabited by gentlemen connected to the Methodist church.

But back to that trip to Carnlough. Aside from the domestic and societal changes that had taken place during the preceding twelve months, the holiday was significant in itself as the family was accompanied by a sixth person, TP's niece Georgina, the eldest daughter of his eldest brother, John. John and his new wife Lilly had left County Wexford in June 1909 immediately after their wedding, relocating to London, where Georgina was born two months later. It would appear that once they realised Lilly was pregnant, John and Lilly decided to flee to England and begin a new life in a place where no one would know just how long they had actually been husband and wife. Consequently, they would have been able to pass the impending birth off as a long-awaited and much anticipated one. By the time TP found himself in a similar position two decades later, his brother was dead, succumbing to TB in 1925. Although she was his niece, Georgina was just four years younger than TP. Lilly had kept in contact with the Pakenham family after her husband's death, and somehow in the summer of 1946, it was decided that Georgina should join her uncle on this holiday, both for the pleasure of fresh sea air, and to help with his children. It is likely that TP and Georgina had met as children, as no doubt John had brought his wife and youngsters to visit his family at Pakenham Hall on one or two occasions. But they would not have seen each other for many years, and Georgina certainly wouldn't have met his children before. Nevertheless, whilst TP had managed to navigate the previous two summer trips by himself, assistance would no doubt have been gratefully accepted, perhaps even sought. Jack, still bursting with energy and mischief, was what might be affectionally termed as 'a handful'. Ted's sensitive stomach was always a concern on holiday. And with Joan now almost sixteen and Kathleen about to celebrate her thirteenth birthday, the girls were on the cusp of becoming young women. An adult woman on hand to help with any child-related matters that might arise would have been a tremendous relief for TP.

Another noteworthy thing about this holiday was that TP hired a car. This could have been at his own initiative, or it may have been a demand set down by Georgina: *provide a car, or I'm not coming*. She was just sixteen when her father died, her younger siblings fourteen, thirteen and eleven respectively. Their mother, who had trained as a nurse before leaving Ireland, resumed her career following her husband's death. She had also been left reasonably well cared for thanks to a military widow's pension as John, a chauffeur by trade, had enlisted with the British Army at the start of World War One. Georgina herself had worked as a jeweller in a respected establishment, and lived with her mother in Harpenden, Hertfordshire. She was thirty-seven when this holiday took place, an unmarried woman, classified as a spinster at that time, who, whilst by no means wealthy, was refined and perhaps a little bit haughty; certainly used to the comforts in life. She would have travelled by train from London to Liverpool and taken the overnight boat to Belfast, quite enough public transport to deal with. The car would have been an enormous deal for the children too. TP didn't own a car when they lived in Dublin, it wasn't he who had driven them to Lurgan, or to Childhaven. It wasn't his car they had posed in for photographs at Millilse beach. They would have been delighted at this unexpected, exciting development, and might even have allowed themselves to imagine, if only for a week, that they were a normal family with a regular father and their very own car on their annual summer holiday. They may even have been forgiven for pretending, if even quietly to themselves, that Georgina was their mother. The holiday was a great success, all of the children remembering it fondly. In fact, they would return again the following year, with Georgina's mother Lilly joining the party. And for Jack, that first trip to Carnlough would be life changing, in a very small, but ultimately enormously significant way.

Of the four children, Jack was the one who struggled the most at school, more out of a restless disinterest than a lack of academic ability. Joan had put her previous learning anxieties behind her and found her academic stride. Kathleen was doing well too. While not just as conscientious as her sister, she liked the rhythm and routine of school and took her lessons seriously, and would be joining her sister at Wesley College that coming September. Ted was also displaying academic ability with a natural propensity for mathematics, Mr Palmer's favourite subject. He was studious and loved to learn. But maths and science didn't make sense to Jack, and he had yet to fall in love with words in the way that he would eventually do. Unlike his brother and sisters, he showed no interest in learning, he just didn't see the point of it, and consequently was a difficult pupil to teach. The cane often came out for Jack Pakenham, even after Joe Culbert's brave intervention. The one thing that did hold his attention in class was art, and that was only because he liked the teacher, Miss Boyd, one of the additional staff members who arrived at Millisle National School after the Blitz. And the real reason he liked Miss Boyd was because she would set the class tasks to draw different items, like her bicycle, or her chalk duster, or a piece of food. And if the item in question was food, a carrot perhaps, or an apple, then Jack would make sure he drew the best carrot or apple that he could, a better carrot or apple than anyone else in the class. Because when food items were the subject matter in art class, the pupil who produced the best likeness got to take the item home. So when food was the prize, Jack would sharpen both his pencil tip and his focus and do his damnedest to win it. And he often did, his only real competition being Ted, who to Jack's unending frustration was actually better at drawing than he was. Ted was precise and focused, his ability to draw an accurate copy of just about anything quite remarkable, although he was less driven to win Miss Boyd's competitions than his little brother. But other than the lure of the prize, Jack had no real interest in art. Until the holiday in Carnlough, that is.

One particular sunny afternoon, the family and Georgina left their boarding house, piled into the car, and drove an hour or so up the rugged coastline to the picturesque Ballintoy Harbour. Known as a painter's paradise, the harbour is accessed via a steep and narrow road that winds down to the sea from Ballintoy village. On the twisty drive down to the harbour, they passed an artist sat at his easel, then, just around the bend they saw another one. With almost every turn in the road they seemed to pass a painter. Jack was fascinated. When they parked the car, he could see more people dotted along the beach and the harbour walls, easels facing out towards the Irish Sea. As the family stretched their legs, Jack ran over to take a closer look at one of the artists who was painting with watercolours. Another was using oils, and yet another chalk. He had no idea such things existed: different types of paints, coloured chalks, canvas boards, special paper, paintbrushes, easels. This was a new and entirely magical world to him, and though just eight years old, it was a world he knew he wanted to be part of.

"I'm going to be an artist when I grow up," Jack told the rest of the family that day. Whether they took him seriously or not, or patronisingly indulged this sudden new fantasy, or laughed at him, or made a silent hopeful wish that maybe, just maybe he would be, from that day on, the only gift that Jack would ever ask for at Christmas and on his birthday, was a small tin of paints and a brand-new brush.

The trips to Bangor and Carlingford and Carnlough helped to bond the children, for the duration of the holiday at any rate. Outside of Childhaven they were a family, inside the orphanage walls, not so much. They all slept in different rooms, they didn't walk beside each other in the crocodile lines, they didn't sit next to each other in the classroom, and they didn't play together in the playground, or the garden, or inside the house. Of course that's not entirely unusual for siblings, however growing up in such a tense, dysfunctional, unloving environment, one might imagine that they clung to each other for support. Kathleen was the one who kept an eye on everyone. Though not the eldest, it was she who developed a sense of familial responsibility. She knew that the relentless bulling and intimidation by Davy Barr and his gang was responsible for Joan's timid demeanour and her low-level anxiety, and Jack's default fight or flight mode, though it would be very many years before she understood the full extent of the horrors that her sister in particular was subjected to. She did her best to protect her older sister and youngest brother, standing up to Davy and co., demanding they leave her siblings alone, reporting bad behaviour to the staff. But while her bolshiness probably protected her from the bullies' clutches, it didn't dilute their behaviour towards Joan and Jack and the others on their target list. And reporting to the staff was mostly a waste of time as usually they did nothing. Joan spent a lot of time alone, her head in a book or keeping up with her studies, trying to make herself invisible. Ted expended his energy and frustrations by running, or kicking a ball, or climbing trees. Physical activity was his way of dealing with the situation he was in, that and an innate understanding that it wasn't forever, that there would be a life after Childhaven. He just needed to keep his head down and plough forward. He didn't have much of a relationship with his little brother, but on occasion he would pull him up from the ground after yet another fight left him lying face down in the gravel, or challenge whoever was giving Jack grief to a race or some form of physical challenge. And once or twice, when it was required, he would step in to fight on his brother's behalf. A natural pacifist, Ted recalls that the only fights he ever got into in his life were ones that Jack had started. Jack, meanwhile, continued to barrage his way through the Childhaven years, an unremitting rage rumbling inside him; rage at the injustice of both his own circumstances and the plight of others, rage at the harassment and victimisation he witnessed on a daily basis, rage that he had to learn ridiculous things like maths and algebra at school, and rage at the constant hunger he felt. Jack's rage, Ted's frustration, Joan's anxiety, and Kathleen's vigilance were amplified when they returned to Millisle after one of their holiday trips. Being the only children in the orphanage with a living father who visited them regularly was one thing, that father taking them on holiday was quite another. Following each trip the siblings would experience taunting and cold-shoulder exclusion from their fellow housemates at best, physical torture at worst.

The children did not discuss the difficulty of their circumstances or the reason for their current living arrangement with each other. They did not talk about their mother, did not collectively grieve her, they didn't even have a single photograph of her between them, any lingering visual memory fading with each passing year. The younger three did not ask Joan what she as the eldest could remember about their mother, or knew about her passing. They did not openly wonder about their grandmother in Cashel, or their uncles in Dublin. They rarely asked their father any questions: the past was a taboo subject not to be mentioned, the future unknown, not to be questioned. And they certainly never voiced the one question each one of them quietly, privately pondered as they waved their father off on his bicycle at the end of his Saturday visit, or on the bus when he had delivered them back to Millilse after a trip away: if their father loved them enough to visit them so regularly, if he could bring them on a holiday each year, why could he not find them a home? Why could he not take them out of Childhaven for good?

The children did love those holidays though. They lived for them in a way. And there were other snatched moments of joy during those years too. A man from the church in Donaghadee playing Charlie Chaplin films on his cinecamera. The excitement of the concerts at the Grosvenor Hall. Jack setting the Childhaven record for walking the circumference of the long dining table on his hands. Ted winning all those races. Joan finding solace in God. There were the fortnightly visits from their father, and the outings to Mrs Moffat's for tea and buns, and the occasional new coat. There was the day that Davy Barr left the home, that was a day to celebrate. And then there was the end; the end of Childhaven at any rate. Finally, for each one of them, there would come a time to leave too.

CHAPTER 19

Joan was the first to leave the orphanage in November 1944, after receiving that bursary to Wesley College shortly after her fourteenth birthday. Davy Barr had departed some months earlier, to the relief of pretty much everyone at Childhaven, children and staff alike. There were others waiting in the wings after he left, vying for the position of chief bully, but they didn't do the things to Joan that Davy had done, they didn't persecute her in quite the same way. Still, she had remained ill at ease and hyper vigilant, and was relieved and thankful to be leaving Millisle and the unhappy years there behind. In truth though, she would probably have preferred to stay closer to home, to have been given the opportunity to sit the academic scholarship exam she had been preparing for and then move to a more local school. The thought of Dublin unnerved her, because although she was escaping the orphanage and relocating to the city she had been born in, she was returning as a Protestant with a Northern accent and not a word of Irish on her tongue. The Irish that she had learned back in Dublin in her early years of schooling had by now completely deserted her, something that would curtail her studies at Wesley. But that wasn't her initial problem. As she was late to begin the term, arriving at Wesley more than two months into the new school year thanks to the sudden and unexpected bursary she received, friendships had already been made and alliances formed, and Joan found herself alone and friendless, on the periphery of her class.

We're not entirely sure how the bursary came about, but knowing what we do of TP's thinking and decision making in those years, we can present a fairly solid theory. When Mr Palmer put Joan forward as a potential candidate for a scholarship to secure her continuing education after primary school, TP suddenly realised that he needed to consider his children's future. They were growing up. They could obviously not continue at Millisle National School beyond the age of fourteen, nor could they remain at Childhaven forever. If Joan was successful in securing an academic scholarship, she would no doubt be offered a place at a suitable boarding school in the North. But what if she didn't pass the examination? What then? TP was still living in digs and he couldn't house his daughter there with him. And he either wasn't yet in a financial position to rent a home for his family, in spite of seemingly earning a half decent wage by that stage, or wasn't emotionally ready to do so. So sending her to a regular state school in Belfast was not an option. Boarding school was the only plausible route, and he couldn't leave the possibility of Joan getting a place at private school to the chance of a scholarship exam. He may have already known of Wesley College in Dublin, or one of his methodist friends might have told him about it, but somehow, he became aware that the Methodist Orphanage Society of Ireland offered bursaries to the school for suitable orphaned children. Though his children were not orphans, they did reside in a methodist orphanage, and that was most likely enough to put forward a recommendation for Joan to receive a bursary. Strings were probably pulled by contacts at the Grosvenor Hall to both acquire a place for Joan, and facilitate her late arrival halfway through the autumn term. TP must have been hugely relieved. Looking forward, he could confidently assume that Kathleen would be offered the very same bursary when it was time for her to leave Millilse school and the orphanage, and Ted too. He may not have thought as far ahead as Jack's post-primary education at that point, but he could breathe easy for another three years at least.

There was no prior discussion with Joan, no warning. She was going back to Dublin, and that was that. On her first day, as well as being a late addition to the class, she was immediately set apart from her contemporaries when she was introduced as "the little orphan girl from Belfast." The other girls had already been informed of her impending arrival, her status as the orphan girl from up North solidified before she even got there.

Wesley College, which was then located on St. Stephen's Green, the historic park in Dublin's city centre, was a Methodist version of TP's beloved Wilson's Hospital. Established by a contingency of Methodist clergymen for the purpose, according to the school's website, of "*affording a thorough literary, scientific and commercial education, with a sound, religious, and moral training, in strict accordance with the principles of Wesleyan Methodism*" it opened its doors in 1844. The school was a boys-only establishment until 1911 when it became one of the first Protestant co-educational institutions in Ireland, although boys still outnumbered girls tenfold in 1944 when Joan arrived. Boys and girls were educated separately, and the boarders were housed in different buildings. For her first year, Joan was placed in Tullamaine House on Upper Leeson Street, the residency for junior female boarders a short ten-minute walk from the school, but any hopes she had of a fresh start with new friends in a more civilised, refined environment, were quickly dashed. On a positive note, the beds were better and the blankets were softer, so she was warm and comfortable. The food was tastier and there was much more of it, so hunger was no longer a daily distraction. Good manners mattered, and there were rules and order. And possibly best of all, there were no boys in her living quarters, which meant no unwanted attention and no physical bullies. However, from the outset Joan was marked as different; as the poor little Northern orphan girl. The new rules and etiquettes, whist welcome, were not straightforward. Joan already knew from Childhaven that girls could be unkind too, but she didn't expect to become an instant object of ridicule at this new home, so when she didn't fully understand at first that she shouldn't request the salt but rather wait to be asked by someone else if she wanted it, or when she placed her cutlery in the wrong position, or ate her food in the wrong order, she was subjected to sneers and cruel comments. And when the hand of friendship was eventually extended, an unkind adult thwarted it. From the outset once again poor Joan struggled to fit in, as she heartbreakingly recalled in one of her letters:

> *"At Childhaven manners were a little rough but here we were expected to behave like young ladies. So of course everything I did wrong at the table was corrected in front of all the girls. As a result I developed an inferiority complex which took many years to overcome. One of the girls invited me to stay at her house for the weekend holiday the following term, but Miss Cooke, the head teacher, would not allow me to accept in case I disgraced myself. Was it any wonder I felt inferior to the others who had money and position."*

There was another issue to contend with too. Before she left for Dublin her father told her to keep a low profile, to reveal nothing about her past, to never mention the O'Beirne family name or disclose that she had received her First Communion in a Catholic church, and one in Dublin at that. So her first few months at Wesley were anxiety ridden ones: inadequacy at not knowing how to behave, shame at forgetting the language she was once fluent in, fury at being viewed as an orphan, and fearful of exposing her true identity or being spotted by a member of her mother's family. Her memories of her grandmother in Cashel and her uncles and aunts in Dublin had become hazy, and she may have doubted the validity of the happy ones she did retain, because although TP never discussed Ciss with his children, he did paint a vivid picture of Kate. And it was not a pleasant one. Referring to her as The Old Woman, he refused to call her by her name or even use the term 'your grandmother', creating an image of an evil witch-like character. While he didn't give the children full or proper details about their mother's death or what had transpired afterwards, he would occasionally let slip some angry, bitter scraps of information: the Old Woman wanted to steal Jack from them and keep him for herself; he had to rescue the poor baby from her wicked clutches; Pat and Bernie were Catholic bullies who ran him out of Dublin and prevented him from selling their possessions. He insisted it was the Beirnes' fault they were all in this position, the letter that he wrote in October 1939 forming the framework of his narrative. There are many choices that TP made over the years that we can question, many decisions he took that looking back at now from this pedestal of hindsight we are standing on, appear completely baffling. Sending Joan back to Dublin five years after he had smuggled her and the other children out of the city, five years in which he had apparently gone to great lengths to keep their whereabouts secret, must surely be one of the most perplexing. Two years later Kathleen would indeed join Joan at Wesley, and a year after that Ted would enrol at the school; three of his children returned to Dublin. Did TP simply believe that the security of a bursary was worth the risk of them being spotted by a member of the Beirne family? After all, the reassurance that his children would be afforded both an ongoing education and a roof over their heads absolved him of the responsibility of finding a family home for a little bit longer.

As Joan struggled to settle into this latest abrupt and unexpected change imposed upon her, she found herself missing her sister and brothers, even though they had not had a normal sibling relationship at Childhaven. She missed seeing her father every other Saturday too. For the first time in her life she was completely and utterly alone. The irony of having family members living just a mile or so across the city may have been lost to her then, but if she had been able to have contact with them, perhaps her first year at Wesley would have been a happier one. To add to the isolation Joan initially felt, she wasn't reunited with her siblings or father at the Christmas break, as there was nowhere for her to go. Retuning to Childhaven wasn't an option, neither was staying with TP at his Cliftonpark boarding house. And so TP called on another family member for help, this time his brother Edward. Eddie had by now left Pakenham Hall and was working as a gamekeeper on a country estate in Portaferry on the tip of the Ards Peninsula, just twenty miles south of Childhaven, where he lived with his wife, May, and their children. One of their daughters, Georgina, was a similar age to Joan and the two girls hit it off. Finally Joan had found a friend, another girl to be at ease with. She would see her own family again during their summer holiday trips in 1945 and 1946, but other than that, school breaks were either spent with Uncle Eddie and Auntie May in Portaferry, or else she remained at Wesley.

By the time Kathleen joined her sister in Dublin in September 1946, arriving for the start of the new school year term, TP getting the timing right for once, Joan was much more settled. She still struggled with feelings of inadequacy and anxiety, but she had finally made a few friends and was enjoying her studies. She had moved from Tullamaine House to Epworth Hall, the new accommodation for girls, which Kathleen was housed in too, and it was here she began to relax into boarding school life. She still missed her family dreadfully though, so was delighted to finally be living under the same roof as her sister again. Kathleen took to life at Wesley like a duck to water. She was not tarred with the same orphan girl status that Joan had been. Although everyone knew the girls were sisters, it no longer seemed to be an issue. Kathleen was ecstatic to have left Childhaven. She did worry about leaving her brothers behind, especially Jack, but was delighted to be reunited with Joan, and excited to commence boarding school life. The dormitories in Epworth Hall were small, with just four to six girls per room. They would form secret societies, and play cards, a forbidden activity, and read under the covers by torchlight. It was a million miles away from their bedrooms at Childhaven. Their routine was still regimented. The rules were austere and the staff and teachers were stern and strict, but compared to Childhaven, Wesley was a doddle. Kathleen felt an immediate sense of ease and freedom, something she hadn't experienced in years. In her first few days she made firm friends with a girl from Cork called Fen. Fen hated Wesley. She was used to her own bedroom at home in Cork, to driving around the countryside in her mother's car, to going out to play when she felt like it and into town when the fancy took her. To Fen, Wesley was a form of imprisonment and she couldn't understand her friend's enthusiasm.

Joan's adjustment was slower, but it did come, and she particularly enjoyed her third and last year at the school with her sister by her side. By her final term she had even started to interact with boys, as some of her classes were now mixed. To her surprise she enjoyed their company, delighted to realise that not all boys were like Davy Barr and her distant cousin from Lurgan. She was shy on a one-to-one basis, but would readily join in with class discussions and joint social activities involving the opposite sex. The girls began to enjoy a cultural life for the first time too. Organised visits to Dublin's museums and art galleries were regular weekend activities, and there were occasional trips to the theatre and organ recitals at the cathedral. Joan took piano lessons, they both joined the school choir, and enjoyed attending the Wesley Debating Society events as regular audience members. They played hockey and tennis and practised Swedish Drill, a form of physical exercise popular at the time. Naturally, religion was a prominent feature of life at Wesley too. A Christian attitude permeated through every element of the school and the boarding facilities, which was a great source of comfort to the sisters, especially Joan.

The girls also enjoyed their studies. The most usual course of study at Wesley was a six-year period of schooling from the age of twelve to eighteen, culminating in the Leaving Certificate examination. To complete the Certificate however, they would need to be fluent in Irish, which Joan had all but forgotten and Kathleen had never learned. While they were both forced to take Irish classes, it was clear they would never catch up sufficiently to pass an exam in the subject. In addition, sitting the Leaving Certificate would require a guarantee that their bursaries would be extended until they were both eighteen; a guarantee that was not forthcoming. Thankfully, the school provided the option for certain pupils, particularly those attending on bursaries, to take commercial studies, which both girls elected to do. Alongside most of the standard subjects, they studied bookkeeping, shorthand, and basic business methods, and just as they had been at Millisle National School, the girls were enthusiastic pupils; studious, bright, and diligent. In Joan's leaving report, the headmaster wrote:

> "...she has shown herself to be a consistent, capable and diligent student, both anxious and able to improve. As a boarder she had

> *proved to be adaptable to people without losing in strength of character and leadership. She is willing and helpful. I have pleasure in recommending her for any position of trust."*

And when it was Kathleen's time to leave the school, she received an equally positive endorsement:

> *"...she is a girl of excellent character and Christian principals, sociable, cheerful, conscientious, and entirely trustworthy."*

In the autumn of 1947, Ted would also make the move to Wesley, leaving Jack as the last remaining Pakenham in Childhaven. Kathleen would still be in Dublin when Ted arrived, but Joan would not. For at the end of the school year in June 1947, she would leave Wesley and return home. The question was, where would that home be?

CHAPTER 20

With every passing day there was a risk that one of the children might be spotted in Dublin by a member of the O'Beirne family. Granted they were now teenagers, a far cry from the two little girls and toddler boy who had been removed from the extended O'Beirne family several years previously. From that perspective they would have been unrecognisable, and yet, they were undeniably Beirnes. Kathleen was the spit of her grandmother Kate as a child, while Joan bore more than a passing resemblance to her mother. And Ted was his uncle Albert's double. The familial similarities may not have been enough to stop Pat or Bernie or Albert, who by then was also living in Dublin, or even Jack's godmother Mollie in their tracks if they had happened to pass the children on the street, but they might have triggered a second glance at least. Dublin was a small city at the time, the galleries and museums that the Pakenham children visited all located in the same general area. And St Stephen's Green has always been a popular destination for a weekend stroll, a park that Mollie Winters especially would have frequented on a regular basis.

A few months after Joan arrived in Dublin, she began to receive invitations to tea from some of TP's old Wilson's associates. The invites were extended to Kathleen, and then, in turn, to Ted. Some of these tea outings took place at the Dublin homes of the gentlemen in question, some in popular tearooms such as Bewley's Café on Grafton Street, the busiest shopping area in the city. It is difficult to believe that Ciss's brothers, Pat in particular, would not have kept an eye on Mr Sharman, Mr Hick, Mr Johnson and Mr Cox over the years. They were his only source of possible connection to TP and the children, and if anyone knew their whereabouts, if anyone harboured TP's secrets, they did. And as well as the afternoon tea engagements, there was other social interaction with the gentlemen, or at least with one of them. By the time Kathleen arrived at Wesley in September 1946, Mr Cox had taken ownership of a guesthouse in Bray on the south Dublin coast, and the girls began to stay there during mid-term breaks, until they discovered their father was paying his friend for the favour. Outraged, they told him not to waste his money, and from then on stayed at Epworth Hall during the shorter school breaks, and at Portaferry for the longer ones. It begs the question, just how much of a friend was Mr Cox to TP? How much of his willingness to help the family escape Dublin in 1939 was driven by genuine friendship, and how much by a determination to ensure the Catholic church would not claim the Pakenham children? But regardless of Mr Cox's motivations, sending the girls to Bray was another potential risk, as the seaside town has always been a popular daytrip spot for families who live in the city. Pat or Bernie could easily have gone there on a family outing during mid-term breaks or on a spring Sunday afternoon.

The O'Beirnes, of course, would never have expected their sister's children to attend a Methodist run school in the heart of Dublin city. They could never have imagined that their eldest niece would arrive back on her true home turf five years after her disappearance, followed in turn by her sister and one of her brothers. But if they had randomly happened upon one of TP's former associates sitting in Bewley's café with a couple of teenagers who looked vaguely familiar, well, the game may well have been up. Whilst Joan was initially reluctant to venture out, scared to be seen, she relaxed in time, especially when Kathleen was with her. Kathleen was less anxious, Ted not concerned at all. TP travelled to Dublin himself on a few occasions, bringing each of the children down to the city when they first started at Wesley. Perhaps his own anxieties about the children being spotted lessened over time. Or perhaps he believed that by the time Kathleen arrived in Dublin and seven years had passed, they would have been forgotten; that Kate and Pat and Bernie and all the other brothers and cousins and aunts and uncles would have moved on with their lives, Ciss and her children a sad but distant memory.

Of course the children had not been forgotten. Far from it. They would never be forgotten; certainly not by their grandmother. When we last checked in on Kate it was 1941. She had suffered two further bereavements, the deaths of her sons Michael and Terence just a year apart. The Blitz had destroyed much of Belfast where Kate suspected her grandchildren might have been living, and while there was still no news of them, she had not given up hope. By November 1944 when Joan, her eldest grandchild, the girl who had initially been passed off as an orphan, moved back to Dublin, Kate had been blessed with three more grandchildren. Yvonne was born to Bernie and Nancy in 1941, a sister for four-year-old Irene. John arrived in 1941, the third child of Pat and Agnes. And in September 1944 another John was born, this time in Cashel, the firstborn of Ned and his new wife May. But just before the Cashel John's birth, tragedy had struck the family once again. A baby girl, Anne, Kate's tenth grandchild and Bernie and Nancy's third child, died. She was two months old. In all probability, Kate never even got to hold the little girl. Five dead children, a deceased baby granddaughter now, and one stillborn, her husband dead too, and four grandchildren still missing.

Kate had suffered multiple other losses throughout her life. Her twin sister Elizabeth of course was the first, followed three years later by her older sister Mary Anne. Though she would have had no conscious memory of her sisters, the trauma of their deaths would have lingered within the family for many years. Three of her brothers had also died: Pat in 1903, and Michael in 1931, both of whom lived close to her in Cashel, and Thomas in New York in 1906. She would have keenly felt the loss of her brother Michael's only two children, Michael Thomas and Johnny, who died in 1901 and 1911 from whooping cough and meningitis respectively, as well as her niece Lillian, Thomas's daughter, who also passed in 1901. And in 1920, Annie Winters, her cherished sister-in-law and neighbour, my grandmother, had died, a year or so after giving birth to Mollie. By the autumn of 1944, Kate Beirne had suffered seventeen close family bereavements in her sixty-seven years; what a load to carry. It was as though she had been born into death and trailed the curse of it with through the years. Yet still she breathed. And still she prayed, every day.

On 2nd August 1943, Ned, the only Beirne son still living at home, married May Molloy of Cloonturk, a townland not far from Cashel. The couple had been courting for several years and planned to wed long before this date, but due to the custom at that time of not marrying during a period of mourning, their wedding had been pushed back several times due to the five close family deaths in four years. When the wedding eventually did take place, May moved into the farmhouse with her new husband and mother-in-law, all too aware of the dark shroud of grief that enveloped it. She had empathy for the older woman, stooped and wracked with grief, dressed only in black, who prayed every day that her missing grandchildren would be returned to her; or at least for news that they were still alive. With Ned's surviving brothers Pat, Bernie and Albert in Dublin, and Thomas in Liverpool, it was up to Ned and his new wife May to care for Kate. Kate was still active, despite the curve of her spine. She was still walking, still cutting potato splits, still boiling the comfrey. But life was hard and bleak and sad. Kate probably saw her Dublin grandchildren from time to time when Pat and Agnes and Bernie and Nancy brought them to the farm, though those visits would have been fleeting. And after Ciss died, she most likely never returned to the city herself. Then Ned's son John was born, and Kate had joy in her life again. She still prayed for Joan and Kathleen and Ted and Jack every day. She still loved her grandchildren in Dublin, every one of them, but John was special. He had been born with something called Erb's Palsy, which is essentially a dead arm. In those days there was no hospital treatment plan for such a condition, no physiotherapists working in rural areas, and so Kate took it upon herself to heal her grandchild. She massaged the baby's arm several times a day for months on end, until finally his arm began to respond. By the time he celebrated his first birthday he had regained full movement, and his arm never bothered him again. John would soon be joined by four sisters, two of them twins, and there would be more grandchildren in Dublin, and Liverpool too, but it was he who gave Kate Beirne reason to live again.

If only Kate had known, as she rocked her precious new baby grandson to sleep in the winter nights of 1944, that her firstborn grandchild who she prayed for every day was back living in Dublin, just a hair's breadth away from her sons.

CHAPTER 21

Joan's departure from Wesley College in June 1947 was not a surprise. She had known it was coming as her bursary was expiring and the commercial course she was studying would be concluding at the end of that school year. Her father knew that it was coming too. His eldest daughter would be seventeen at her next birthday. She was a young lady now, yet also still a child, and he was still responsible for her. Until this point, he had survived on a combination of his own wit, the generosity of others, and a healthy dose of luck. He had managed to cajole certain family members into taking in the children at various points in time, and relied on the kindness of strangers at others. He shared his story readily, keen to lay out the truth as he believed it to be, at pains to not be perceived as the villain of the tale. Moving into the boarding house on South Parade had perhaps been TP's greatest stroke of good fortune, because everything that transpired in the coming years stemmed from there. The Methodist friends he made in that house and his introduction to the Belfast Central Mission changed the course of Thomas Pakenham's life, and by association, the lives of his children. Childhaven, Wesley College, Jack's foster family, his own conversion to Methodism: it all happened because of the connections he made during those first few weeks in Belfast. In the eight years since TP had fled Dublin with the children, while they were passed from pillar to post, put into an orphanage, sent to boarding school, he had lived the life of a bachelor man. His digs were comfortable ones, inhabited by educated gentlemen and members of the clergy. His work at Edison Swan was steady if sometimes dull. It suited him. His stint as an Air Raid Patrol Warden had given him a sense of pride and responsibility, a belonging of sorts, and he resolved to continue with community work of some nature once the war was over. His increasing involvement in the Methodist Church and with the Belfast Central Mission in particular would give him that opportunity, introducing him to the merits of the Boys' Brigade. TP quickly immersed himself in the organisation, devoting the rest of his life to helping the hundreds of young boys, many from underprivileged backgrounds, who would pass through its ranks during his tenure.

Of course through all of this, TP was still a father. His first responsibility was still his four children. Childhaven had suited him. The Magills and the Jenkins and the Porterfields had suited him. Wesley College suited him. That he loved his children is unquestionable; he wanted them to be safe and cared for and educated, and if he could not directly manage those things himself then he made sure that others did. He would see them when he could and he would cry when he left them. And yet, the situation suited him. TP had never taken steps to remarry, unusual perhaps for a widower at that time. There was talk on one occasion of a lady from his congregation who was interested in stepping out with him, but TP showed no desire to pursue his admirer. And his sister Florrie tried to set him up with her friend May, to no success. May, as it turned out, went on to marry TP and Florrie's brother, Eddie, also a widower: the May and Eddie from Portaferry. As we know, TP had also never taken any steps towards finding a home for himself and his children to live in together, preferring the comfort and camaraderie of digs. But suddenly the time had arrived when he could no longer wholly rely on schools or institutions or the church or other people to care for his children. Joan was about to leave Wesley. Kathleen would not be long behind her. And then what?

Nevertheless, as the spring of 1947 turned to summer, and the end of the school year approached and then arrived, and as Joan packed up her belongings and prepared to leave Dublin once again, her father had still not addressed the question of what would happen to her next. Joan had nowhere to live. The summer break provided TP with a short stay of execution to resolve the dilemma. He would send Joan and Kathleen to Portaferry to stay with May and Eddie again, then the five of them would go back to Carnlough for their family holiday. After that, Kathleen would return to Wesley, and the boys to Childhaven, and Joan would … well, something would come up. And luckily for TP, something did. As it happened, Georgina invited Joan and Kathleen to spend six weeks with her in England. It was a holiday of sorts, but essentially Georgina decided it was her responsibility to make young ladies of the girls, to complete their education in manners and etiquette. She took them to London for a few days where they visited all the sights, attended a debate in the House of Commons, took afternoon tea in fancy hotels, and went to a performance of *The Gondoliers* at the Savoy Theatre. It was an eye-opening experience for Joan and Kathleen; a step up from the culture they had enjoyed in Dublin, and a world away from the confines of life in the orphanage. When the six weeks were up, Georgina and her elderly mother Lilly returned to Belfast with the girls, joining TP and the boys for that fortnight's holiday in Carnlough. Then Georgina and Lilly boarded the boat back to England, and Ted and Jack returned to Millisle, and Joan and Kathleen went to May and Eddie's until it was time for Kathleen's school term to start. The summer was over, and Joan's new life as an adult was about to start. She would move to Belfast, she would find a job, and, crucially, she needed somewhere to live. Finally, TP had run out of time.

TP could potentially have helped his daughter find long-term digs and secure a job, and then leave it at that, seeing her when he could, just as he would continue to do with her siblings. But he realised, perhaps with the input and persuasion of others, perhaps entirely of his own volition, that after eight tumultuous years it was finally time that he and his children became a proper family again. Still, the epiphany didn't quite come in time for Joan's move to Belfast to take up the position she had secured with a solicitor's firm in the city. Armed with her high achieving commercial certificates from a top-class boarding school, she had no problem in getting a job. Realising too late that acquiring a family home to rent (purchasing one was still out of the question) wasn't something he could do overnight, TP found temporary digs for his daughter until he could find somewhere suitable. Joan agreed to help her father look for a house, but it wasn't easy, and the pressure of the search coupled with her anxiety at living alone in digs led her to leave the solicitor's firm before her probation period was up. Finding a house, then acquiring furniture, then moving into the place and making it into a home became Joan's full-time job instead; not quite the role she had imagined for herself ahead of her seventeenth birthday.

The house in question was a large five bedroomed terrace on Cliftonpark Avenue – just across the road from the boarding house that TP had been living in for the previous couple of years. He had forgotten what it was like to live in his own home, so used had he become to the boarding house bachelor lifestyle where his meals were prepared for him, where his laundry was taken care of, where he had no domestic responsibilities or household decisions to make. Joan had no real memory of living in a proper house herself. She had been too young in Dublin to have been given proper household duties, and though she had her chores in Childhaven, such as sweeping the floors and scrubbing the tables, and had to make her bed and clean her shoes at Wesley, tasks like cooking and laundry and grocery shopping were beyond her. She had no idea what to do or where to start. She had no mother to teach her, no grandmother either, no one to watch and imitate. There was no aunt, no older cousin on hand, no female role model at all. The closest was Georgina, but Georgina's brief teachings in London had been centred around behaviour, not practicalities. And yet, regardless of her obvious inexperience her father expected her to take on the role of housekeeper without argument. While Joan struggled to adjust and maintain her father's standards, he, unsurprisingly, settled into his new home environment with relative ease.

There was, of course, the issue of the other children to deal with. Kathleen would stay at Wesley for a further two years until she was sixteen, and TP remained determined that Ted should attend the school too. However, an unexpected spanner fell into the works. Now that his father had acquired a family home, Ted was no longer eligible for a bursary from the Methodist Orphanage Society. For some reason, a clerical one perhaps, or possibly due to strings being pulled by TP, Kathleen's bursary remained secure for the duration of her tenure at Wesley, in spite of the registered change in her "orphan" status. However, as TP would now be expected to take his sons out of the orphanage and bring them to live at Cliftonpark Avenue once the house was ready, Ted could not avail of the same philanthropic funding that his sisters had been given. Undeterred, TP vowed to find another way. He made an approach to Sir William Robinson, a prominent Belfast businessman and dedicated Methodist who, TP discovered, had previously provided a personal bursary for a Methodist boy from Belfast to attend Wesley College. A couple of weeks into the new school term, twelve-year-old

Ted, still resident at Childhaven, took a bus from Millisle to Belfast to attend a meeting with Sir William at his city centre office. A week or so after that he was on a train to Dublin accompanied by TP, his bursary from Sir William successfully secured.

Ted wasn't nervous about starting at Wesley. He knew that if he could cope with life at Childhaven, he could cope with anything. But the fact that he, like Joan, was coming late into the term did not make for the smoothest of transitions. Once again, alliances were already in place, friendships well underway. Even worse, the other boys, who had all been preparing for their first year at Wesley for months beforehand, had all arrived with the requisite sports gear. Ted had none, and as TP apparently didn't have the funds to buy him any, poor Ted had to wait six weeks for free coupons to come through so he could at least secure his rugby kit. During that time, he was forced to stand on the sidelines and watch his classmates play the game, desperate to join them on the pitch. He had heard about rugby but had never seen it played before, and as he stood on those sidelines, Ted instinctively knew he had found his sport. His contemporaries knew nothing of this new boy's background, save that he had come from Belfast, so he at least escaped the orphan tag that his eldest sister had been given. And for the duration of his stay at Wesley, Ted never told a single soul that he had spent the previous eight years in an orphanage. On his first day at the school, a boy from his class pushed him up against his locker and snarled into his ear

"I hope you're not going to be a stoolie, boy."

Ted couldn't help but laugh to himself. *If only you knew where I've come from,* he thought, *I'm going to survive this place better than any of you.* As far as Ted was concerned, he was simply swapping one boys' dormitory for another. But once he settled, he fell in love with Wesley. After the slightly awkward start, his easy manner soon attracted friends, and his prowess on the rugby field helped him to fit in. Like his sisters, he was not eligible to sit the Leaving Certificate due to his lack of Irish, but he excelled academically regardless, particularly at maths, Baldy Palmer's teaching paying dividends. Of the three of them, Ted was the one who got the most out of Wesley. He enjoyed everything about the school, and relished the freedom he had at weekends to wander around the city and discover Dublin, completely unperturbed by the suggestion from his father that he should keep his head down. He didn't see much of Kathleen during that first term, if anything at all, until it was time for them to travel back to Belfast for the Christmas holiday.

When Ted left Childhaven, Jack had just turned nine. He was too young to go to Wesley, and it's unlikely that TP would have managed to acquire another bursary at any rate. But while Ted and Kathleen were in Dublin, and his father and Joan were now living together in Belfast, Jack remained at Childhaven, the sole Pakenham left in the orphanage. He must have wondered at this perceived abandonment. He must have questioned why, when his father had now acquired a house, an actual house with multiple rooms and only he and Joan to fill them, his home was still the orphanage. He must have thought, if only fleetingly, that he wasn't good enough; for why else would he have been separated from the rest of his family yet again? Obviously, TP wasn't going to leave his youngest son at Millisle indefinitely, but his focus, at least initially, was on moving into the house and getting Ted sorted with a place at Wesley. Jack would have to wait. There would have been no malice in his thinking, no intended cruelty. He simply couldn't navigate too many changes at once, and wouldn't have paused to consider how this latest development would affect his youngest son.

Eventually, in November 1947, almost two months after TP and Joan had moved into Cliftonpark Avenue, Jack was brought to join them. He was enrolled into the Model Public Elementary School, a state primary school close to the house. Just like Joan and Ted, he arrived late in the term, and struggled to fit in at his new school and bond with his classmates as a result. His new-boy status aside, Jack's small frame and County Down country accent immediately set him apart from the other boys in the class, and he was an instant target for mockery. His natural inclination was to retaliate with his fists, and when on his very first day another boy laughed at the cumbersome black boots he was wearing, the standard orphanage foot attire, he grabbed the boy in an armlock and rubbed his face against a rough brick wall, marking his card with both his fellow classmates, and his new headmaster.

Once more TP's decision making comes into question, his inability to get his timings right impacting negatively on his children's wellbeing. As we have noted, Joan's departure from Wesley was not a surprise. He could have made sure she had a home to live in when she left. He could have arranged Ted's bursary to Wesley in advance of the new school year, and registered Jack to start at the Model in September. He could have taken the boys out of Childhaven together at the end of June, orchestrating things so that all four children moved into the new house at the same time, spending the summer there, as a family. But for whatever reason, be it a predisposition towards disorganisation, or an inability to realise the importance of structure and security in the lives of his children, or the hope that someone else would step in to take care of things, he misstepped yet again.

By the end of that year, however, the house was in order, or at least halfway to being so. There were beds in each of the bedrooms, a table for the family to eat around, and chairs for them to sit on. Some curtains had been hung, some linen had been purchased, and adequate cutlery and crockery acquired. Joan had not yet returned to work, helping her father with an anxious reluctance. Still feeling overwhelmed by the task of keeping house, she was doing her best to make a home for the family, determined that the coming Christmas would be a happy one. TP, to his credit, wanted that too. This would be the first Christmas he had spent with his children since 1937, a full decade previously. Ciss was still alive then. Joan was seven, Kathleen four, and Ted two. Jack was yet to be conceived. By the following December, everything had changed, so TP wanted this first Christmas together again to be special. He bought gifts and decorations and drafted in help for Joan with the food preparations. He got a tree, and thought of games to play, and he even made an episcope projector from wood and mirrors for their post-dinner entertainment.

Ted and Kathleen took the train together from Dublin to Belfast for the Christmas break, not quite knowing what to expect. Kathleen had yet to even see the house. Ted had spent one night there in October before going to Wesley, Joan sewing name tags onto his uniform and few basic clothing items late into the evening. It had been sparsely decorated then, with basic furniture and curtainless windows. It certainly didn't feel like home, not that he had any real concept of what home should feel like. But when they walked through the front door of Cliftonpark Avenue on that cold December evening, they almost stopped in their tracks. The smell of Joan's freshly baked wheaten bread wafted out from the kitchen. A roaring fire crackled in the drawing room grate. Jack lay on his stomach in front of the hearth listening to *Dick Barton Special Agent* playing on the radio. Ted looked around the room. His sisters were hugging. His brother rolled over and waved up at him. His father smiled and nodded slowly, there may even have been a tear in his eye. *Well*, thought Ted, smiling himself, *so this is what family life is.*

PART 3
HOME

"The ache for home lives in all of us, the safe place where we can go as we are and not be questioned"

~ **Maya Angelou**

CHAPTER 22

It took some time, but gradually the Pakenhams did become a proper family again, and an extremely close one at that. Although it had taken him eight long years, signing the lease papers on Cliftonpark Avenue was one of the most positive things that TP ever did for his children. They finally had somewhere to call home again, the pledge he had made to his dying wife at last fulfilled. Naturally there were still some bumps along the road, and TP's questionable decision making would continue to play a pivotal part in the trajectory of each of their life journeys for some time to come.

With Joan and Jack and TP all living together in the Cliftonpark house, and Kathleen and Ted back in Dublin for the spring school term at Wesley, January 1948 should, in theory, have been the happiest start to a year for almost a decade. But Jack was struggling to adjust to his new life, and Joan was struggling to cope with hers. Although Jack was ecstatic to leave the orphanage he so deeply detested, he had become somewhat institutionalised during his four years at Childhaven, as indeed all the children had to a degree. He was used to sleeping in a dormitory with up to twenty other boys. He was used to poor table manners, to questionable hygiene, to secretly stashing food and constantly looking over his shoulder. And he was used to living in a constant state of high alert, always at the ready to defend himself. Sleeping alone in this big ramshackle three storey house with just he, his father and Joan to fill it, was disconcerting. The doors creaked, the windows rattled, wind whistled through the rooms. These noises weren't new as such, they would have been present at Childhaven too, but masked or softened by the sounds of communal sleep: snoring and coughing and mutterings in dreams, beds squeaking, chamber pots being used, occasional weeping. To his bewilderment, Jack missed those sounds. He missed the dormitory. He missed the other boys, even, irrationally, the bullies. He missed Matron scolding him, and Mr Young shouting at him, and Baldy Palmer sneering at him. He missed Childhaven and his life there, because that was the only life he had ever really known, or at least could properly remember. He felt frightened and lonely at night in his bedroom all by himself, confused about why he wasn't happy, about why he missed the hell on earth he had been so eager to leave behind. And he resented his father and his sister, both of whom he still felt he barely knew. His whole life long he had yearned to live with his father in a proper house with their very own kitchen and their very own table and their very own front door, and now that it had finally happened, he didn't want it. And to make matters worse, the sister who had rarely interacted with him when she was at the orphanage, who he had scarcely seen for the past three years, was now bossing him about and telling him what to do, like she was Matron, or trying to hold his hand when they walked to church, like she was his mother. Well, she was neither, and Jack wasn't having it. He was filled with a burning rage he couldn't process, a new sense of injustice to rail against. And so Jack did the only thing he truly knew how to do, he fought. He fought boys at his new school, he fought boys on the street, he fought boys he met through the church he was now forced to go to, the Belfast Central Mission, and at the Life Boys, the junior division of the Boy's Brigade in which his father had immediately enrolled him. He didn't know how to be a son to his father, or a brother to Joan, and they, in turn struggled to fit into their own new roles of fulltime parent and dutiful daughter come supportive big sister.

By the start of 1948, Joan was working once again. That fleeting week she had spent at the solicitor's firm back in October was an unfortunate false start, so with the house now established and furnished to a degree, she wanted to properly commence her working life, and found an office position in Kelly's Coal Yard at Belfast Docks. TP approved of both the company and the salary, as an additional household income would be most welcome. Indeed over the coming years, Joan would contribute towards the ongoing education of her siblings, helping with uniform expenses, stationary, and travel costs. Joan had previously been offered an office job at the Guinness headquarters in Belfast, but TP most certainly did not approve of that. No daughter of his was going to work for a company that sold alcohol. Kelly's was much more respectable. Job or no job, however, he still expected Joan to keep the house too. He wanted his naive and anxious seventeen-year-old daughter to both earn a living and step into the shoes of the landladies he had become accustomed to. Try as she might, Joan still struggled with domestic chores, and found the stress of combining a full-time job with keeping house too much to bear. She was exhausted, and frustrated, and lonely. She had yet to bond with her new work colleagues, or with the girls at the Belfast Central Mission's Christian Endeavour Society that her father had insisted she join, her inability to accept any offers of social excursions in the evenings or at weekends due to her commitments at home not helping. Living in Belfast, becoming a working woman, and experiencing true family life were not at all as Joan had expected, and she yearned to return to Dublin and Wesley. As Joan's unhappiness deepened and her anxiety exacerbated, the memory of the broken little girl he had taken from Charlie Pakenham's house in Lurgan no doubt triggered in TP's head, and he realised he had to act. And so he did what he'd become accustomed to doing in delicate situations involving his children; he turned to others for help. He wrote to Georgina with a proposal. She, as it transpired, was already aware of Joan's predicament as her young cousin had written herself. An agreement was reached, the ins and outs of which we do not know, and in early 1948, Georgina arrived at Cliftonpark Avenue, tasked with completing the job of turning the house into a home, and teaching Joan how to manage it. There may have been a timeframe suggested, there may not have been, but the assumption most likely was that Georgina would stay for a few months, until early summer, perhaps. As it transpired, she stayed for three years, long enough to see both Kathleen and Ted return from Dublin and settle into their new Belfast home too.

With Georgina under its roof, the house truly began to take shape. More furniture was purchased, more curtains hung, more kitchen essentials acquired. Ornaments and soft furnishings appeared, flowers were put into vases, pictures were hung, clocks placed. Provisions were ordered from local grocers and butchers and bakeries, only essentials or emergency supplies would be bought in an actual shop. That was not Georgina's way. She taught Joan to steam vegetables and baste meat and stew fruit for jam, to fold eggs into flour and bake breads and cakes; Kathleen too, when she was at home on a school break. Though the girls, Joan in particular, were her focus, with lessons in laundry, and dusting, and general housework also on her rigorous agenda, the boys didn't get off entirely scot-free. Georgina was so very traditional in many ways, but ahead of her time in others, and did not hold firm to the notion that cooking and baking and household chores were exclusively female tasks. So she taught Ted and Jack to sew and knit and bake too, the latter of which Ted in particular took to. She showed them how to peel potatoes and carve the Sunday roast, to clear the table, and wash the dishes, and light the fire. They were dispatched on errands that needed to be run and offered up for interior decoration on occasion too, helping the men whom TP had enlisted from church to paint walls and hang wallpaper. TP observed and instructed, but rarely participated in the inner workings of this home that was being built around him, reserving his energy for and dedicating most of his spare time to the Boys Brigade.

Joan gradually eased into her new role of a working teenage girl come apprentice homemaker. She was both relieved by Georgina's presence, and resentful of it. Any hopes she had harboured that her cousin's arrival would allow her to neglect all domestic duties and focus entirely on work and building a social life were quickly abated, and she realised she was undertaking some kind of unspoken apprenticeship. But at least there was structure to it now, at least there was someone to guide her. Georgina taught her well, but without the natural love and nurturing that her own mother would have. Joan also had a little more free time, and so was able to make a friend or two and attend some church related social events, but she was not as carefree as many of the new young people she was meeting were. Georgina had high expectations and demanded a great deal of attention, and Joan knew that whenever she left them, as she inevitably would, it would all be up to her again. Slowly she began to absorb her older cousin's ways and habits, Georgina's insistence on routine and the proper way of things subconsciously rubbing off on her.

Kathleen, Ted and Jack, while not quite adoring of Georgina, were fond of her. She brought structure to their lives, even if that structure was sometimes bewildering, and she almost singlehandedly made the house into a home. She was a tough taskmaster, a perfectionist with ideas that were seemingly above her station, and by association, theirs. She instructed Jack to stand straight and respond to visitors in the appropriate polite fashion. She told Ted to adopt a Dublin brogue as it was preferable to his hard, northern accent. Manners and etiquette were paramount. Everything had to be entirely proper and just so. When money was tight, as it mostly still was, fish knives and fancy coffee sets would be purchased regardless, or an afternoon tea party for TP's friends from church would be organised, with all the trimmings. The children, excluded, would peek through the dining room door, and wait for the leftovers, a memory perhaps of Childhaven triggered. But at least there *would* always be leftovers on these occasions, and there would be supper too, and proper Sunday lunch. They would eat together at a table adorned with a crisp white tablecloth, a small vase of flowers, and cutlery precisely placed in the correct order. There would be pies and roasts, and delicacies like tongue, and dishes they had never heard of before, like kedgeree. It was a far cry from the fatty slops they were forced to eat at the messy communal table at Childhaven, and the hunger that had haunted them for years would never return.

Georgina never tried to parent the children as such. She didn't shower them with affection, or mother them, or help them with their studies. She didn't read to them or play with them or provide counsel. Her cousins did not become her substitute children, but there is no doubt that she cared about them deeply. It is no great leap to surmise that if Georgina had not come to Belfast when TP asked her to, if she had been disinclined to help her uncle, or had commitments of her own in Harpenden, or if her mother Lilly had been incapacitated and required her daughter's attention herself, then life at Cliftonpark Avenue may have worked out very differently.

As for TP, he and Georgina enjoyed a cordial relationship, the narrow age gap making them more like contemporaries than uncle and niece. She bossed him around a little and indulged him too at times. He let her get on with things, the less he had to do with the running of the house and the organisation of the children's day to day lives, the better. He would have seen how she was coaching the girls, especially Joan, and it would have no doubt brought him great satisfaction. Not only would he be well cared for himself when Georgina returned to England, but he knew too that his daughters were becoming able young women prepared for married life, if that is what they chose. And he must, on occasion, have thought about Ciss as he watched Georgina teach Joan and Kathleen how to stuff a goose, or griddle potato bread, or steep the fruit for the Christmas pudding. He must have considered how different their lives would have been if she had lived, if they had stayed in Dublin, if the children had remained Catholic and he had not discovered Methodism. Almost nine years had passed since he had written that letter absolving himself of any wrongdoing in how things had panned out after her death. There was no sense of guilt in his words then, no acknowledgment of responsibility, no mention of an orphanage. In those intervening years had guilt ever arrived, nudging at his conscience? Did regret ever penetrate his soul? Or did he hold firm to the belief that everything he did was for the best; that, guided by God, his actions, his decisions, his motivations, were entirely justified. And perhaps they were. He had never completely abandoned his children after all, and although it had taken the best part of a decade, had finally found them a family home once again.

CHAPTER 23

Kathleen left Wesley in June 1949 and following her summer break began a bookkeeping course at Belfast Technical College. She adjusted well to life in Belfast, settling into her new environment with more speed and ease than any of her siblings had. Even though she missed her friends at Wesley, her outgoing chatty manner ensured she quickly made new ones. She was very happy to be finally living permanently in the house that had gradually become home over the previous two years, to have the luxury of her own attic bedroom, and to eat Georgina's home-cooked meals every day. She readily pitched into the running of the house, accepting the chores she was given with grace and good humour, easing the burden of responsibility that Joan had been carrying just a little. But there was never the same expectation of Kathleen from either TP or Georgina. TP still viewed his eldest daughter as the natural homemaker, and Georgina focused most of her attention on grooming Joan for that very role. Kathleen obviously learned the same skills and domestic practicalities from Georgina that her sister had, but she felt less pressure to emulate her cousin, less inclined to replicate her ways. She was especially delighted though to be living under the same roof as Joan once again. Although the differences in their personalities and mannerisms had become more evident over time, the two sisters adored each other. She also began to bond more with Jack, though she found herself pulling him out of scraps once again, still on the alert for potential bullies and aggressors, just as it had been at Childhaven. And for the first time, Kathleen began to form a proper relationship with her father, though he was often absent from the house, tied up with one church related activity or another. Kathleen quickly became involved in the church herself, joining Joan at the Christian Endeavour Society where she enthusiastically embraced the organisation's social activities, and also at the Girl's Brigade, the female equivalent of TP's precious BB. Kathleen's faith had come to her more slowly and less intensively than Joan's had, but by the time she became an active member of the Belfast Central Mission church, she knew she shared her sister's commitment to God. All in all, Kathleen threw herself into this next phase of her still-young life with enthusiasm, positivity, and a hope for her future that just a few years earlier she would not have dared to contemplate. The further she moved away from it, the smaller Childhaven and the horrors it contained became, and, consciously or otherwise, she began to pull a curtain around the memory of those dark, cold, hungry, frightening, years.

Down in Dublin, Ted had already begun to block out Childhaven and everything that had happened there too, perhaps subconsciously at first, and then very much deliberately. He was enjoying life at Wesley so much that a determination not to sully the experience by reflecting on his life at the orphanage meant he rarely thought of it. None of his classmates knew he'd lived in an orphanage, not even his closest friends. Even though Ted spent more time at Childhaven than any of his siblings, he had always inherently known that his time there would pass, that eventually he would be free of it. The certainty that there would be more to his life than the perimeter of the orphanage grounds and Baldy Palmer's classroom was what got him through those eight long years. And now he was free. He had survived. He was living in an exciting city and attending a wonderful school. He was learning interesting subjects, gaining new knowledge every day, playing the magnificent game of rugby that he loved so much, and enjoying new close friendships. He had a comfortable bed in a small dormitory with enough blankets to keep him warm, and he was never hungry. Yes, his Irish teacher clearly detested him, and yes there was a more widespread distaste from some other staff at the school towards Northern children who did not speak the native language, but compared to the life he had been used to previously, dealing with a few condescending teachers was a breeze. Overall, Ted felt confident enough to embrace thoughts of his future, and that was something to celebrate. Any emotional scars he bore would fade, the bad memories with them. Head up, onward looking, that was Ted. But this predisposition towards positivity and acceptance was tested when Ted's time at Wesley was unexpectedly cut short. During the Christmas holiday of 1949, his father informed him that he would not be returning to Wesley when the new school year commenced in September 1950. The school fees were increasing, and the bursary he was receiving from Sir William Robinson would no longer be sufficient to cover them. TP could not afford to make up the deficit, so there was no option but to withdraw Ted at the end of the current school year in June. But at least there were the spring and summer terms to look forward to, his father told him, and plenty of rugby matches to be played before he would leave. Ted was devastated. He wept, one of the few times he can recall crying actual tears during his childhood, despite all the difficult things he had gone through, and begged his father to reconsider, to find another source of funding. But there was no discussion to be had on the matter. As was the way with TP, a decision had been made, and that was that. Ted returned to Wesley after Christmas with a heavy heart, but a gritty determination too to make the most of his final months in Dublin. However, there was worse news to come. Halfway through the Easter half-term break, TP received a call from Wesley informing him that there had been an outbreak of polio just before the holiday commenced, and very sadly two of the affected boys had subsequently died. The school would not now reopen until September. Ted would never return to Wesley, never get the chance to say goodbye to the friends he had made there, never wear the Wesley rugby kit again. His possessions were packed up by his house master and delivered to Belfast on the train. He was distraught, but his devastation was tempered to a degree by a sense of relief that he had escaped the polio outbreak. Ted had harboured a fear of polio for as long as he could remember, without really understanding why. He told his father this when the news of the Wesley deaths filtered through.

"That's obviously because your mother had it," TP replied. "That's why she had a limp."

More often than not, TP had refused to answer questions from the children about Ciss, batting them off, changing the subject, until gradually they stopped asking. For many years her name was rarely spoken. But he must have mentioned her limp and the polio on one occasion in passing, and though Ted had no memory of such a conversation, it had quietly seeped into his consciousness, becoming one of the few fears he couldn't tame. To make matters worse for Ted, any expectations he held of attending a grammar school in Belfast to complete his education were quickly dampened. Ted was a bright boy, an academic achiever. He wanted to go to university and held aspirations of becoming a teacher. To a casual bystander, the obvious thing for TP to do would be to send his son to Methodist College, a highly regarded Belfast grammar school with links to both Wesley and the Belfast Central Mission. But TP sent him to the same Belfast Technical College that Kathleen had attended, a further education establishment with a lower academic element. Perhaps he believed it would be better for Ted to pursue a practical qualification, a solid apprenticeship in bookkeeping or accountancy, just as he himself had done. Something that would see him land a nice steady job in a reliable profession at the earliest opportunity. Ted hated the technical college. He resented having to participate in carpentry and metalwork classes when he had so recently been studying literature, history, Latin and Greek. And once again he found himself the odd one out, starting the course in the last term of the year with other boys with whom he shared nothing at all in common.

Somehow, Ted managed to convince his father that he should be allowed to take the Queen's University matriculation module that the college offered, but even though he passed the exam with flying colours, when the time came, his pleading to actually go to the university fell on deaf ears. They couldn't afford it, TP told him. Ted would not become a teacher after all. He fared better with his new domestic situation though, enjoying the dynamics of family life, even happy to be back saving Jack from his scraps once again. It was not uncommon for Ted to be summoned by a neighbour to save Jack from a fight on the street with a boy twice his size. Ted was the last of the children to officially join the family, so to speak, and he adapted fairly easily to the house rules and routines that had been established by Georgina and his father. He had always liked Georgina, she intrigued him a little with her ladylike ways, and he admired how she had sorted the house out and pulled his father and siblings into line. But he was not broken hearted when the time came for her to return to England, nor indeed were the rest of them.

Towards the end of 1950, almost three years after she had swept into Cliftonpark Avenue with her plans and ideas, Georgina decided her job there was done. Her mother was keen for her to return home permanently. Lilly had visited Cliftonpark Avenue on several occasions, forming a particular bond with Jack, whom she would regularly dispatch to the corner shop to purchase secret supplies of cigarettes, slipping him a sixpence for his effort and discretion. She would instruct him to buy "proper" cigarettes, not the Turkish Pasha brand commonplace in the war years. More often than not, the shop would not stock anything *but* Pasha, supplies still affected by post-war shortages, and so Jack would return empty handed, only to be dispatched once again for the "better than nothing" option. But age and some health issues, not helped by her heavy smoking, had begun to restrict Lilly's mobility and travel was becoming more stressful. Georgina herself was eager to resume her life in Harpenden, to be invited to afternoon tea parties rather than host them. She was confident that after three years of training, the family could cope without her. The house itself was still a bit ramshackle in places, and most likely always would be. There would always be walls to paper and ceilings to repair, draughts to block and drains to unblock, but it was presentable and comfortable and clean. There were systems in place and each of the children knew what their responsibilities were. The girls to cook and clean and take charge of the shopping, the boys to tend the fire and empty the grates and polish the floors. Their father would continue to issue instructions and enlist help from the church and the BB if something requiring attention was beyond the capabilities of his children. Georgina was pleased with Joan in particular. She had been an excellent pupil; diligent, meticulous, and precise, and had even adopted some of Georgina's mannerisms. She had no qualms whatsoever about leaving her in charge.

And then, finally, it was just the five of them. Twelve years after TP had smuggled his four little children out of Dublin, away from their home and everything that was familiar to them, to begin a new life in an unknown land with strangers to care for them and a precarious future and multiple separations and reunions, they were at last all living together under one roof. Just them. The children had grown, Joan now twenty, Kathleen seventeen, Ted fifteen, and Jack twelve. They had lived as orphans, and attended a prestigious private school. They had known hunger and fear and cruelty, and snatched moments of joy. They had encountered bad people and good people and many in between. And they had become Protestant Methodists with Northern Irish accents, the Catholic youngsters that Ciss O'Beirne gave birth to all but forgotten.

CHAPTER 24

Back in Cashel, Kate was now seventy-three years of age and living in the new house that Ned had bought not far from the original dwelling. It was a veritable palace compared to the old farmhouse. Though still small, there was a little more space too to accommodate its nine inhabitants: Kate, Ned and May, their children John, twins Catherine and Nuala, Olive, and Angela, and six-year-old Brian, the youngest child of Bernie and Nancy. In the latest tragedy to befall the Beirne family, Nancy had died in March 1946, a year after the birth of Brian. One year previously in January 1945, Edward's brother Hugh, who still lived with the family and helped on the farm as much as his advancing years would allow, had passed away. And six months after Nancy's passing, Kate's beloved brother and close neighbour, John Winters, my own grandfather, left this world. Twenty close losses now for poor Kate Beirne, and her four grandchildren still missing.

After Nancy's death, Brian was brought to Cashel. A heartbroken Bernie could manage with his two other surviving children, nine-year-old Irene and five-year-old Yvonne, both of whom were of school age. But the baby was too much for him. He had to work, his busy job running the Liffey Bar providing no time for grief or family adjustments. And even with Pat and Agnes and his youngest brother Albert and his cousin Mollie Winters all in Dublin, and Nancy's family too, keeping Brian at home simply wasn't feasible. Despite her ongoing barrage of grief, and though the house was already full, Kate took the baby in, and reared him until his seventh birthday. And she loved him fiercely. Just a year apart in age, John and Brian grew up more as brothers than the cousins they actually were, both now the apples of their grandmother's eye. But still Kate thought about baby Jackie, and little Ted, and Kathleen and Joan, and still prayed for them every day. Though they remained as children in her mind's eye, she knew exactly what age they all were. She remembered each of their birthdays every year, silently marking them with a prayer, just as she remembered with agonising clarity the anniversaries of her deceased children's deaths. She knew that Joan was now a young woman of twenty, perhaps even a mother herself. She could be a great grandmother now, and she would never know it. Kathleen would soon be of marrying age herself, the boys still, hopefully, at school. She must have wondered about their lives relentlessly, visiting and revisiting multiple scenarios and possibilities in her head. Were they academic children, or practical ones? Were they serious or free-spirited? Healthy or sickly? Had they inherited their mother's kindly nature or her own work ethic? Had they become country folk, working on a farm somewhere in the rolling hills of county Antrim, or remained as city dwellers, settling in Belfast? Knowing their father as she had, the latter was surely the most likely. Had he taken another wife, that Protestant housekeeper who had accompanied him to the farm they day he snatched back baby Jack, perhaps? Did the children have a new mother, more siblings? Were they safe, were they happy, were they healthy, were they together? Did the girls resemble their mother, or did they look like Kate herself? Did the boys favour the Beirnes, tall and dark like her sons, or take after their father, small and slight and fair? Would she recognise them if they walked down the Cashel Road? Would she be able to pick them out in a crowd? Most definitely she would, in a heartbeat. They were her blood, they lived in her heart; but, she must have asked herself time and time again, did she live in theirs? Did they remember her, think of her, and more importantly, did they remember their mother? She must have agonised too about the children's religion, hoping and praying that somehow their father would have abided by their mother's dying wish and permitted them to stay within the Catholic faith, whilst knowing in her heart that he would almost certainly not have.

The rest of the family would think about the children too from time to time, but their own busy and stressful lives meant their anguish and curiosity diminished over the years. They had their own sorrows to deal with, Bernie in particular, a widower himself, with one deceased child and one absent one. The pain he must have felt on giving his baby son to his mother to rear must surely have brought thoughts of TP and Jack into sharper focus, a frustration rising up in him: why in God's good name had the man not accepted their offers of help? Why had he not left the baby in Cashel with his grandmother, and focused his attentions on the older children, as he himself was now doing? Or perhaps he admired his brother-in-law for keeping his family together in spite of the pressure he was under. Perhaps, for the first time, Bernie understood Tommy's decision to flee Dublin and the South, determined that the children would not be separated from him nor each other. Of course he did not know about the orphanage and the foster carers, or the boarding school that his two nieces and one of his nephews had attended right under his nose. And he never would do.

By 1951, Pat and Agnes had four children of their own. Pat was still working for CIE alongside his cousin Mollie, who had become a busy career woman. The shock and tragedy of Ciss's death and the children's disappearance had been replaced by the shock and tragedy of Nancy's death. Bernie and his girls were now the ones they must focus on, and they helped out as much as they could, leaving little room for contemplation about their missing nephews and nieces and ongoing worries about their likely religious conversion.

Albert, now twenty-eight, was living in Lower Baggot Street and working for Imperial Chemical Industries (ICI), rapidly making his way up the ranks of the company's Dublin office. He was courting a young woman named Nellie Bohan. Nellie also lived in Dublin, though she was born and grew up close to Cashel in the adjoining townland of Derreen, and the two would marry in 1953. Growing up there had been a considerable age gap between him and his siblings, the closest in age being Terence, who was eight going on nine, when baby Albert was born. Ciss, his only sister, was twenty-one, Hugh, the eldest brother, twenty-four. Kate herself was forty-six and Edward fifty-three, verging on elderly for parents of a newborn. And not long after Albert arrived, the litany of close family deaths began, Hugh the first to go just ten weeks later. Albert was born into a grief that grew denser with each new family loss, and it must have affected him. That and the extremities of age must surely have influenced his relationships and shaped his standing within the family. Perhaps, being so much younger, he always felt somewhat separate from the rest of them, more like a nephew or young cousin than a brother, more like a grandson than a son. Albert also went to boarding school for a period of time as a teenager, the only member of the family to receive such an education. Clearly a bright boy, he was awarded a prestigious scholarship to St Mel's College in Longford after sitting the challenging academic entrance examination. Most Sunday's, Kate would insist that Ned make the twenty-four-mile round trip from Mohill to Longford on his bicycle to deliver a food parcel to his youngest brother, a chore that even mild-mannered Ned was not always happy to do. By the early

1950s, Albert was a busy young career man, about to marry and start his own family, and any lingering resolve he might have had to track his sister's family down had been paused. For the time being, anyway.

Apart from Kate, the ongoing agony of Ciss's missing children was most heavily borne by Ned. Living with his mother was a daily reminder of their absence. In the twelve years since their disappearance, he had witnessed her grief on a daily basis, heard her prayers, watched her light candles for them each time he took her to mass. Each subsequent loss would weaken her further, press down a little more on the curve of her spine. He would have remembered the woman his mother was before darkness first descended on his family; strong and feisty, fearless even, an organiser, a doer, the no-nonsense matriarch of the Beirnes of Cashel. She was principled and loyal and courageous too. He might have thought back to the time when she looked after a former solider from the Irish National Army who was hiding out in a derelict house behind the Beirne's farm. Paddy Keville was the soldier's name, a familiar face in Mohill, a regular drinker in Fox's pub, Edward Beirne's local. At the end of the War of Independence, when the Irish Free State was established, Paddy joined the army full of bravado and hope for the future. But by November 1922, with the Civil War now in full flow, he had left. We don't know why he left, nor why he went into hiding, but for whatever reason, he believed his life was in danger, and bedded down in an old, abandoned cottage used to store thatch. Kate was the one who fed him, quietly delivering three full meals a day to the cottage for nigh on six months. Times were tough. She had nine children at home to feed, her husband and brother-in-law too, and money was scarce. Yet she somehow made sure that Paddy Keville was fed and tended to like one of her own. On Thursday 24th May 1923, a ceasefire was called. The war was over. The very next evening, believing he would now be safe, Paddy ventured across the bog to Michael Diffley's house in Currycramp where he knew a game of cards was in play. He was welcomed inside, a glass of something placed in his hand and a chair pulled out for him to sit at. A short time later the door latch knocked again, but this time the visitor wasn't welcome. The stranger pulled Paddy out of the house, walked him a short way up the road, told him to get on his knees and say a prayer. Then he put a bullet in the back of Paddy's head. Kate was distraught. All those months she had cared for this young man, who was just five years older than her eldest boy Hugh, all that time she had shielded him, and for nothing. A rage flew out of her the like of which Ned had never seen. "His poor, poor mother," she cried. In a couple of weeks, Albert would arrive, the new life providing a welcome distraction. And then, just two months after that, her Hugh was gone, and Kate became the poor, poor mother herself for the first time. Ned would remember not just Kate's grief, but her strength too. He admired his mother for what she had done for Paddy, and he admired her for rallying after Hugh died, for holding the rest of them up and pushing them through. And through all the subsequent losses and the increasingly heavy burden of grief, his admiration for her never wavered. But it pained him to see her so diminished, to know that neither the most recent deaths, nor the joy of new grandchildren, would dilute the ache she felt for the ones she begged God to give her news of.

Even if Ned had not shared a home with Kate, he would have found the grief of separation from his sister's children impossible to escape for two key reasons. Firstly, he felt partly responsible for what had happened at the farm on that fateful day in February 1939 when TP had snatched baby Jack from Kate's arms. He always believed that if he had been at home that afternoon, he could have prevented it. Perhaps he could have reasoned with his brother-in-law, sat him down at the table and had a chat about the situation, man to man. Perhaps he could have convinced him that leaving the baby with them, for the time being at any rate, was best for everyone, TP included. Perhaps he could have reassured him that they, Ciss's family, meant him no harm, that their offers of help and assistance were genuine; that they all loved the children, that yes, they wanted them to remain within the Catholic Church, and while he could see how that might present issues for TP, it was surely what Ciss would have wanted? Ned was a gentle man, a quiet man, not one to raise his voice or a hand to his children, or confront a neighbour, or row with a stranger. If anyone could have reasoned with TP, calmed him, sought a compromise, a resolution that worked for everyone, it was Ned. But in all probability, even his placid temperament would have been tested that day if he had in fact been present, and the outcome would have been the same. Especially as TP was not alone. He would, I am certain, have displayed empathy for his brother-in-law, who was grieving and so evidently under pressure, and after all, he was the boy's father. But his sympathy would not have extended to TP's companions. The second reason that Ned would never, could never, forget about his nephews and nieces was because his own wife had been through a similar experience herself as a child, and it had utterly shaped the woman she had become. At the age of twelve, May's mother Mary died, leaving three small children and a broken husband. Knowing she was dying, Mary pronounced that their youngest child, seven-year-old Roseanne, should be sent to her sister, also named Roseanne, in America. She would have a better life there, Mary reasoned, and her husband Paddy would be more able to cope with two children rather than three. And in turn young May, would be better placed to help her father if she had just one sibling to care for. And so early one morning, before dawn had broken, Paddy and his children made their way through the narrow roads of Cloonturk in their horse drawn cart to a pre-arranged meeting place, where a lady who was to be Roseanne's travelling companion was waiting. The handover was made, a terrified Roseanne crying out in despair. May begged her father to let her go too, to not leave Roseanne alone. But although the man collapsed on the ground, distraught and inconsolable, the arrangement had been made, and that was that. Roseanne and the stranger took a car to Cobh in County Cork where they boarded a ship bound for the United States. On arrival in America, already traumatised, the little girl's name was changed to Patricia, her aunt deeming it too confusing to have two Roseannes in the home. The sisters would correspond regularly for the rest of their lives, but they would only meet once again in person, when Patricia visited May in Cashel. May missed her sister every day, and when she met and married Ned and became part of the Beirne family, she felt her mother-in-law's grief as though it was her own, not begrudging her a second of it. When John her first born came along, May's joy was not contained to herself and Ned alone. It extended to Kate too. She knew, whilst not replacing the grandchildren she had lost, the new baby would be a distraction for her mother-in-law, and she was happy to let Kate tend to him and fuss over him; happy too when little Brian joined the family, and when her four girls came along. That was May's nature, benevolent, compassionate and utterly selfless.

So Kate was surrounded by love, and by children, and she adored every one of them. But in her dying days, it was Joan, Kathleen, Ted and little Jackie who she called out for. On a cold winter's day in February 1954, Kate Beirne took to her bed. She had enough of life and all the death that it had brought her, and was ready now for her own. It took five months to come for her. Five months in which she wailed and ranted and railed and pleaded for news, for reassurance that her grandchildren would not be waiting at the gates of heaven for her when she arrived. Ciss she was prepared to meet, and her sons Hugh and John Joe and Michael and Terence. Edward her husband too. But not the little ones. Please God, not the little ones. Kate Beirne died on 30th July 1954, two full weeks after her seventy-seventh birthday. For thirty years she had lived in a state of deep grief, the last fifteen of which were spent in the emotional wilderness of not knowing. The news she had prayed for so relentlessly, so desperately, so faithfully, never did come. Not for Kate.

CHAPTER 25

Back in Belfast, Kate Beirne's grandchildren did not know that their grandmother had just died. How could they have. As young adults with busy lives they would rarely have thought of Kate at all. On the rare occasions that their father spoke of her, he painted such an unappealing picture that if she did in unexpected moments wander into their minds, their question would more likely have been, *does she ever think of us?* As the years had passed, TP did not become any more forthcoming about his wife and her family, and when on occasion his children's curiosity would stir, and one or other of them asked a question, he would mostly either deflect or ignore them. On occasion though, if his patience was particularly tested, he would rant again about the Old Woman who wanted to steal Jack from them, the brothers-in-law who harassed him, the O'Beirne conspiracy to break up the family and raise the children as Catholics, omitting the crucially significant detail that they had in fact been baptised in the Catholic church. And so, while the children were aware of the bare bones of the story, of *their* story, they did not know the details. For a long time they believed that Pat and Bernie, the evil Dublin brothers from whom Joan, Kathleen and Ted were supposed to 'hide' during their years at Wesley, were their mother's only siblings, any memory that the girls may have had of other uncles at the farm soon deserting them, although Joan did still retain a quiet, unspoken notion of her uncle Ned. Gradually the children stopped asking questions, for a while at any rate. They would come again, but in 1954 they each had their own distractions.

Joan was now working at the Eagle Star insurance company as a shorthand typist. Her time at Kelly's Coal Yard had been marred by that surprise visit from an unwelcome caller from Lurgan. The incident had unsettled Joan, and while she enjoyed the work at Kelly's, she never felt entirely comfortable there afterwards. The job at Eagle Star was much more to her liking, with better pay and more chance of promotion. She would go on to run the Eagle Star office, and was also by default now in charge of running Cliftonpark Avenue. She now took her role as housekeeper extremely seriously, determined to maintain Georgina's high standards, demanding the same level of table manners and general etiquette from her siblings as their cousin had. Indeed, she amplified Georgina's yardsticks, developing a sharp and unyielding ritualistic perfectionism. Juggling shopping and cooking and cleaning with work left her little time to live the life that a young single woman in her early twenties should have been living. She became quite regimented in her routines, with certain evenings reserved for specific chores. Laundry, for example, may have been assigned to a Wednesday evening, ironing to a Thursday, baking to a Saturday morning, and nothing short of an earthquake would have derailed Joan's carefully constructed timetable. Any social activities Joan did embark on were connected to the church, and in every club or society she joined, she was persuaded to take on an administrative role. At the Christian Endeavour Society, she became first secretary and then governor. With the Girl's Brigade she progressed from lieutenant to captain. And when she joined a badminton club, she almost immediately became its secretary. Joan found it hard to say no. Perhaps it was an inherent desire to keep everyone around her happy. Or perhaps it was her way of maintaining a sense of control in her life. She never allowed her responsibilities outside of the home to overshadow her domestic responsibilities though, the family and the house remaining her priority. There were other things she missed out on because of those commitments. She would have loved to join the National Youth Hostel Association with her friend May from the Christian Endeavour, with whom she often enjoyed a Saturday afternoon bike ride to Helen's Bay beach for a swim and a picnic. May was an enthusiastic hosteler and hiker and tried to persuade Joan to join her, but Joan knew her father would never let her leave the family for a full weekend, let alone undertake something as frivolous as hiking or hostelling on a Sunday. Sundays were sacrosanct to TP. The only acceptable activities on the Lord's Day were worship and eating. No play, no sport, no socialising outside of church. No games at home, no housework beyond cooking and clearing the Sunday meal. Even the radio use was restricted to news bulletins or, at a push, classical music. Joan was also extremely keen to become a Sunday School teacher. The problem was, Sunday School at the Grosvenor Hall was held at two thirty on a Sunday afternoon, making the timing impossible for her. As the family returned home from morning service at one o'clock, she would not have enough time to cook, serve, and clear Sunday lunch, the most important meal of the week, and make it back to the Hall for the start of the class. Located in the centre of Belfast, it was a thirty-minute walk, or a twenty-minute bus ride from Cliftonpark. TP was keen to help. He could see how much being a Sunday School teacher meant to his eldest daughter. But rather than gather his other children around and inform them that Joan would no longer be responsible for Sunday lunch, that they must all play a greater role in the cooking and serving and clearing of the meal, himself included, he volunteered Joan's services at a nearby church instead. Carlisle Memorial Methodist Church was just a ten-minute walk from the house, and its Sunday School started slightly later in the afternoon. It was the perfect solution. Joan could still carry out her daughterly duties, and become a Sunday School teacher. Although she kept her links with Belfast Central Mission and the Grosvenor Hall, over the years Joan would become more involved with Carlisle Memorial. Its proximity to home was a happy convenience for her, reducing her stress levels around timekeeping, and opening up the opportunity for new friendships and social events. Despite enjoying a few dates however, mostly with young men from one church or another, Joan did not embark on any serious romantic relationships, perhaps, for a time at least, believing that love was not in God's plan for her, that her duty, her destiny, especially as she was the eldest child, was to look after her father and siblings. And so she watched on from the sidelines while one by one her sister and brothers embarked on their own romantic journeys.

Kathleen naturally helped Joan in the house, but she was much more relaxed than her older sister, not allowing household duties to interfere too much with her social life, which was also mostly connected to the church. If Kathleen wanted to do something, she generally did it. If she wanted to go somewhere, she usually went. She possessed a sense of adventure and spontaneity that her sister did not have, and was much more at ease in social situations. After leaving Belfast Technical College, Kathleen secured an office job at Broadway Damask, one of Belfast's long established linen manufacturers, where she befriended a girl called Edna Hazzard. Edna also happened to come from a Methodist household, and the two girls began to attend some social events together at each other's churches. One evening Edna invited Kathleen to her house for tea before a talk they were going to at her church, Lynn Memorial Methodist, not too far from

Cliftonpark. Edna had an older brother, Watson, who rolled his eyes when his mother instructed him to change into something more respectable when he arrived home from Mackies, the manufacturing firm where he worked operating heavy, sometimes greasy machinery.

"There's a wee orphan girl coming for tea," she told him.

Kathleen wasn't used to the 'wee orphan girl' tag. It had been used to refer to Joan at Wesley, but not to her, and eight years on from her time at Childhaven, she no longer felt the weight of the word that wasn't even true. Yet here it was in 1954, rising up again. She didn't take to Edna's mother, not one bit, but she did quite fancy her brother. And as it happened, when he saw the little orphan girl, Watson's head and his rolling eyes were turned too.

Nineteen now, Ted was working for the Belfast Corporation, the precursor to today's Belfast City Council, as a clerk. He had pleaded with his father again to be allowed to study for a teaching qualification, but TP was not for turning. There was no spare money to facilitate such a whim, especially as TP was about to embark on an exciting new business venture. He and a work colleague called David Bruce, were to open a small electrical wholesaler's shop at the bottom of their street. The premises had been identified and plans were in motion. Kathleen was to leave her job at Broadway Damask and work in the office doing the books, and TP and David would work in the shop. As Joan would be the only person left in the house with a regular wage, not only would there be no excess cash to pay for university fees, but it was crucial that Ted now entered the workplace too, and as soon as possible. A second steady household salary was imperative. Ted was initially very upset. Since leaving Wesley his life had not exactly panned out the way he had imagined it would do. But his inherent optimism and stalwart determination shone through.

There were other ways to succeed, he decided, and he would find his path. He applied for a clerical job at British Airways. There might be travel perks, he thought, or decent opportunities for promotion. At his interview it was revealed that occasional Sunday work may be required, and his heart sank. There was no way his father would allow that, and he was right. TP put his foot down, and once again Ted's plans were thwarted. His next application was to the Corporation and he passed through the interview process with flying colours, securing a position in the building surveyors department. Though he enjoyed the work, he knew it wasn't enough for him. He needed more. He needed a challenge. And so Ted made a quiet pledge, a pact with himself to take every opportunity within the Corporation that came his way, and to resume his studies alongside his job. He moved from the surveyor's department to the electricity one, and from there to education, all the while studying for his Chartered Institute of Secretaries exams. Outside of work, when he wasn't studying, he played rugby and took up tennis. And of course he was heavily involved in the BB, whether he wanted to be or not. Both he and Jack had no option where the Boys' Brigade was concerned.

When Jack left the Lifeboys he told his father that he didn't want to progress to the BB, he'd prefer the Boy Scouts, thank you very much. They were a much more interesting prospect. They went on proper camping trips to forests and mountains, not the front lawn of an orphanage, and carried knives, and sang songs that were not hymns. And therein lay the problem. The Scouts were not Christian enough for TP. His boys would both become members of the Boy's Brigade, and that, once again, was that. Although they didn't exactly hate it, neither Ted nor Jack loved the organisation either. They certainly never became as embroiled in it as TP was. But for several years during their teens and into young adulthood, it was the main way, sometimes the only way in which they could fully connect with their father. Ted did however love the Christian Endeavour. As with his sisters, his social life mostly centred around the society, with talks and debates, picnics, and treasure hunt games, and even some trips away. There was one trip in particular that everyone wanted to go on; the big Easter excursion to Craigmore House, which, yes, was the holiday home on the grounds of Childhaven. All four of the children went on at least one Easter outing to Craigmore. They were more like mini holidays really, lasting anything from five days to a week. And if being back at the orphanage, or at least a stone's throw away from it, caused them stress or anxiety, it seems the excitement of being on an adventure with friends, and more importantly people of the opposite sex, sufficiently diminished the fear. Ted found himself there in the April of 1954, Wednesday 14th April to be precise, a date etched in Ted's memory. He hadn't really wanted to go though, perhaps the concept of returning to Childhaven, orphanage or not, was pulling at his subconscious. Perhaps, in spite of his pragmatism about the years he spent there, he had a niggle of worry that the memory box locked and buried deep inside him would spring open and rise to the surface, the ghosts contained within it released. But he did go. And so, as it happens did a young seamstress from Belfast named Noreen McLarnon.

In the summer of 1954, while Kate Beirne was dying in Cashel, baby Jackie who she still cried out for night after night and would do so until she took her final breath, was fifteen. He would be sixteen that coming September. Sixteen years without Ciss. Sixteen years since the lightning bolt that fractured the Pakenham and Beirne families and sent the children up North with their father. Jack was still at school, though reluctantly so. After passing his 11-plus exam he had gone to Grosvenor High School in the city centre. He was bright and intellectually capable, but unlike Ted, did not harbour any academic aspirations. He still enjoyed English lessons, literature in particular, and art remained his key passion, but at that stage of his teenage life he had no ambitions to pursue either subject at a higher education level, never mind as a career. Although Grosvenor High was a grammar school with a natural feed to both Queen's University and Stranmillis Teaching College, many of Jack's contemporaries were leaving school that year to embark on trade apprenticeships in carpentry or electrics or plumbing, or accountancy. Or even at Harland & Wolff, the famous Belfast shipyard in the east of the city. Jack wanted to join them. In truth, he most likely assumed that he would be joining them as none of his siblings had stayed at school beyond the age of sixteen. He even took himself down to the shipyard one day to see what apprentice jobs were going, but as he looked about twelve at the time was shooed away. At any rate, TP was having none of it. For some reason, he was determined that Jack would be the one to stay at school and complete his General Certificate of Education. He had no apparent plan for what might happen after that, but school, he decided, was the best place for his youngest son. Jack wasn't pleased. School had continued to be a struggle for him, not academically, but procedurally. Rules antagonised him, teachers antagonised him, other pupils antagonised him. He was almost expelled on multiple occasions for scrapping, or giving out cheek to a teacher, or some other misdemeanour. On one occasion, he hit a girl in the playground for moving a ladder he was using to retrieve a football from a roof. He was halfway down the ladder at the time, having successfully recovered the ball and thrown it back to his friends in the playground below. When the girl pushed the ladder, Jack lost his footing and tumbled down onto the tarmac, the ladder landing on top of him. The girl and her friends found the whole thing hilarious, and Jack saw red when he looked at their laughing faces staring down at him. A memory of Childhaven and the bullying he witnessed and experienced there flashed into his head, and on instinct he leapt up, and slapped the girl across the face. It was an incident that haunted Jack for years, one he was not proud of, but he gradually came to accept the psychology behind it. TP would regularly have to plead his son's case with the headmaster, or call on one of his Methodist contacts with a connection to the school to speak on Jack's behalf. The pent-up anger that had plagued Jack throughout his childhood and the Childhaven era was amplified during puberty, and his teenage years were just as troublesome. At home, it was his relationship with Joan that was most affected. Joan struggled more than any of them to deal with Jack's rages and his seemingly untetherable energy. Ted mostly ignored his brother. Kathleen may have tried to reason with him. TP had never really learned how to discipline or teach his children, and besides, he was mostly too busy with church and the BB to deal with domestic matters. So he opted out as much as he could, and left Jack to Joan. She took his behaviour to heart, torn between wanting to calm and placate her youngest brother, and shake the waywardness out of him. The two clashed constantly. They did not understand each other, Jack's propensity towards chaos and questioning utterly alien to Joan, her meticulous perfectionism a source of immense frustration to him. And yet they were the two siblings who still wrestled with their memories of Childhaven; the two who were most affected by their time at the orphanage. But as they did not talk about it, to anyone, neither knew what the other was feeling. Jack was not inherently a bad boy. In today's world he might be diagnosed with something or other, post-traumatic stress perhaps, or even ADHD. But in the Belfast of

1954, Jack was just a confused and spirited teenager who had yet to find his path in life. He still had difficulty with relationships of any nature: with his father and siblings, teachers and classmates, and his few friends outside of school, instinctively believing that ultimately everyone in his life would either let him down, or harass him. Or worse, they would leave. And so trust was inevitably an issue. At fifteen, he was developing an interest in the opposite sex, but there was no way he could talk to a girl he liked, never mind ask one out. They would laugh in his face, especially Ethel Howard, the girl he'd harboured a secret crush on since he'd seen her two years previously at a church event. Ethel was beautiful. Tall and slender, she looked like Grace Kelly, and all the boys fancied her. But she was a world away from Jack and he knew he didn't stand a chance, so he kept his crush quietly tucked up inside his heart. Perhaps if he had known Kate, if he had been allowed to maintain a relationship with his grandmother, even from the distance of Belfast, the two might have spoken to each other on the telephone in the weeks before she died. Or written letters. Or a visit to Cashel might have been hastily arranged. And maybe Kate would have taken her grandson's hand in hers and asked him did he have a girlfriend, just as Ciss on her own deathbed had asked Annie Kate if she had a boyfriend. And Jack would have said, *well Granny, there's this girl Ethel, but she'd never look at me*. And Kate would have replied, *and why wouldn't she? Sure aren't you a catch. Now get away out of that and ask her out, and we'll see what happens*.

CHAPTER 26

Of course Kate Beirne wasn't the Pakenham children's only grandmother. When Kate died, Annie, their father's mother, was still alive. She was ninety, about to turn ninety-one, and preparing to move out of the cottage on Tullynally Estate that she had lived in since her husband Edward's death half a century ago. It must have been a wrench to leave her home and the estate. She had moved to Tullynally from Armagh as a young bride in 1886, almost seventy years previously, birthed ten children there, buried two of them in the local Church of Ireland cemetery, and mourned a third from afar. She had watched some of them marry and bear children of their own and held many of those babies in her arms. But she had not been present when her youngest son Thomas got married, may not even have been aware that the wedding was taking place until after the event. A staunch protestant, Annie would not have approved of Ciss Beirne, or the marriage, nor the Catholic children the couple bore; not the children themselves, but their baptised religion. She did at least meet them, though. We can't be certain how many times TP brought his wife and family to Pakenham Hall to visit his mother, but we believe it was a rare event. Neither Joan nor Kathleen held any memory at all of Tullynally or their grandmother Pakenham, but we know they did visit on at least one occasion not long after Ted was born. There is a photograph taken outside Annie's cottage on a sunny summer's day. Ciss is holding baby Ted in her arms and little Kathleen by the hand. Joan stands beside her grandmother, another younger woman, possibly her aunt Florrie, is behind her, her hands resting on Joan's shoulders. So there was some contact. Ciss and the children were known, and we must assume loved, by Annie, if not entirely accepted in her heart.

Ciss and TP visiting Pakenham Hall with his mother and children, Joan, Kathleen, and Ted (1935)

We can only speculate about TP's relationships with his mother and siblings as we don't know the full truth. But we do know that after Ciss died, TP did not seek solace with any of them, or if he did, it was denied. Although Florrie did spend that short while at Errigal Road in the aftermath of the tragedy, it was very temporary, and it seems none of his other sisters nor Edward his brother made the journey to Dublin to lend their support or see the children. And neither did his mother. And when he fled Dublin, it was not a sibling he ran to, at least three of whom were then living in the North, but a distant cousin. When he needed a home for baby Jack, it was initially a cousin of his mother's who took the child in, his sister Etta only doing so when TP had run out of options, and temporarily at that. The family must have known that first three and then all four of the children were in an orphanage, yet they did not visit nor write to them. On the face of it there seems to have been an absence of empathy for TP's situation from his immediate family, a lack of concern for the wellbeing of his children. They would however have strongly encouraged him to reverse his children's religious status and withdraw them from the Catholic church. Perhaps the idea that he should flee the country and relocate to the Protestant North was even planted by one of them. But there was no apparent practical, or emotional, or indeed financial support. Indeed, not one member of his family is mentioned or referred to in TP's letter of testimony, the only relative who does feature is his distant cousin, Charlie. And in later years he would write in another letter that he had "no one to turn to". TP would never offer any explanation as to why his family did not furnish him with comfort or assistance. Perhaps the overriding sentiment from his mother and siblings was that he had got what was coming to him by marrying a Roman Catholic in the first place, a sort of *well, you made your bed Tommy, and now you can damn well lie in it.*

Alternatively, this hypothesis may be entirely inaccurate. The family might indeed have proffered their support, offered him money, suggested options; to place one child here, perhaps, and another there. Annie herself could have proposed that she take in all or even one of them, at least in the short term. His brother and married sisters all had expanding families themselves and wouldn't have had the room to house four more, no one could have expected them to, but one additional child might have been manageable. But TP had made that deathbed promise to Ciss, and while he may not have been wholly able to fulfil it, surely keeping three of the kiddies together, albeit in an orphanage, was better than splitting them all up. Whatever the truth of it, he did what he did, and his family relationships, which were never especially close, remained distant for the rest of his days. Aside from his children, the church became his family, Belfast Central Mission and his beloved Boys Brigade filling any theoretical void. But he would still call on his brother and some of his sisters for help, when help was needed. Etta to take in Jack that time in Poyntzpass, Eddie and his wife May to look after the girls during the Wesley school holidays. And once a year, TP would make the journey down to Westmeath to stay with his mother for a few days. In later years, when the children lived with him, he would pack a freshly baked fruitcake in his suitcase, made by Ted. Annie, delighted with her gift, would send back half a crown to the grandson she didn't know. Ted can't recall if he baked the cake as an act of love, or in pursuit of recognition from his grandmother, or simply for the coin he would receive in return. In reality, it was most likely a combination of all three.

By her ninety-first birthday in September 1954, Annie had moved out of Pakenham Hall and in with Etta. Etta and Willy had moved to Armagh a few years previously, and for a while it looked as though Annie's life had turned full circle. She was back in her homeland, close to her home county, where she would surely die. But 1954 rolled into 1955, and Annie was still breathing; mostly bed-bound but still as sharp as a pin. And as 1956 approached, Etta had enough. She declared to her siblings that her duty was done, and it was time for someone else to take the baton. One by one they all presented their excuses, some valid, some not, but TP had none to offer. His house was big enough to facilitate Annie, he had no health issues of his own, and best of all, his adult children were living at home and would happily look after their grandmother, the grandmother that Joan and Kathleen and Ted had zero memory of, and whom Jack had never met.

Annie wasn't the first house guest to stay at Cliftonpark Avenue, nor would she be the last. Over the years, a collection of people would come and go. There had been Georgina, although her residency was somewhat different. Then there was Bill Wills, a friend of TP's from his boarding house days. Bill was in the RAF and stayed at the house for a while in the late 1940s, leaving behind his treasured set of Encyclopaedia Britannica, which Jack devoured. Those books both ignited his curiosity in the world, and fuelled his frustration with it. Jack's first friend Wesley Porterfield, Etta's son, also stayed with the family for a time in the late 1950s before moving to the bright lights of London. His older sister Jean would be a frequent weekend visitor too, often with a friend in tow to attend a dance at Belfast's famous Floral Hall, not too far from the house. There would be the odd lay preacher, or a visiting minister, or someone connected to the church or the BB who needed temporary accommodation for one reason or another. Georgina would return for the odd visit and occasionally Florrie would stay, and eventually there would be spouses too. And if there were no guests staying there would invariably be guests visiting, for dinner, or afternoon tea, or one committee meeting or another, or even a party - without alcohol, of course. The house was always busy and rarely occupied by just the five of them. TP thrived on company, so long as he did not have to make the food or clear the dishes or prepare the beds. Perhaps this relaxed sociability stemmed back to his time at boarding school, and then the Dublin Boy's home, and then the Belfast boarding houses; days when he was not just used to having everything done for him, but to company. Perhaps he also viewed it as incumbent of his Christian faith; his home would be a place of sanctuary for those who needed shelter. Or perhaps it was his way of paying back the help that he himself had received in the years following Ciss's death, whether that help had been benevolently offered, or not. Regardless of his reasoning, life at Cliftonpark Avenue, whilst a million miles away from the orphanage at Childhaven, was never that of an average family home. So, in spite of there being no close relationship between TP and his mother, and no relationship at all between Annie and her grandchildren, offering to take her in was a completely normal and unsurprising gesture. The children did not blink an eye, or if they did have reservations, they remained unspoken and unseen. Under TP's instruction, Ted and Jack and the girls, and some boys from the BB who he enlisted to help, transformed the sitting room into a bedroom for Annie. And in the spring of 1956, at the age of ninety-two, she met her Catholic-born grandchildren for the first time in twenty years. They were all good Methodists by now, of course. Church of Ireland would have been preferable, but at least they were Protestants. Annie lived out her days in Cliftonpark Avenue, forging a bond of sorts with her newly acquainted grandchildren. Ted in particular took to her, the connection already made through his cakes proving useful. Kathleen liked her too, finding, unexpectedly, that the old woman had a sharp sense of humour. Joan most likely found her grandmother's arrival stressful from a practical perspective, but would have done everything she could to make her feel welcome and comfortable. Jack remembers her as fiercely religious, more so even than his father. They had become used to reciting grace before meals and saying prayers at bedtime, something that was commonplace too in both Childhaven and Wesley College, and to respecting TP's strict Sunday rules, but Annie's commitment to God and the Protestant faith seemed extreme, to Jack at any rate. He was still at odds with his own views about God, unsure how he felt about religion in general, questioning God's existence. He enjoyed the peripheral social elements of the church, CE, and even BB to a degree, and some of the other youth activities, but not really church itself. From this respect he was definitely the odd one out in the family, and for a while, perhaps in part precipitated by Annie's presence, he began to wonder if they were all right, and he was wrong.

Annie lived with her son and his children for almost a year, finally meeting her maker on 4th May 1957 aged ninety-three. There is an irony to the fact that the four children who had for so long been denied a grandmother, were present with one of them at the end of her life, and on the other's lips at the end of hers.

CHAPTER 27

In early 1957, a few months before Annie died, Kathleen found herself pregnant. She had been courting Watson for almost three years, and the couple were due to get married that coming September, but regardless, they knew the news would not be welcomed with open arms. It was a case of history repeating itself. Twenty-seven years on, the stigma surrounding pregnancy before marriage was still flourishing. In the mainly Protestant North, such an event was considered just as shameful as it was in the mainly Catholic South when Ciss O'Beirne had found herself pregnant with Joan in 1930. And neither North nor South had softened their attitudes. As we know now, in the late 1950s, the practice of removing babies from their unwed mothers at birth and placing them up for adoption against the mother's wishes, was still thriving on the island of Ireland. But as with her mother before her, Kathleen was determined to keep her baby. Naturally she felt anxious about telling her father, and Watson too would not have relished breaking the news to his own deeply religious parents, but the couple reiterated that they were in love and were to be married that September anyway. They would simply fast track their wedding plans. They married at the end of March, and moved to Greenisland on the outskirts of Belfast. To begin with, TP wasn't pleased. He liked Watson, and was happy to have him as a son-in-law, but couldn't hide his annoyance at the situation. Perhaps he thought the young couple should have been more careful, forgetting that he and Ciss were once that same young couple themselves. Well, almost. At least Watson was the same religion as his daughter, and the same denomination at that. All that TP really had to suffer when Kathleen became pregnant out of wedlock was a little bit of social embarrassment, not the outright discrimination that he and Ciss had to deal with. But when his first grandchild, a girl named Norma, arrived on 10th September 1957, all feelings of irritation, or shame, or frustration fell away. Perhaps he recognised the privileged position he was in: he had his family, he had a home, he had his church and his health, and Ciss had not lived to experience any of this. Ciss, who he rarely mentioned but still carried in his heart, would never get to hold her grandchildren, or see her children wed, and here he was doing both. Norma was the first of ten grandchildren that TP would welcome. He would get to hold, and know, and love them all. And though he wasn't aware of it at the time, something in TP shifted the day that she was born.

Jack, now nineteen, was a student at Queen's University, following the path that Ted had so badly wanted to walk himself. He had flirted briefly with the idea of going into the ministry, triggered perhaps by his grandmother Annie's presence and a desperation to bring God into his life in the same way that his father and siblings had. But his first term at Queen's put paid to that, introducing him to a world of philosophers and poets and artists. Finally Jack had found his tribe, yet he almost didn't go to Queen's at all. Although TP had insisted on that return to school to complete his General Certificate exams, the principal wasn't quite so enamoured and provided no encouragement. He tolerated Jack, but didn't nurture him in any way. There was no discussion between father and son, nor father and school principal, or any of the teachers for that matter, about university, or a potential career path. Jack was just left to his own devices, by all of them. He passed his exams with marks high enough to secure him a scholarship to university had he applied, which he hadn't. When the results came out, he took himself down to the job centre in town to see what jobs were going, where a bemused assistant on hearing of the grades this young lad had just achieved, convinced him to phone the university. One phone call led to another, and by the end of the day, Jack had a confirmed offer to study Philosophy, Spanish and French at Queen's and a full scholarship grant into the bargain. The problem was, TP was away at a mission event in County Clare in his capacity as a lay preacher, and the university needed his approval. Joan managed to get hold of their father that evening and explained the situation, emphasising the scholarship. She knew there was no way that TP would finance a degree, and though she was still helping with Jack's schooling costs at that time, her contribution would not see him through university.

"So what do you want to do?" asked a nonplussed TP when Joan put her brother on the line. "Do you want to go to university?"

"Well," said Jack, shrugging his shoulders "I suppose I might as well."

Poor Joan, still having to sort out domestic concerns on her father's behalf. Poor Ted too, having to watch his younger brother walk through the door of opportunity that was denied to him.

During his second year at Queen's, two weeks before Annie died, Jack went to the Christian Endeavour Easter week at Craigmore House, just as Ted had done three years previously. He was more keen to go than Ted had been, relieved perhaps to get away from Cliftonpark Avenue for a while, aware that death was hovering on the doorstep. And he had previously attended a couple of CE events at Craigmore, so any reservations he'd had about returning to Millisle and Childhaven had already been dealt with. Ted had ventured into the Childhaven house the weekend he met Noreen. At one point, Noreen developed a nasty headache, and, pushing down any nudging misgivings, Ted took her into the big house to seek assistance. There was a new matron, and different staff, and the place was lighter and brighter, and to his surprise, not packed to the gills with undernourished, unhappy children. It was being run as a children's home now, the stigma of the orphanage word dropped, and he felt uplifted on seeing the place. When the new matron heard that this kind and thoughtful young man was a Pakenham, she told him with glee that he and his siblings were held up as exemplary past residents of Childhaven, and were cited as examples of the home's success when additional funding was required. Even though Ted and Noreen had only just met, they both bonded with the matron that day, a lady named Lucy Kirkman, and stayed in contact with her for several years. Indeed they would go on to bring some of the children from the home out on day trips, at Lucy's request. It may not have been his intention, but Ted most likely laid some residual ghosts to rest that day. Jack would have been aware of his brother's visit, so perhaps the first time he went to a CE event at Craigmore, any fear at seeing Childhaven may have been diluted a little. He didn't venture inside the house though, as his brother had done. That was several steps too far.

As it happened, Ethel Howard was also attending the event at Craigmore that Easter. Jack still carried a torch for Ethel, but had never asked her out, still believing she was too far out of his league. Ethel knew a little bit about Childhaven and what life had been like there, because her elder sister Joan was engaged to be married to none other than Joe Culbert, Ted's old chum and running adversary and hero of the classroom. She also knew that Jack Pakenham was Ted Pakenham's brother. Joe and Joan and Ted and Noreen had become quite the foursome, playing tennis, going to the cinema, and attending dances together, so Ethel had heard some stories about the orphanage. One evening during the trip, the group walked into Millisle to get some fish and chips. Ethel walked beside Jack, chatting easily with him, and somehow, on the way home, they found that they were holding hands. They had their first kiss that night, Jack not quite believing his luck. The problem was, he now had a life plan, and it didn't involve Ethel. He was going to be a famous artist and travel the world, and never imagining for a second that he and Ethel would ever get together, she didn't feature in the scenario. He wrote her a letter explaining that he simply didn't have space in his life for love, and that was that. Until five months later when the two met again at a mutual friend's birthday party. Jack did become a well-known Irish artist, and he did travel the world. He wrote poetry, and attended soirees with Seamus Heaney, Michael Longley and Paul Muldoon. Their writing style wasn't quite to his taste, but he valued their friendship and counsel and, as with his art, developed his own unique approach. He also became an English teacher, fulfilling another of Ted's ambitions. And, after reuniting with Ethel at that birthday party in September 1957, he never let her go again.

Jack graduated from Queen's in the summer of 1959, and one year later, in September 1960, embarked on a one-year postgraduate course at Stranmillis Teacher Training College. Unlike his brother, teaching had never been on Jack's radar and he wasn't initially enthused. During his time at Queen's his passion for art was solidified after a chance meeting in Swanage, Dorset, with the renowned Irish artist, Pádraig Mac Miadhacháin. Jack and a friend had gone to the south of England during the summer break looking for work, and happened upon Mac Miadhacháin's gallery. His work resonated with Jack, and Paddy, as Jack would call him, became both his friend and mentor for many years to come. Jack returned to Swanage every summer during his university years, and on completing his final exams, with no idea about what he was going to do next, Paddy suggested he spend a few months at an artist's retreat in Ibiza. It was an eye opening and moving experience for Jack, but when he returned to Belfast the following spring, he realised that his art would not sustain him financially, at least not for some time. It was Ethel who suggested Stranmillis, and Jack, with no other options on the table, half-heartedly agreed. But by the beginning of 1961, a few months into the course, he had discovered his inner teacher and decided teaching would be a good career choice after all. Decent pay, job security, and best of all, long summer holidays to dedicate to his art. Then, just as he was beginning to contemplate his new plan for the future, Ethel became pregnant. As with Kathleen and Watson, the couple had planned to wed at some point, but with Jack still a student, the timing was tricky. And then there was the moral, or immoral, dilemma to deal with. Ethel's parents adored Jack, but as good Christians they weren't best pleased with the situation. And neither was TP, forgetting himself once again. There was no fatherly conversation, no sense of, *"it's okay son, these things happen. Look at your sister, look at me and your mother for goodness' sake. You love each other, and that's all that matters."* Words of comfort along those lines from TP would have meant a great deal to Jack, but while they didn't come, he did welcome Ethel into the family with open arms. The wedding took place in February 1961, and the new Mrs Pakenham moved into Cliftonpark Avenue. Everyone agreed that Jack should continue with his studies, and as Ethel would soon have to leave her job at the computer firm ICT, the young couple could not support themselves financially. So, moving into one or other family home was the only option, and as Cliftonpark Avenue had more room, it was decided they should live there with TP and Joan. But the dynamics didn't work. Jack, unsurprisingly, clashed continually with

Joan. Ethel, not understanding her sister-in-law's very particular ways, struggled to meet Joan's high standards. She was fond of her father-in-law, but he wasn't at all like her own father, and as her pregnancy progressed, she realised she didn't want the baby to be born and reared at Cliftonpark. So, shortly before their firstborn Michael arrived, on 30th July 1961, Ethel and Jack relocated to Ethel's parent's home at Orby Drive in the south of the city. Michael was quite poorly after his birth, so for Ethel, having the hands-on support of her mother while Jack was at college was a blessing. A few months later, Jack graduated from Stranmillis and got a job teaching English at Ashfield Boy's High School in East Belfast. And shortly after that, the couple bought a house in Carolhill Park, just a short walk from the school, where they would live out their married life together.

Ted and Noreen had married on 25th September 1958. Ted was twenty-three, still working for the Belfast Corporation, but now as a law clerk at the Town Solicitor's Office in Belfast City Hall. He had covered some legal modules while studying for his Chartered Institute of Secretaries exams, and enjoyed that element of the course. When the opportunity came for him to move to City Hall as a law clerk, he jumped at it, and before long knew he had found his calling. It was too late now for Ted to go to university. He had missed that opportunity, and had to watch from the sidelines as his brother studied at both Queen's University *and* Stranmillis College. But though he may have been irritated by Jack's apparent easy passage, and perhaps felt a little wistful too, Ted being Ted held no grudges against his brother, or indeed their father, whose plan to open that electrical business never got off the ground. And by the time Jack took up his teaching position at Ashfield High, Ted had a new life plan in place. Jack was welcome to his teaching job; he would become a solicitor, and he would do it internally. He moved from the Corporation to the Civil Service, gradually working his way through the ranks to become the Chief Law Clerk, all the while studying in his spare time for his Solicitor's exams. Ted would eventually become the Solicitor in Charge of Property Development at the Department of the Environment for Northern Ireland, fulfilling the potential he first displayed as a little orphan boy in Baldy Palmer's classroom.

As with Jack and Ethel, Ted and Noreen had moved into Cliftonpark Avenue on returning from their honeymoon, as the sale of the house they had been hoping to buy fell through. Though Noreen's experience of living under the same roof as Ted's father, his eldest sister, and his younger brother was a much happier one than Ethel's would be two years later, the couple desperately wanted the privacy of their own home. It took almost two years, but in the summer of 1960, they finally found a house fifteen miles down the road in the seaside town of Bangor, where TP had taken the children on holiday during the war years. They would make a happy life for themselves in Bangor, and were blessed with two daughters.

For a short time, when TP had first rented Cliftonpark Avenue back in 1947, it had just been he and Joan living there, and now, fourteen years later in 1961, it was just the two of them again. Joan was thirty-one now. She had watched as her sister and brothers fell in love, got married, bought houses, and began to have families of their own. She must have wondered at times if she was destined to remain living with her father in the big house, which he had now bought from the landlord, for the rest of his days, just as her mentor Georgina was doing with her mother, Lilly. A spinster woman, an old maid. The status carried almost as much derision and scorn as that of an unmarried mother. A bachelor man was perfectly acceptable, but an unmarried woman in her thirties raised an eyebrow or two. But while Joan wanted love and marriage and children for herself, and quietly prayed for them, her life was happy. She loved her job at Eagle Star, where she was now running the typing pool. With just her father left to care for, she had more free time to devote to her roles at the GB and the CE and the badminton club, and to other church related organisations and activities. For years, from the start really, the house had been noisy and busy, always full of people coming and going, and Joan had felt responsible for them all. She loved her two sisters-in-law dearly. They were good Christian girls from good Christian families, and they made her brothers happy. But living with them, living with married couples, had been difficult. Still, she probably missed the chatter and the company a little bit, and she definitely missed Kathleen, who had recently moved to England when Watson relocated there for work. But there was still the occasional house guest, and Joan and her father still hosted the extended family's Christmas dinner. A couple of years previously, when the house was at its peak of activity, with girlfriends and boyfriends and work friends and church friends and visiting relatives, TP had employed a housekeeper to help Joan with the cleaning. Mrs McGrath still came twice a week, despite the decreased requirement for her, and Joan was glad that her father had not dismissed the older lady, and returned full responsibility of the house to her. The TP of ten years earlier might have done so, or even five years, but that slight shift in attitude that had begun with Norma's birth, was becoming more evident as each additional grandchild arrived. And so, when Joan announced that she was going on holiday to Lloret de Mar on Spain's Costa Brava coast with some girlfriends in the summer of 1962, instead of putting his foot down and telling his daughter that a Spanish holiday resort was no place for a young single woman to visit, he gave her his blessing. It was probably the most courageous, adventurous, and possibly nerve-wracking thing that Joan had ever done for herself. But the leap of faith was worth it, because a couple of days into the trip she met a young man from Feltham in Middlesex called Mark Ison.

CHAPTER 28

By the end of the 1960s, TP's ten grandchildren had all been born. Norma had been joined by sister Shona and brothers Kenneth and Gary. Michael had acquired a brother, David. Ted and Noreen had their two girls, Julie and Gail. And in 1966, Graham Ison was born to proud parents Joan and Mark, his sister Angela completing the family two years later. Mark and Joan fell in love on that holiday in Spain. In a serendipitous coincidence, it transpired that Mark was also a committed Methodist who had a difficult childhood, brought up by his mother after his father left the family. The two clicked immediately, and on their return home they began to communicate through precisely timed weekly phone calls and regular letter writing, sharing their life stories with each other on the pages. It is those letters, at least some of the twenty-odd that Joan penned to Mark, that have informed much of this story. The couple married in Belfast in 1964, and Joan moved to Feltham to join her husband, immersing herself in her new English life. Her prayers had been well and truly answered. She only agreed to marry Mark however, when Kathleen announced that they would be relocating back to Belfast. She was homesick, and struggling to raise three young children without a support network around her. When Watson was made redundant, they decided to return to Northern Ireland, and would, initially at least, move into Cliftonpark Avenue. Joan rejoiced at the news. She had been too worried about how her father would cope on his own to accept Mark's proposal of marriage, knowing that it would be she who must make the geographic move. TP was by now serving on Belfast City Council as a Labour Councillor, and was very active in the Northern Ireland Labour party. He was also still working full time. There was absolutely no way he would relocate to Bangor to live with Ted and Noreen. And moving in with Jack and Ethel just wasn't plausible. Joan was as certain of that as she was that tea came from China. It didn't occur to her that the man might just manage by himself. He had Mrs McGrath to help in the house, after all. And as he now owned the house, he could have sold it to downsize, to a nice new bungalow perhaps. But the notion of TP not being "looked after" by someone was inconceivable. And if Joan had shared her dilemma with her father, or any of her siblings for that matter, the idea that he was perfectly capable of fending for himself would not have struck any one of them either. Kathleen and Watson's exquisitely timed return to Belfast was the perfect solution. Joan married Mark and moved to England, and Cliftonpark Avenue was filled with noise and people and the chaos of family life once again.

The little change that had started to gently nudge at TP when Norma was born increased in intensity as each new baby came along. It was as though his grandchildren were softening him in some way, thawing a hardness that had settled deep inside his soul after Ciss's death. It wasn't just that he adored them, which he did, but his rigid, hardline attitudes began to ease too. He no longer believed that children's playparks should be locked on a Sunday. He decided it was acceptable to buy ice cream cones from an ice cream van. Music other that classical was allowed to be played on the radio. These were small things, but enormously significant ones too. As time passed and more grandchildren arrived, he would read them bedtime stories, and take them paddling in the sea, and kick a ball around a garden with them, even on a Sunday. He would bounce them on his knee and kiss the tops of their heads and play peekaboo and pull funny faces. He loved them all, and they loved him back, the grandfather role seemingly effortless for the man who struggled so much with the fatherly one. Joan especially must have watched Graham and Angela playing with their grandpa in the garden of their Feltham home when he came on one of his regular visits with an ache in her gut, thinking about the days when he used to do the same with herself and Kathleen in the garden of Prince Edward Terrace. She was the only one of her siblings who really remembered their father as a daddy. The sight must have uplifted her soul and hurt her heart in equal measure, sad for what could have been, but thankful for the here and now.

Perhaps TP had been reflecting on the same memories himself, feeling similar emotions. Perhaps when Norma was born the memory of Joan's birth, of holding his baby daughter in his arms and loving her from that very first second, the angst of all the pregnancy and wedding drama suddenly forgotten, flipped a switch inside his own heart, and the TP that Ciss had fallen in love with slowly began to re-emerge. Joan remembered him as a fun and loving father back in her early childhood. Ciss's dear cousin Annie Kate recalled to her daughter Annette that *"Tommy was a lovely man, a good man"*. Liam Keogh, the young next-door neighbour at Errigal Road who became Jack's emergency Godfather, would tell his daughter Helen in later years that the Pakenhams were a loving family, a close family, but that Tommy changed after the tragedy of Ciss's death. He became suspicious and paranoid. He stopped playing with the children and kept them indoors, refusing all offers of help. And then he simply disappeared. TP never stopped loving his children, but without Ciss by his side, he lost the ability to be that hands-on daddy that Joan remembered, the religious tug of war he unwittingly found himself the centre of not helping. But now here he was two decades later, a happy man, surrounded by his family, embracing the new generation, accepting love easily, and giving it in return.

The sense of community involvement and social responsibility that TP had felt during his days as an Air Raid Patrol Warden had fed into his devotion to the Boys Brigade and his dedication to Belfast Central Mission. These in turn led him to explore socialism, one of the bedrocks of Methodism, and ultimately to join the Northern Ireland Labour Party. He became a Labour Councillor for North Belfast in 1966, preventing, to his delight, a certain Mrs Eileen Paisley from winning a seat for the Protestant Unionist Party, the forerunner to her husband's Democratic Unionist Party. TP was not a fan of extreme loyalist politics, and as the 1960s progressed he became increasingly despairing of the direction his adopted country was headed in. In 1969 he was made a Justice of the Peace, possibly his proudest achievement, although in truth that accolade may belong to his role within the BB. By the end of the 1960s, Thomas Pakenham was an almost entirely different character to the broken, paranoid, grieving man who had smuggled his children out of Dublin in March 1939, the man who had no solid plan, the man who spent more than a decade making questionable decisions, the man who had placed his children into an orphanage. Almost.

Mrs Paisley did eventually win a seat on Belfast City Council in 1967, and her husband launched his DUP party in 1971 amidst the increasingly unstable political situation in the North. A year later, following the events of Bloody Sunday in Derry/Londonderry in January 1972, a catastrophic car bomb in Donegall Street less than a mile from the Belfast Central Mission, and the IRA bombing of The Abercorn, a popular Belfast City Centre café on a busy Saturday afternoon in March, TP, Kathleen and Watson decided it was time to leave Belfast. Jack and Ethel had been in the Abercorn that afternoon, leaving just twenty minutes before the bomb exploded. Fate was on their side that day, but the close call rocked the entire family, and would haunt Jack and Ethel for years to come. The area of East Belfast where they lived with their boys was considered relatively safe in comparison to the city centre and North Belfast, so they would stay put. But Cliftonpark Avenue was close to an interface section between the predominantly Catholic Ardoyne and predominantly Protestant Lower Oldpark areas, and one of the early infamous "peace walls" that were erected throughout the city during the years of The Troubles wound its way through several of the adjacent streets. Kathleen and Watson could not subject their children to the increasingly terrifying violence that was erupting around them. And so, after twenty-four years at Cliftonpark Avenue, TP sold the big house to the Northern Ireland Labour Party for use as their offices, and together with his daughter, son-in-law and their four children, moved to a modern semi-detached house in Bangor, just around the corner from Ted, Noreen, and the girls. The scourge of Irish politics and religious divisions had once more intervened in TP's life.

That said, the move to Bangor was ultimately a positive one. TP and the Hazzard family joined Carnalea Methodist Church where Ted and Noreen were already active members of the congregation, and TP immediately immersed himself in the Carnalea church family. There was one downside of his new community however, the church did not have a company of the Boy's Brigade. Nor did the local Church of Ireland, with whom the methodists shared a building. The upside, though, was that TP could start one from scratch. He liaised with some like-minded members of both congregations and established the 11th Bangor Boys' Brigade, becoming, naturally, the company's very first captain. Though he lived with Kathleen and her family, he could now spend more time with Ted and Noreen and his granddaughters, and would regularly make the twenty-minute drive to east Belfast to visit Jack, Ethel and their boys. He continued to work for the first few years, taking the train to Belfast every day until he eventually retired in 1975 at the age of 70. Although he was reluctant at first, retirement suited him. Fit and sprightly he would walk for miles, a common sight and popular figure in Bangor. Always impeccably dressed, he would tip his hat politely to passers-by, and stop to chat to anyone who would indulge him. He was still active within the church, still captain of the BB, and still a lay preacher, delivering a version of his testimony to audiences and congregations on mission trips and church excursions throughout Ireland. And with more time on his hands, he was free to visit Feltham more regularly too. He also began to take an annual winter sun holiday in Cyprus or southern Spain, swimming and walking and reading in the sunshine, befriending other guests and enjoying their company.

Throughout these years, thoughts of Ciss were never far away, for all of them. Marriage and parenthood had triggered long buried emotions for Joan, Kathleen, Ted and Jack. They had no idea what it was like to have a mother of their own. As children, they missed having a mother, *any* mother, rather than missing the one they had actually had. She was so very quickly lost to Ted and Kathleen. Jack had never known her, Joan the only one with any sense of a memory at all. But she had found holding onto those memories more difficult with each passing year, and by the time she gave birth to Graham all that remained was a hazy sensation of Ciss's touch and smell, a scent she frustratingly could never quite place. Becoming parents themselves made the siblings think about Ciss; about what she had missed, and what they had missed, and yes, what their father had missed too. Naturally, they would have thought about her on many occasions through the years, sometimes fleetingly, sometimes with yearning. There would no doubt have been wistful wishes that she could have stood by their father's side at their respective weddings, or witnessed the progressing pregnancies, as Joan and Kathleen's babies grew inside them, Noreen and Ethel's too. But it was when those babies were born that thoughts of their mother truly surfaced. As they held each new child in their arms, their own-born and their nephews and nieces, brimming with love and joy and pride and hope, there would be an intake of breath, a sharp stab in the heart, a clutch of grief at the throat when the thought of Ciss arrived, as it inevitably would. She was more present in their lives now than she had been for years, the need for her more desperate. Ted in particular felt a deep rush of pain when he realised that he had no memory of calling Ciss *mum*. And as a young man, Jack struggled with the notion that the loss of their mother was his fault. That his life took her life. *If I had not been born*, he reasoned, *she would not have died*. It is no doubt a common sentiment in children whose mothers have died during or shortly after their birth, and a difficult sorrow to navigate. And in some way perhaps, it explains both the weight that Jack carried on his shoulders, and the thread of darkness that would run through his art and poetry throughout his life. The fear of loss and abandonment clung to him, and when Michael and then David arrived, and Ethel survived both births, his relief was immense. She had not gone the way of his mother, who he now finally allowed himself to mourn.

So, as their own families took shape and began to grow, the questions inevitably came; questions they had stopped asking long ago. *What was mum like? How did she die? What were our grandparents like? How many siblings did she have again? Are they still alive? Exactly why did you take us away, Dad?* And there were some new ones too. *Can we visit her grave, Dad? Can we try and find our family?* Just as he used to do, TP mostly batted the questions away like irritating little midge flies. But they were more persistent now, spurred on by a new ache for information, and curious spouses, and grandchildren who were growing up with questions of their own. So he divulged new bits of information here and slivers of detail there, handing out pieces of a jigsaw puzzle he didn't ever want them to complete. Though he didn't read them his testimony, nor recount the events leading up to their departure in the detail recorded within it, he did continue to use the letter as the basis of his story, sticking carefully to the narrative contained within it. Kate was still a wicked, threatening character, her brothers all religious bullies. And then suddenly, in 1963, he declared that they were all dead. He had happened upon an old friend of Ciss's during a mission trip to Longford, and she, apparently, had told him as much. The lady in question was one Lily Connolly who we believe Ciss had met in the sanitorium during her treatment for polio. Lily owned a sweet shop in Longford town and had kept in touch with Ciss until her friend's untimely death, so it's possible that TP had sought her out during his visit, rather than randomly bumping into her on the street. Whatever the circumstances of their meeting, there was of course an element of truth in Lily's words. Kate had died almost a decade previously. Michael and Terence had followed Ciss to their graves in the 40s, Bernie's Nancy too. So much grief for one family, Lily might have said, and TP would have agreed, and nodded gravely. And when she had asked about his own family, he would have replied that they were well and healthy and then expertly deflected the conversation to some other topic, or excused himself and tipped his hat. TP used the information he had acquired from Lily to proclaim to his adult children that there was no point in trying to track down their mother's relatives as there were none of them left. And when his grandchildren began to quiz him on the subject, he said the same thing to them; knowing that this was not the case, that they were not all dead. At least in 1963 they weren't. He knew that Pat and Bernie were still in Dublin. He knew that Ned was running the farm. And he knew Albert was working for ICI, in a senior position at that. And the reason he knew about Albert was because he had seen and spoken with him in person, on several occasions.

CHAPTER 29

The contact between Albert and TP is a conundrum; a bewildering mystery we simply cannot solve. We don't know exactly when these encounters took place, or how many times the two men met, but we do know that as Albert progressed through the ranks at ICI, he began to make frequent business trips to the North to meet with the company's Northern clients. Somehow, he managed to track TP down to his own place of work and went to his office. It may have been a lucky guess. TP had worked for Edison and Swan in Dublin after all, though that had been years before he left the city. But Albert may have taken a punt on the electrical company as a starting point, and hit the jackpot. Or he may have received a tip-off from someone, one of TP's Dublin friends perhaps, who saw Albert as less of a threat than his older brothers. Ted remembers hearing his father mention Albert's visits, but he is unclear about when this was. It is likely Albert began working with ICI after graduating from the National University of Ireland with a general academic degree. In 1951, at the age of twenty-eight, he moved to England for a year to take a Mathematics and Organic Chemistry course at Bolton Technical College, returning to Dublin and ICI in 1952, with a new qualification and a bucketload of ambition. This would have been when his professional career truly began to flourish, and perhaps coincided with the first of his visits to the North. It may have been later, but it's unlikely he had his first encounter with TP before 1953.

This hypothesis is really just for scene-setting, as regardless of the timing, nothing about Albert and TP's interactions make sense. TP told the children about their uncle's visits, when in truth he had no need to. If he was set upon keeping Albert at a distance, why even mention that he had made contact in the first place? And when he did tell the children, he suggested that the man was trouble making, interfering, sniffing for information. But they were safe, he reassured them, because he refused on each occasion to divulge any details about their whereabouts. If this first conversation did take place in 1953, almost fourteen years had passed since the Beirne family had last had contact with TP and the children. Joan would have been approaching twenty-three, Kathleen twenty, Ted eighteen, Jack fifteen. The eldest three were young adults, all now working, while Jack was in his fourth year at secondary school. So what exactly was TP keeping them safe from? No one was going to steal them away back to Dublin or Leitrim. No one was going to insist on them reconverting to Catholicism. No one was going to make a scene. Not now. TP was in a better position financially than he had been since leaving Dublin. He had made a home for his family. The children were settled and happy, indeed they weren't even children anymore, they were young adults. What harm would it have done to give Albert their address, invite him for tea, ignite a reconnection with his children's mother's family, reassure the Beirnes in Leitrim and O'Beirnes in Dublin that all was well. And if their first encounter was before 30th July 1954, well, Kate Beirne could have died with peace in her heart.

Or the first meeting between the two men may have happened later, when Albert held a more senior position at ICI, 1962 perhaps. Kate had died not knowing of her grandchildren's whereabouts, but Ned was still alive and praying for them, his wife May too. And Pat and Bernie and Annie Kate and Mollie. Kathleen, Ted and Jack were all married, grandchildren had started to arrive. What would TP's fears and motivations have been then? There was even less chance of any repercussions for his children, but what if it was actually himself that he was worried about? Not of reprisals or revenge or violence, but of judgment. What if he did not want the story of the preceding two- and a-bit decades to be exposed to the remaining Beirne family because it would shed him in a very poor light; because he feared that none of them would understand the choices he made or forgive him for placing the children in an orphanage. The most feasible scenario, however, is the first one: Albert arriving as an unexpected visitor at TP's office around 1953 or 1954, as that timeline fits more into Ted's hazy recollection.

Why TP refused to tell Albert anything about the children or what had happened to them over the years is one curiosity, but what was Albert up to? When Albert made one of his uninvited visits to the Belfast office of Edison and Swan, TP told his children about it, proudly reiterating his refusal to divulge any information. Albert on the other hand told no one. Well, he may have told Nellie, his wife. She would have known about the series of tragedies that had befallen her new husband's family, so it's possible Albert confided in her that he'd met with TP. He didn't tell anyone else though, even though he would have been well aware of the anguished desperation that had plagued his mother for years. After Kate's death, Ned continued to carry the burden of his missing nieces and nephews, never fully shaking off the feeling that if he had only been at home the day Tommy had come for Jack, he could have reasoned with him, done something to prevent things from turning out the way they did. Just like his mother had, he prayed every day for news of them, and he never stopped. He talked to his own children about their aunt and cousins on a regular basis, in fact on most Saturday evenings, as they sat around the fire, he would regale the family with stories about Ciss and her babies. Even in the early 1960s, when the Pakenham children were all adults and married, some with children of their own, Ned was still asking questions. On one occasion during a mission event at the church in Bornacoola, he held back a visiting priest from the North after mass and asked to speak to him privately, telling May and the children to go on to the car. He told the priest the story, explained that he suspected the family were up North, the children probably Protestant now, confided that all these years on the sorrow was still a heavy burden to bear. *Could you help me trace them?* he asked. But the priest shook his head and said there was nothing he could do. Ned returned to the car crestfallen, a sadness settling on him for days to come. When RTE launched its flagship chat show *The Late Late Show* with presenter Gay Byrne in 1962, it featured a segment that reunited long lost families. Ned thought he should write to the show, thinking this might be his golden ticket, so to speak, but was dissuaded from doing so by some other family members. *They know where we are*, he was told. *Let them come to us if they wish to.* Even if Albert wasn't involved in the *Late Late Show* conversation, even if he hadn't heard about Ned speaking to the priest from the North, he knew what finding the family meant to his brother. He knew just receiving the news that the children were all alive and well and thriving in their lives would satisfy Ned, even if he never set eyes on them again.

If we are perplexed by TP's reaction to being found by Albert, Albert's own actions on finding TP are equally puzzling. Why he chose not to tell anyone in the family that he had found TP, that the children were all alive and well and happy, remains a mystery. Perhaps his silence was at the behest of TP. Perhaps TP begged him to stay quiet, convinced him to let sleeping dogs lie. If that was the case, the sleeping dogs did indeed lie, because by March 1975, all five of the Beirne brothers were dead. Thomas passed in 1964 aged fifty-three. Pat died next, in May 1971 aged sixty-seven. Albert himself followed in February 1973. He was just forty-nine, and in the prime of his career. Two months later, it was Bernie's turn. Then, on 16th March 1975, Ned collapsed at the farm and died later that evening in Sligo Hospital. All five died as their father had done, from a sudden and catastrophic heart attack. The Beirne family of Cashel was no more.

There were others in the family who still held Ciss and the children in their hearts, of course. Ned's widow May and his children John, Catherine, Nuala, Olive and Angela would continue to carry their father's torch, albeit a much dimmer one. They had their own grief to deal with. In Dublin, Mollie Winters would occasionally visit Mount Jerome Cemetery to place flowers on her cousin's grave and pray for news of her godson and his siblings. But her visits were quiet and personal, and she was one step removed from the immediate family. In Leitrim, Annie Kate Conboy would tell her daughter Annette, and sons JJ and Thomas stories about her dear cousin Ciss and the lost children. But Annette and her brothers grew up, and married, and had families of their own. We don't know if Pat talked about his sister and her children to his own family, or if Bernie did, although his son Brian would undoubtedly have known the story as he grew up on the farm. In Albert's home however, their names were never spoken. And so, inevitably, in the wider family circle, the memory of Ciss gradually dwindled, and as time passed and the years rolled by, the story of her four lost children became lost itself.

CHAPTER 30

We don't know if TP was aware of Albert's passing. He may have read about the younger man's untimely death in a newspaper obituary, or he may have heard nothing about it at all. The two men might have still been in contact at the time, or they may not have spoken for several years, Albert no longer dropping into Edison and Swan, bored with trying to elicit information from TP, or satisfied with the details he had managed to ascertain. But we know that Albert's visits unsettled TP, as did the renewed questioning from his children. And when some of his grandchildren began to push him on the past, thoughts of Ciss and her death filled his mind. Julie, Ted's daughter, and Michael, Jack's son, were especially interested in their heritage and their fathers' backstories. They pressed their respective dads, who still knew very little, and they pressed their grandfather, who remained tight-lipped and selective, sticking to his well-rehearsed narrative. *They're all dead*, he repeated, knowing perhaps that the brothers were indeed all dead by then, or maybe not. *They can't all be dead*, Julie and Michael countered. *What about their children? And their children's children, our second cousins?* When Julie was in her late teens, she suggested that she and Michael go to Dublin to do some research. There must be records, she reasoned. There must be O'Beirnes still living in the city. Surely it couldn't be that hard to find them. And then there was their grandmother's grave. That at least was worth a visit.

We can't be entirely certain, but we suspect that TP never returned to Ciss's grave after her funeral. He may have done so of course. He might have hopped on a tram out to Mount Jerome on one of his quick trips to Dublin to bring Joan or Kathleen or Ted to Wesley, but the temporary marker placed on her burial site in October 1938 had never been upgraded. At some point in the early to mid 1980s, more than forty years after her death, he decided to change that. It may have been his grandchildren's burgeoning curiosity, the realisation that at least one of them, most likely Julie, would seek the grave out one day. Or it may have been a sense of responsibility to his wife finally catching up with him, an acknowledgement that he owed her the dignity of a proper memorial. And perhaps there was also an awareness of his own mortality clipping at his heels, a feeling that he was running out of time to make at least this one thing right. In truth, it was probably a combination of all three scenarios that led TP to contact the cemetery and arrange for a limestone surround to frame the perimeter of Ciss's grave. There was no pomp or ceremony attached to the event. We don't believe TP visited the cemetery himself to inspect the sculptor's handiwork, or place a fresh bouquet of flowers on the stone, or say a prayer. Indeed, he did not even tell his children, or his grandchildren, what he had done. He most likely assumed that some of them, or one of them at least, would come across the newly spruced up grave at some point in the future, long after he himself was gone. And he may have believed that any of his wife's relatives who were still alive would have ceased visiting her grave years before, if indeed they had ever visited at all. But if that is what he thought, then he was wrong to.

By the age of sixty-seven, Mollie Winters had given up hope of ever hearing news about the fate of the Pakenham children, never mind setting eyes on them again. Retired now from CIE, her life was full and busy, travelling throughout Europe and attending cultural events in her adopted city. Her visits to Mount Jerome had dwindled over the years, but every so often she would take the bus out to the old cemetery to pay her respects to the cousin she still thought about. On a cold January morning in 1986 she made such a trip. It had been a while, and although was certain about the location of Ciss's grave, she thought she had got her bearings wrong to begin with. Only when she knelt to read the short inscription on the new surround did she know she was indeed at the correct site.

In Loving Memory - Mary (Ciss) wife of Thomas Pakenham departed this life 4th October 1938.

Mollie contacted May as soon as she arrived home, assuming it was she who had arranged the spruced-up grave. As May replied that no, she wasn't responsible, a chill ran through her blood and a choke caught in her throat as it dawned on her who was, who it could only be: Tommy, or one of the children. *Surely this is it*, May thought. *Surely, we have found them.*

PART 4
THE REUNION

Change depends on the questions we ask. Always providing we are willing to ask them

~ From *A Journey with Two Maps* **by Eavan Boland**

CHAPTER 31

25/2/86

"Dear May

> *What a wonderful, pleasant surprise to get your letter. Yes – I am still alive. I will be 81 this Friday, 28th. Still active in youth work in this area and still driving my own car. I never married again and so have been a widower for over 47 years…"*

When TP received a letter from May Beirne in February 1986, his instinct was to put it in the bin, or at least ignore it. He would have known of May Molloy when she was courting Ned back in the late 1930s before everything changed, although it's entirely possible that the two had never met. Albert conceivably might have filled him in; told him that Ned had married May, that they had five children, that Ned had bought a new house for his family close to the old farmhouse, and that Kate had lived with them. Or he might not have told him anything at all, Albert reluctant to impart any information about the family, or TP unwilling to receive it. Regardless, when TP read May's letter for the first time, he was not best pleased. For a start, he hadn't considered that by placing a new surround at Ciss's grave he was in effect scattering fresh breadcrumbs. So the letter was a shock. Then there was the outrage he felt that the memorial company had given his personal address to a complete stranger. And on top of that, he was most put out that May had signed off the letter as Beirne.

If TP had been living on his own, the letter might have remained undetected, thrown onto an open fire or tossed out with the rubbish. But someone in the Hazzard household had noticed the delivery of a handwritten envelope with an Eire stamp addressed to Mr Tommy Pakenham. Questions were asked, questions which naturally TP tried to deflect. But Kathleen read the letter, and hurried phone calls were made to the rest of the family. It was May's use of the surname Beirne that TP used to justify his decision not to reply.

"Your mother was an O'Beirne," he said, "not a Beirne. This May is not her family."

His children were horrified, his grandchildren too. And this time they weren't letting him off the hook. *But you must reply*, they told him. *You absolutely must. And if you don't, we will.*

It had possibly taken May a few weeks to write and post the letter to TP after Mollie contacted her with the news of her discovery. Mollie had spoken with the memorial company, probably begging them to give her the contact details of the person who had paid for the new surround. It's unlikely they would have relinquished an address as easily as TP suspected, but when they heard the story, well how could they resist reuniting this very smart lady with her dead cousin's long-lost children. Mollie would have known that it was up to May now to make contact with the Pakenhams, if she so wished. What a moment it must have been for May to hold TP's address in her hands, decades of grief and pain reduced to the small square of paper declaring that Tommy Pakenham was indeed still alive and living in the town of Bangor, County Down. He must be eighty now, at least. The children would all be in their fifties, no doubt with families of their own. How she would have wished that her husband was standing by her side, her mother-in-law too, but all she could do now for Ned and Kate was bring those children home.

We don't know exactly what May said in her letter. It was probably friendly but not emotional, neither long nor short, and balanced an equal amount of information - cataloguing Kate and her sons' deaths, listing the names of her children and grandchildren - with a few probing questions, such as how long have you lived in Bangor, how is your health, how are Joan, Kathleen, Ted and Jackie, do you have any grandchildren yourself? She would not have wanted to antagonise TP or scare him off, so there would have been no accusations or recriminations, no sense of *where the heck have you been all these years*, or *my husband and my mother-in-law both died with broken hearts because of what you did*. It would also not have contained any suggestion of a meeting, that would come later. But that first letter opened the door, and to TP's credit, he stepped over the threshold. Persuaded to do so by his children, he replied to May, the opening words of which mark the start of this section. His letter was gracious and warm enough to merit a reply from May containing more information about the wider family circle. We are blessed to have access to most of the letters that TP wrote to May, though sadly the ones she penned to him did not survive. His letters, however, speak so much more than the words contained within them.

In his second letter, TP enquires about three of his wife's family members – and not necessarily the ones you might think. Annie Kate is the first.

> *"Tell Annie I am on the lookout for a letter from her as she was my favourite cousin-in-law."*

This confirms that the Tommy of old, the young husband of Ciss, was fondly thought of by Annie Kate, and probably others. That regardless of the issues surrounding the start of their marriage, and irrespective of the fact that Tommy was a Protestant, he was at least welcomed into his wife's family by some of her dearest relatives. The next name mentioned is Nancy's.

"Is Bernie's wife Nancy, was that her name, still alive?"

This is a strange question. It's unlikely that TP would have forgotten or doubted his memory of Nancy's name, as she is referred to in his testimony letter. And why not ask about Pat's wife Agnes too? It is possible he already knew that Nancy had died in the 1940s, informed of her passing by Albert. For if he felt it was important enough to enquire about her all these years later in his second letter to May, why would he not have asked the same question of Albert during one of their encounters? Was he seeking reassurance that the woman was actually dead? And as for Albert, it is he who TP comes to next, pouring burning hot oil onto that old conundrum.

"What did Albert do before he died? Wasn't he the youngest?"

We can only assume that he was testing the water, sounding May out, attempting to ascertain if she had even a sniff of a notion that the two men had met before Albert's death, and on several occasions, which she of course did not. This must have been such an anxious time for TP. Almost fifty years had passed since Ciss's death and his undercover dash to the North. Any perceived threat from her family had long gone, as were all the real or imagined villains. His children were grown adults, now in the midterm of their lives, all settled and thriving in their various domestic scenarios. None of them were about to upend their lives and suddenly move back to Dublin or Leitrim. And yet, he was nervous. Perhaps he was worried about his version of the events that happened back in 1939 being challenged, although he now remained the only living witness. Or perhaps he believed he would be judged for the decisions he made; for placing his children into an orphanage, for turning his back on their Irish Catholic heritage. Or he may have felt a niggling sense of guilt that he never reached out to anyone in Ciss's family to reassure them that the children were safe and well. Perhaps he was finally seeing that they had at least deserved that, and oh how easy it would have been to send just one letter. He was bound to be challenged by someone, bound to be questioned, bound to be shamed, and so it was imperative that he get his story straight.

His children were delighted at this unexpected turn of events, thrilled to finally have a connection with their mother's family, as were his grandchildren. They unanimously encouraged the correspondence and some began to write themselves. And so more letters were exchanged, family news and updates shared, photographs sent and received. There was tentative talk of a visit sometime, lots of ifs and buts and maybes, May insisting they would all be made most welcome. And then it happened. As chance would have it, Kathleen and Watson had already been planning a touring holiday in the South of Ireland that summer, although Leitrim was definitely not on the agenda. But after reading the third of May's letters to her father, and on writing and receiving one herself, Kathleen decided they should make a detour. And so, in July 1986, she became the first of her siblings to return to Cashel. As the car crossed the border and headed through County Cavan towards Leitrim, Kathleen felt a mixture of nerves and excitement. They had arranged to stay with May, her son John, and his wife Lily at the family farm in Cashel for just one night, everyone privately acknowledging that for the first visit, one night was of ample sufficiency. But as Mohill approached, Kathleen realised they had no idea where the farm actually was. They had the address, but no directions; a quiet assumption from the Beirnes that Kathleen would instinctively know her way. She was coming home, after all. They drew up outside a pub in Mohill and Watson popped inside to ask the bartender if he knew where John O'Beirne lived.

"I think you'll be meaning John Beirne," the barman replied, "we don't have O'Beirnes in these parts."

The couple set off again down the road, but Watson, perplexed by his brief exchange in the pub realised he hadn't fully concentrated on the man's directions. TP had never properly explained the Beirne-O'Beirne thing to his children, and his objection to the use of Beirne, the family's original name, was always confusing to them. Now here it was, rearing its head in plain sight. There was so much, Kathleen realised, that she didn't know about her mother and her family. There were so many questions and vast chasms to be filled, where would she even begin? The nerves that had been rumbling intensified. Exchanging polite, warm letters was one thing, but what if the reality of meeting these people face to face was a huge mistake? After driving for a few miles thinking they must be lost, they came across a house. Kathleen told Watson to stop. She would knock on the door and ask directions herself this time. As she climbed out of the car, the front door of the house swung open and a dark-haired woman ran out, enveloping Kathleen in her arms.

"Kathleen Pakenham, you are the absolute spit of your grandmother," cried May Beirne, "I would know you anywhere."

Kathleen cried herself to sleep that night, her heart broken not by admonishments or reproaches or unkindness from the people she had met, but by love and by loss; by the realisation that there was an entire living breathing family circle that she and her siblings had grown up without, and by visions of the mother she had stopped herself from properly thinking about decades before. Aside from May, she and Watson met John and Lily and some of their children, and Annie Kate too, and her daughter, Annette. They were regaled with stories about her mother and her uncles and her grandparents, Kate especially, each new tale a revelation, a piece of that jigsaw puzzle her father had never wanted them to complete. It was like jumping into a storybook you were supposed to be a leading character in, only to find you had been written out instead. Kathleen hadn't been bombarded with questions herself, not about her father or her childhood years at any rate. She was asked about her children, and grandchildren, of whom she had two by then, and how her father and sister and brothers were doing. It would have been strange not to acknowledge them, not to bring them into the conversation, but she was not pressed at all about what had happened to them in those missing years. As she cried herself to sleep that night, she allowed herself to wonder, for the first time ever, how their vanishing had affected this big new family they were finally part of once again.

CHAPTER 32

TP was the next to visit, driving himself down to Cashel just a matter of weeks after Kathleen and Watson's trip. He too met with May, John and Lily, and Annie Kate. What a reunion that must have been, as aside from Mollie and Babs, Annie Kate was the only person left in the family circle who knew Tommy from before. As we know, the two were fond of each other back then, a lifetime ago, but Annie Kate must have harboured some feelings of anger towards the man who had absconded with her beloved cousin's children, one of whom, Kathleen, was her goddaughter. She, no doubt, would have been the person TP was most anxious about meeting. She would have been the one he found it difficult to look in the eye. We don't know what happened at their reunion. We don't know if TP was asked questions by his hosts; if he was asked to explain himself, asked why he left, or pushed on what had happened to them all in the early years following their departure. Or indeed if, just as with Kathleen, he wasn't really quizzed at all, the family perhaps agreeing to let him reveal details as and when he was ready. But if he was questioned then he must have expertly deflected, for we do know he didn't reveal a single thing. Not then. He returned to Bangor in high spirits, delighted at how the visit had played out, proclaiming to his family that they were extremely nice people and he had been very well received. But when pushed for more details, true to form, he remained resolutely tight lipped. There is a photograph taken on that visit of TP sitting on the couch at May's house, one arm around her, the other around Annie Kate, Lily perched on the end with a baby in her arms. They are smiling, happy. A genuine warmth radiates from the image. It would be the first of several visits TP would make to Cashel in the coming two years.

Ted and Noreen made their first visit in September. On throwing her arms around Ted, just as she had done with Kathleen, May was astounded by how much he resembled Albert.

"There's definitely another Beirne in the parish today," she declared.

That Sunday morning they accompanied May to church, where Ted was introduced to an abundance of cousins and second cousins. Word would have spread throughout the parish by then that Ciss Beirne's missing children had been found, yet still, for reasons I simply cannot fathom, this momentous event was not discussed in my own family circle. We had all left home by then, my siblings and I, but we were close, and in regular contact. And my parents had remained close to May after Ned's death. Indeed, they often accompanied her to mass, and would undoubtedly have witnessed Albert O'Beirne's lookalike enter the chapel on that particular Sunday. Perhaps they did not mention anything about this unexpected turn of events because nothing had ever been mentioned before, and really, where would they even start?

As with the others, Ted and Noreen were warmly received. They did not know how much TP had told the Beirne family about what had happened in the 1940s, as he had refused point blank to discuss it with them, but assumed he must at least have relayed the bare bones of the story. It was only when they went to dinner at Olive's house that they realised he hadn't. Olive, May and Ned's fourth child, was warm and welcoming. She laid on a delicious home cooked meal and was clearly delighted to meet her cousin and his wife, but both Ted and Noreen detected an underlying sadness in her demeanour. Throughout the course of the evening, they gradually became aware that Ned and Kate had both experienced a prolonged and agonising grief for the remainder of their lives, a grief that carried them to their graves. It was Olive who revealed to Ted that their grandmother had cried for him and his siblings each night and prayed constantly to the Lord for news of them, from the day they left Dublin to the day she died. It was she who told how her own father had carried the burden after Kate's death, how he'd thought about going on the *Late Late Show*, how he'd spoken with the priest from the North, how he'd even asked his own brother Albert who sometimes worked in Belfast to help track them down. But no one could help and nothing could be done. It was clear too to Ted and Noreen that not just had Olive and the wider Berine family suffered unresolved trauma because of TP's actions, but they had no knowledge whatsoever of the sorrows that Ted and his siblings had been forced to endure themselves. As Ted and Noreen listened to Olive talk, they empathised with her pain, neither daring to look at the other. Ted's heart was quietly breaking for his grandmother and the rest of his mother's family, for this cousin he was meeting for the very first time, and for himself, Joan, Kathleen and Jack. None of them had deserved this pain. Noreen's heart was quietly breaking for her husband. They both realised with growing dismay that TP had divulged nothing at all about the truth of those dreadful years, and had either deliberately or inadvertently allowed the Beirne family to believe that after leaving Dublin, their lives had been easy and carefree. Caught in a quandary, Ted decided to remain quiet himself. Perhaps if Olive had asked him directly what happened to them all after the move North, he might have felt compelled to reveal the unsavoury truth, or at least some of it. But she didn't, so neither did he. The evening ended with hugs and gratitude, and genuine promises to meet again soon.

On their return to Bangor, Ted and Noreen recounted the details of their dinner with Olive to the rest of the family, who were all eager for news. Ted can't recall if he quizzed his father about the lack of information he had seemingly bestowed upon the Beirnes; if he suggested it was time he told them the truth, or if he didn't press him on the matter at all, assuming it would make no difference. His father would do things his own way, just as he had always done. But Ted's experience that evening at Olive's house must have nudged at TP's conscience, for a few weeks later he wrote again to May, the fifth time he had done so. If this contact with the Beirne family was to continue, and it seemed that everyone on both sides of the border very much wanted it to, then it was time for him to write his testimony for the second time.

To do both TP and his letter justice, it is only proper at this point to reproduce his words in their entirety.

9th October 1986

Dear May,

> *I was glad to hear from Ted & Noreen about the wonderful time they had with you, especially that they were able to go to church with you.*
>
> *I feel it is time I told you why I behaved the way I did so many years ago. You remember I asked you in one of my letters if Nancy were alive. Here is the reason. One evening she came to see the children and asked me if I were going to Cashel for the baby. She then said "there will be murder, you won't get him. He will be kept until he's reared."*

So I went down. When I told the mother-in-law that the other three children were looking forward to seeing Jackie she said several times, "he will not leave this house except by force". You know what happened then.

Let me say here that I never blamed her. She believed that I was a heretic and therefore going to hell and naturally wanted to save the children from the same fate. Thank God good Pope John changed all that by saying we were not heretics merely "separated brethren".

I never wanted to leave Dublin. With a good job and house, why should I? It was a visit from Pat and Bernie, Alderman Martin O'Sullivan, Kevin Bunyan, and a letter from Pat setting out how they wanted things to be done and planning my whole future. This I could not accept, and so leaving job, house, furniture, I went to Belfast and for some years had a real tough time – not much change out of my wage of thirty shillings a week!

Pat thought that I was a member of an organisation that was exerting pressure on me, but he was wrong. I never believed in any of these and never had any inclination to join.

I sincerely hope that I have not caused you any pain by giving my side of the unfortunate story. Ciss & I were very happy together and I often thank God for her. When she was in the hospital I said to her "what about the children"? She replied, "you are well able to look after them, you always have." I trust that I have carried out her wishes faithfully.

Why didn't we get in touch with each other before this? Well remember that in 1963 Lily Connolly told me - "They are all dead". I enclose a few verses from Ecclesiastics verse 3-8 which sums up what I think.

Hope to hear from you.

Love, Tom

PS - I have a feeling that Olive should read my letter. Why? I don't know.

~~~~~~~~~~

For everything has its season and for every activity under heaven its time:

A time to be born
A time to plant and a time to uproot
A time to kill <u>and a time to heal</u>
A time to fall down and a time to build up
A time to weep and a time to laugh
A time for nourishing and a time for dancing
A time to embrace and a time to refrain
A time to seek and a time to lose
A time to tear and a time to mend
A time for silence and a time for speech

~~~~~~~~~~

The letter is a much-condensed version of the one he wrote for his own consumption in October 1939, but this time there is a softening of tone, an underlying sentiment of loss and heartache, and an acknowledgement of the part he played in the sorry story. And there is a note of regret too that things worked out the way they did. And yet, and *yet*, he does not tell May just how tragic that sorry story became. He readily cites his own hardships, but does not mention the sufferings of the children, does not refer to the years they spent in an orphanage or to Jack's multiple foster homes. *I trust that I have carried out her wishes faithfully*, he says. But Ciss would never have wished an orphanage upon her children, surely that much we can be certain of. And then there is that reference to Olive. Perhaps he sensed that Olive would be the one to push for details, while her mother and siblings and aunt were content to simply have the Pakenhams back in the family fold again. And so he decided to pre-empt any direct questioning by offering up his version of events, carefully choosing his words, ensuring that she would read them. He must have known how heartbroken May and Annie Kate would have been to hear the full truth of the matter. He may have feared for his own reputation which had seemingly, unexpectantly, been magnanimously restored. Or perhaps he truly believed he was doing right by his children, saving them from the pain of mentally returning to those dark days in Millisle. Whatever his motivation, he sent the letter not knowing if May would reply, or if this would be the end of it.

May did reply. Her response did not come as quickly as her previous letters had done. No doubt she needed time to digest TP's words and discuss the matter with those in her family closest to her. And possibly the turn of events had triggered memories of her own childhood trauma, when she was separated from her darling sister, her father left a broken man. The decision he had made was to separate his family, and the consequence was a lifetime of pain for May and Roseanne. TP's decision was to keep his family together, regardless of the hardship to himself. Of course she didn't know the truth of the story then. She never would. But May Beirne was a woman of great compassion, and it is not a stretch to imagine that TP's letter moved her. We don't know what she wrote in reply, but it must have been supportive, because on 11th December, TP penned a very short response himself, the sixth letter he had exchanged with May that year.

Dear May,

Yes, it was a sad letter which I wrote. I spent a long time pondering whether I should write it or not.

One thing, because I had no one to turn to, it put me on my nerves more than normal.

I trust that God will spare me so that I can visit you all next year.

Love to all,

Tom

TP never admitted to any of his children that he was emotionally affected by their mother's death and the subsequent events. He never spoke of any loneliness or sense of isolation he experienced in the following months and years. He never hinted that his decision making may have been affected by his state of mind. He rarely spoke of Ciss, never painted a picture of her for his children, never told them what books she liked to read, or what her favourite colour was, or her favourite flower, or what perfume she liked to wear. He stubbornly refused to talk about her family, and persistently deflected questions about what really happened back in 1939. And now here he was almost five decades later, an elderly man of eighty-one, finally exposing the crack that had opened inside his heart when Ciss died to the widow of her brother. Finally offering us a true glimpse of his mental disposition back then. Finally providing an honest explanation as to why he took his children away from everything they knew and plunged them into years of turmoil. *I had no one to turn to, it put me on my nerves more than normal.* How lonely TP's grief must have been through all those years, how sad that he either believed he could not turn to his own family for support, or that he attempted to but was rejected, how unnecessary the suffering that he and everyone else involved endured.

CHAPTER 33

God did indeed spare TP for another visit. Indeed, over the next two years, he would make the drive to Leitrim on a number of occasions, usually staying with Annie Kate as she had a spare bedroom. May lived with John and Lily and their children, and their farmhouse was full and busy, and while she would happily give up her own bedroom when any of the Pakenhams came to visit, it simply made more practical sense for them to stay at Annie Kate's house. They all grew to know each other, a bond of sorts tentatively forming. Even Annette's children became fond of their "Uncle Tommy" as he would play with them in the garden and accompany the family on daytrip outings.

A few months after Ted and Noreen's first visit to Cashel, they returned with Julie in tow. Gail, their youngest daughter, wasn't quite as fascinated by her father's family history and his Southern Irish relatives as her sister, but Julie was euphoric about this new development. A young woman of twenty-two now, she had recently embarked on a management programme with Marks & Spencer based in Sussex, but she flew home to accompany her parents on a weekend trip to meet the Beirnes and the Conboys. They were everything she had imagined them to be, as was Cashel and Mohill. She fell in love with the place and the people, and they with her. But Julie knew there were more people to meet, more branches of the family tree to explore, more stories and secrets to uncover, both in Leitrim and Dublin, and she vowed to return. *There might just be a book in this you know*, she told her parents.

Joan and Mark went to Cashel in the summer of 1987, eighteen months after May's first letter to TP. While she was delighted at this renewed contact with her mother's family, Joan was also extremely nervous about meeting them. Of all her siblings, she was the one who remembered Cashel the best, the one who had the clearest recollections of the farm and the fields and their grandmother. Those memories had both dimmed and become distorted through time, thanks in part to her father's portrayal of Kate as a wicked old woman, but she still carried them with her. Ted and Jack of course had no memory of Cashel whatsoever. Kathleen had maintained some vague recollections, and one exceedingly clear one, that memory of being brought into a bedroom in the farmhouse by their father to be told that their mother was dead. She had been relieved on her first visit to discover that the old farmhouse had long been demolished, as stepping inside it may have been too much of an emotional trigger to bear. But it was Joan who recalled her uncle Ned, albeit very vaguely, this unexpected twist of events nudging that distant, shadowy memory of him at the farm all those years before into her peripheral vision, and the prospect of meeting his widow and her children was both wonderous and terrifying. She was aware of the unsettling feeling that Ted and Noreen had experienced on their first trip to Cashel, and although they were much more relaxed on their second visit with Julie, and while Kathleen and Watson had been welcomed by everyone with open arms, and in spite of their father enthusiastically embracing the family he had both smeared and disregarded for decades, she was quietly worried that these relatives might not take so kindly to her. Perhaps she felt a weight of responsibility being the eldest of the children, believing that she should have tracked her maternal family down many years before and not left the reunion to a twist of fate in a Dublin cemetery. Or perhaps she felt a sense of betrayal to her mother. As a child, she was the only one who had received her First Holy Communion the second big step into the Catholic church, her mothers church, and here she was returning to her mother's homeplace as a middle-aged woman and devoted Protestant. She could not be certain either of exactly what her father had told the family by way of explanation, knowing that whatever account he gave of his actions and their subsequent lives, it would not be entirely straightforward. Joan valued transparency, but she did not want to betray her father, deliberately or unwittingly. As the date of their visit approached, her stress levels intensified. There was no question of cancelling however, this was a pilgrimage she knew she must make.

Joan did not talk much about the trip to Leitrim afterwards, not to Graham or Angela or Kathleen or TP, except to say that it went well, and everyone was kind, and all in all they had a lovely time. Years later she would confide to her daughter-in-law, Karen, with tears in her eyes, that the visit had allowed the circle to finally close; that it had provided her with the missing piece of the puzzle she had been seeking for decades, sometimes consciously, mostly subconsciously.

"But why did we leave it so long?" she said. "Why did we leave it until people had died? It could all have been so very different."

In the immediate days following their return to Walton-on-Thames in Surrey where the family had moved a few years previously, Joan said nothing much at all. She was quiet and pensive, slightly withdrawn. Three weeks later she suffered a massive heart attack. Ted was the one to first make the connection, and whether is it real or imagined, he and Kathleen and Jack, and Joan's children too, believe to this day that her heart attack was a direct result of the visit to Cashel.

Not the visit itself, and certainly not the people she met and the love and welcome she received there, but the stress and worry she felt in the weeks leading up to the trip, and the grief and profound regret she experienced afterwards. Thankfully Joan recovered well, a heart bypass operation two years later restoring her quality of life.

Jack and Ethel did not make the journey to Cashel. Ethel had begun to experience ill health, and Jack's life was busy with his teaching job and his art. He was now a prominent Irish artist, known and respected in particular for his work on The Troubles which were still raging north of the border, and had recently been elected as a Member of the Royal Ulster Academy of Arts. Weekends and holiday periods were devoted to working on new pieces, preparing for exhibitions, or travelling to residencies or events, and Michael had now married and settled in France, so Jack and Ethel had to make time to visit their son and daughter-in-law. It wasn't that he didn't want to meet this new Irish family, the one he had been so desperate to know details about in his younger years, he was simply too busy. He would meet them soon, he told everyone, when he had more time, when life was less hectic. Next year, perhaps, or if not, then the following one. And he absolutely meant it, though in retrospect there was perhaps a suppressed anxiety about confronting the past.

TP paid another visit to Cashel in June 1988. In July he spent a fortnight with Joan and Mark in Surrey. In August, he bought himself a new car, a red Nissan Micra. He told May about the car in a letter. On his last trip to see her he'd notched up almost two hundred miles in his rusting old Mazda, and his next drive down would be much more comfortable. And in November he took his annual winter sun holiday to Cyprus. At the age of eighty-three he showed no sign of slowing down. His life was full and happy, and the demons of grief and defiance and guilt and regret that had chased him for fifty-odd years had nigh on dissipated. He befriended other holiday makers in the hotel, as always, chatting with some of them about politics, religion, and family, proudly sharing photographs of his grandchildren. He settled into a regular daily routine, taking breakfast at nine a.m. and making his way to the hotel beach at eleven thirty, his Boy's Brigade toggle bag slung over his shoulders. He would go for a swim, then walk along the beach, before retiring to his room to sunbathe on his balcony. On the last day of his holiday, the 26$^{th\ of}$ November, he changed his routine slightly as the weather was windy, and walked to a more secluded cove further along the coast. He might have been thinking about his early wakeup call the following morning, or the grim Ulster rain he would be returning to the next day. He may have been wondering when he would see his latest great grandchild, a little girl born to Michael and his wife in France, or looking ahead to Gail's wedding the following year. Rain or no rain, there was a lot to look forward to back home. They thought he had drowned at first, the people who found him, but his family knew that was not what had happened. Thomas Pakenham was a strong swimmer and a fit man for his age. An autopsy confirmed a sudden and catastrophic heart attack, one he would not have survived regardless of the location. Fifty years and seven weeks after his beloved Ciss had left him, the two were finally reunited.

There was grief from his children, of course there was, but it was tempered by an unspoken understanding that none of them had experienced a typical father-child relationship with TP. They had loved him, of that there was no doubt, forgiven him even for some of the more reckless and frustrating decisions he had made, admired him too for the courageous ones. But they still, after all this time, after the reconnection with their Irish family even, had questions they wanted to ask him, and now it was too late. The grief of his grandchildren was more acute. They had only ever known a grandfather who was present and active and entertaining and supportive, a force for nothing but good in their lives. The father he had been to their relevant parent was mostly irrelevant to them, and the parents in question did not begrudge that. In fact, after everything that had transpired throughout their own childhoods and young adulthoods, such an outcome was both a relief and a joyful thing to behold. There was sadness too from friends and neighbours in the area of Bangor where TP had lived with Kathleen and Watson for the preceding sixteen years, from the Carnalea Methodist church community, from the wider Boys' Brigade family in Bangor and Belfast, from his beloved Belfast Central Mission, from former work colleagues and fellow Labour Party activists. And there was genuine sorrow and regret from the Beirne and Conboy families of Cashel and Mohill. The funeral was huge, with people from all of these walks of life joining Joan, Kathleen, Ted and Jack to pay their respects to this enigma of a man. And of all the cards and letters of sympathy they received in the days and weeks following their father's death, one in particular stood out: a note of sincerest sympathy from Frank Pakenham, the 7th Earl of Longford, on the death of his dear friend. TP and Frank had dipped in and out of contact in the decades since their boyhood days at Pakenham Hall. Whether Frank was aware of his old friend and "cousin's" hardships and family circumstances we do not know, but a few years before his death, TP travelled to London to spend an afternoon with the Earl at the House of Lords. It was a proud day for TP, one he would cherish for the rest of his days, and one that it seems was significant for Frank too.

"I am so very pleased to think that he and I came together at the House of Lords after so many years," he wrote, "and that he treasured the memory, as indeed do I."

TP on his 80th birthday with Joan, Jack, Ted and Kathleen.

After TP's death, all tentative plans for future trips to Leitrim were put on hold, not because of his passing per se, although there were obviously the obligatory and often time-consuming post-death legalities to get through, but because 1989 was shaping up to be a busy and eventful year. Kathleen and Watson had already made a couple of return visits to the county to stay with Annette and her husband Sylvester, with whom they had become close, and they looked forward to seeing them again. But Watson's health wasn't too good, and there were work and church and family commitments in the calendar, so it looked like it might be the spring of 1990 before they could make their next journey down to Leitrim. Jack and Ethel were still hopeful they would finally get down soon, but Ethel's health too remained an issue, and life showed no sign of slowing down for Jack. He would admit in later years that he may have been subconsciously avoiding such a visit, concerned about the emotional pain it might educe. Joan would be getting her heart surgery early in the year, and ruled herself out of a return visit for the foreseeable future. And Ted and Noreen had Gail's wedding to plan. Julie was still keen to return, this time with a notebook and tape recorder, determined to start the process of getting her grandparents' story down on paper. But she was as busy as a young woman in the prime of her life should be, rapidly rising through the ranks at Marks & Spencer, newly in love, leading a busy social life, and taking the role of chief bridesmaid at her sister's upcoming wedding very seriously. It would need to wait until next year, she told everyone. Maybe in the summer, or late spring. She was due to go on a skiing holiday to France the following March, so definitely sometime after that.

Julie never returned from that skiing holiday. She and another girl from their party were killed in a freak accident at a popular viewing point on the mountain. She was just twenty-four years old. This time the grief was overwhelming, not just for Ted and Noreen and Gail, although theirs was obviously the most acute, the most vital, but for the entire Pakenham family circle. Julie was beloved by them all, and the shock and repercussions of her loss would resonate for years to come. It changed everything, including the family's connection with Cashel. For although written correspondence with May and Annie Kate was maintained for a while, and although Kathleen and Watson retuned to visit Annette and Sylvester on a handful of occasions, the contact gradually fizzled out. It was nobody's fault. There was no blame, no real reason. It was simply a consequence of grief.

CHAPTER 34

Jack was especially close to his niece and took her sudden passing extremely badly. He retired that year, exhausted by grief and concerned about Ethel's ongoing health issues, but also eager to devote more time to his painting. He had been a teacher at Ashfield for twenty-nine years by then, nineteen of which were as head of the English department. But life was unpredictable, and he didn't want to waste any more years doing trivial things that were not connected to his art. Not that teaching was trivial, but it had been tough at times to keep going through the Troubles in a school that was often touched by the extremism of loyalist paramilitaries. Jack was worn out by the political situation in Northern Ireland, and had become despondent about his role as an educator. His art allowed him to vent the anger and frustration he felt about the Troubles, at inequality in general, and at his own past. It was time to focus on that, and pay more attention too to the poetry he'd been dabbling with since those days with Heaney and Muldoon. He would think about Julie often, and his father, and, on occasion, the family he had never got to meet. He and Ethel had not made it down to Cashel before Julie's death, and he could not see them doing so now. He resigned himself to the fact that door was closed, and the questions he still had about his mother and his grandmother would never now be answered.

Leaving Ashfield school provided no real emotional respite however, as although Jack finally had the freedom to focus solely on his art, it was an intense and all-consuming time. The work he was producing, titled the *Belfast Series,* featured masked and gagged figures, and limbless, decapitated mannequins. The focus and the subject matter and the intensity took its toll, along with ongoing grief and a long-held anger that was finally being released, and in 1993, Jack too had a heart attack.

He recovered, and continued working on the series, and in 1995, BBC Northern Ireland commissioned a documentary about his life and work. The director was Paul Yates, a former pupil of Jack's from Ashfield, who had become a film maker and an artist of some note himself. Jack was his mentor and inspiration, and the film, titled *Return Journey*, was a sensitive tribute to him. It was the first time Jack or any of his siblings had spoken publicly about their childhood and the years they had spent in an orphanage. Paul took Jack back to the Childhaven complex, which by then was empty and derelict, where he reminisced to camera about his time there, recalling the bullying he had endured. Or at least some of it. They also went to Dublin; a city Jack was by now quite familiar with as he had exhibited in some of its premier art galleries. He had never ventured out to Mount Jerome cemetery though, and so Paul and the crew took him there. They found Ciss's grave, thanks to the stone surround TP had paid for a decade earlier. Jack asked for privacy. He needed to speak to his mother alone. Just the two of them. In the film, we see Jack from a distance standing in front of the grave, but this scene was filmed after he had that private moment. It was a profoundly moving experience. Jack still possessed no religious faith. He did not, still does not, believe in an afterlife or that our souls live on after death. And yet he felt the presence of his mother that day, or at least an essence of her. It was the closest he had been to her physically and emotionally since his birth.

"It all turned out okay, Mum," he told her. "You mustn't worry about us. We are all well and happy, and against the odds, we are still a family."

The following year, Jack brought his *Belfast Series* exhibition to the Project Gallery in Dublin. Mollie Winters, then seventy-eight years old, was still living in the city, still frequenting galleries and museums and the theatre. She hadn't seen the documentary about Jack as it was only shown on BBC Northern Ireland, but she heard about her godson's upcoming exhibition. She knew from May that contact had been made with Tommy and the children, and was as relieved and delighted as the rest of the family who were in the loop that they had survived and thrived and were living meaningful lives. She would have known too that Tommy had died, and that Ted and his wife had tragically lost a child, echoes of Kate's losses reverberating with the news. She would have been told of the visits to Cashel by Joan and Kathleen and Ted, but that for a multitude of reasons, Jack had not made it down. Yet here he was now, exhibiting his work in her adopted city, the city of his birth. He had exhibited in Dublin before, but this exhibition was his biggest and most significant to date, and was attracting considerable attention. And so she went along to the opening event, tapped Jack on his shoulder, and introduced herself as his godmother.

Jack was taken aback. The name Mollie Winters was known to him. He would have been aware it was she who had led May to his father ten years previously, but he did not know she was his godmother and could never have imagined meeting her in the surrounds of a Dublin art gallery. Her announcement was entirely shocking to him. Jack had never thought to ask if he had godparents, or indeed if he had even been baptised, assuming perhaps that as he was so young when his mother had died, and with everything that came afterwards, there hadn't been time for a christening. Or maybe he had asked once, but the question, as with so many, had been deflected. Yet here was his godmother, his Catholic godmother, standing in front of him, talking about his mother, her cousin, telling him how close they were, how heartbroken she had been by her death, how wonderful it was to finally, after all these years, see him once again. The gallery was busy, packed with people from the art world, and press, and specially invited guests. So many people wanted Jack's attention and he had to excuse himself from Mollie, promising to seek her out later. His head was left reeling by her revelation. There was so much he wanted to ask her and he found it difficult to focus for the rest of the evening. But Mollie left the gallery, probably not wanting to burden or monopolise Jack on his special night, recognising perhaps the depth of his shock when she told him who she was. Jack was full of good intentions to contact his newly discovered godmother when he returned to Belfast, to see her again when he was next in Dublin. But as is the way, life took over and time passed, and the two never did meet again. Mollie died on 13th January 1998. She may not have met with the other Pakenham children before she passed, but that brief reunion with her missing godson brought at least one strand of their shared story full circle.

Years passed with little contact between the Pakenhams and the Beirnes and Conboys, two decades in fact. The odd Christmas card was exchanged, an occasional letter too, perhaps. But nothing more than that. There were more births, and more deaths. Annie Kate died in August 2001. May outlasted her by thirteen years, passing away in 2014 at the grand age of one hundred and one. She was the last surviving member of that particular generational connection to Ciss.

On TP's side, Georgina was the last to go. She too lived an unusually long life, dying in 2012 at the astonishing age of one hundred and three. She had stayed in touch with her Northern Irish cousins throughout her life, becoming especially close to Ted and Noreen. Jack's darling Ethel passed in 2015, and Kathleen's beloved Watson in 2017. And on 28th January 2010, Kathleen, Ted and Jack lost their big sister. At seventy-nine, Joan was still active, still involved with her church, still riding her bicycle, cycling daily to the nursing home where her precious Mark was being cared for, the Alzheimer's he'd been diagnosed with a couple of years previously too difficult now to manage at home. But her heart was giving her trouble once again, and before she could have another operation, she went into irreversible heart failure. Her younger siblings flew over to be with her at the end, and Jack, that little brother who had exasperated her for years, who had tried her patience and given her cheek and refused to hold her hand or obey her instructions, and continued to wind her up at any given opportunity for the rest of her life, wrote and delivered her eulogy.

I would like to take this opportunity to celebrate the life of my big sister Joan, he began, taking the assembled mourners through the twists and turns of Joan's life journey: the sudden move North at the age of eight, the orphanage, boarding school, Cliftonpark, the church, her jobs, meeting Mark and moving to England, her children, her health issues, and their own relationship. *She loved having family around her*, he concluded, *with all the camaraderie and friendly banter. And of course I still kidded her … what else are young brothers for!*

CHAPTER 35

When Olive began to tell me what she knew about her father's sister Ciss and the missing children, I was astonished. Aunt Brigie was right after all. And when she told me about the all too brief reunion that had taken place in the late 1980s, my shock deepened. I couldn't fathom how this story had passed me by for six whole decades, passed my siblings by too, especially when our father had been in the thick of things when TP took Jack away from Kate and the farm. Ned was visiting my grandfather that day after all, or so we believe. The incident, and the subsequent flight to the North by TP and his children, haunted Ned for the rest of his life, that much we know for certain. It would have been common knowledge in the parish, fodder for local gossip. Ned would surely have discussed the disappearance of his nephews and nieces with my father, his cousin and friend, regularly at first, dwindling as the years passed to the occasional reminiscence over a mug of tea or a nip of whiskey. And May must have spoken about the family tragedy that preoccupied her husband with my mother. Their own children all knew the story, it was part of the fabric of their history, yet we Winters siblings didn't. Perhaps our parents simply considered the matter too painful, or felt that discussing it would serve no good purpose. Even in my childhood years, pregnancy out of wedlock and inter-faith marriage were still contentious issues, and perhaps my mother and father did not want to indulge in local gossip. Or possibly, somewhere through the years it was mentioned in passing to one or some of us, but at the time was irrelevant, the information flitting through one young ear and out the other, lost forever in the business of our busy childhood lives. There is also the possibility that my father harboured a quiet sympathy for TP, a sympathy he couldn't voice to Ned for fear of offending him. After all, his own father had found himself in a similar situation. When my grandmother died and Mollie was separated from the family, my grandfather took her back, just as TP did with Jack. And thank goodness he did, for if Mollie had been raised by someone else, her life would have inevitably taken a different turn. She would not have become my godmother, nor Jack's. She would not have known, or at least been as close to, Ciss. And she would not have found herself in Mount Jerome Cemetery on a January afternoon in 1986, staring at the new limestone surround to her cousin's grave. Of course my grandfather did not flee the country. He and his children stayed in Cashel, accepting help and support from their wider family circle and the community around them. TP chose a different path, but I suspect my father, whilst not entirely agreeing with his actions, especially the ongoing absence of any contact, did not fully begrudge him it either. And very possibly, Mollie felt the same.

I continued to work on the Winters and Conboy family tree alongside my wife, Mary, and Tony Hennessy, a genealogist we had brought on board to help, but I couldn't stop thinking about this newly discovered family. I knew by now that their surname was Pakenham. That Tommy, or TP, was the father, husband of Kate and Edward Beirne's only daughter, Ciss. That he had died in 1988, a couple of years after renewed contact with May and Annie Kate. That Ted, the eldest son, had suffered the most tragic of bereavements in the loss of his daughter less than two years later. That Jack, the youngest son was an artist of note. That Joan lived in England, and Kathleen had lived in Bangor, County Down, with her father. I had no idea if any of these second cousins were still alive, but I desperately hoped they were. I had questions, so many questions. What had happened to the four of them in the years following their mother's death? How had they made the transition from Southern Irish Catholic children to Northern Irish Protestant ones? What were the war years like for them? How had they coped without their mother, this particular curiosity stemming perhaps from my own father's experience of losing his mother, and witnessing the pain my dear sister Lucy's children experienced when they lost her. Olive didn't have the answers. She had only met Joan once, and Kathleen and Ted on a couple of occasions, and their conversations had centred around family life in recent years. I spoke with Annette too, who was also a second cousin to me. She had spent more time with both Kathleen and TP than Olive had, Kathleen especially, and she looked back on their visits with great fondness and a sense of regret that the connection hadn't lasted. But she hadn't pried into their past, she told me, and no real details had been forthcoming. It was perplexing to me why no one on the Beirne side of the family asked any of the Pakenhams what happened to them after they fled Dublin. Where did they live? How did they manage financially? Did TP have hands-on help from his family, or a live-in housekeeper? It seems strange that the big questions, achingly contemplated for so many years, were not voiced. Perhaps deep down Ciss's family were afraid of what they might hear, scared to rip the scabs off old wounds, worried that the truth might make them resent in some way the family with whom they were now reunited. The children were safe, they had found each other again, and ultimately that was all that mattered.

As the family tree grew bigger, more tales and anecdotes and characters were uncovered, some funny, others tragic, most fascinating in one way or another. Mary and I had decided to produce a coffee table style book to accompany the large family chart and debated over which particular stories and events to include. We both knew, however, that Ciss Beirne and her missing children would definitely feature. It was the one story that had truly got under my skin, becoming an incessant itch I just had to scratch. But the information had to be accurate. And the only way to ensure that it was, was to reach out to one of Ciss's children. With Tony's help we found Jack's contact details, and he and I were soon in touch by email. One thing led to another, and Jack liaised with Ted and Kathleen to source some old family photographs. There weren't many, but they were happy to share with us the few that they had for inclusion in the book. He confirmed the details I was already aware of, and shared some new information too; his meeting with Mollie, our shared godmother, in that Dublin art gallery, the fact that he had been unaware until then that he even had a godmother, or that he had been baptised as a Catholic, and the sad news that Joan had died almost a decade previously. His beloved Ethel had also died, and perhaps the time was now exactly right to embark on this journey and see where it would take him. He would love to see the family tree when it was completed, he told me, and the book too. They all would.

By the time it was complete, the family tree chart that Tony produced contained an astonishing 960 names. In early August 2019, Mary and I held a family gathering at our home in Leitrim to unveil the chart and the book. Everyone who came along that evening had a connection to the tree, though none of the surviving Pakenhams were able to attend. Noreen had just been through major surgery and Ted couldn't leave her. Kathleen's health wasn't too good either. And as Jack had never been back to Leitrim in the eighty years since his father had taken him away from the farm, we all agreed that meeting multiple members of his extended family for the first time in one go would be too overwhelming. But a few weeks later, on 28th September, he did make the trip to Leitrim, a CD copy of his *Return Journey* film, tucked inside his bag. He took the bus from Belfast to Enniskillen where Mary and I picked him up and drove him back to Cashel. Jack wanted to get a sense of his mother, to retrace some of the steps she would have taken during her childhood and young adult life, to walk in her shoes for an afternoon. So we brought him to the spot where the old farmhouse had been. We visited the cemetery where his grandparents and four of his uncles were buried. We stopped at the church where Kate went to mass, and where multiple family baptisms and funerals had been held over the years. We took him to his mother's old school, the one his sisters had briefly attended too when they had all stayed at the farm following her death, and to Mohill where she would have taken a pony and trap to buy groceries for the family and to sell sheep and cattle on fair days. We stopped at the narrow-gauge railway station where she and her mother and brothers would have jumped on a train to Dromod, changing from there to the main line train to Dublin. And we even stopped at the local well from which Ciss would have drawn the family's fresh water. It was an emotional journey, distressing at times, contemplative at others, yet ultimately hopeful too. It was as though Jack, who had just turned eighty-one, was meeting his mother for the very first time. At Jack's request, each moment was photographed, each stop at a new location committed to memory. Inside his head, he was painting the canvas of his mother's young life, the details of which he had never been able to visualise. He saw Ciss the child and Ciss the teenager, Ciss the daughter and Ciss the sister, and finally, and perhaps most poignantly, Ciss the young mother too.

That evening, around twenty close family members came to our house, including some of my brothers and sisters, John Beirne's wife, Lily, and Olive. The true story of Jack and his siblings' childhood had unfolded throughout the day, shocking Mary and me to our core. We knew however that the surface had only just been scratched, that there was so much more to reveal. I wasn't sure if Olive knew about Childhaven. I suspected not as she hadn't mentioned it to me, but then again, how could all of those visits have taken place in the 1980s without such a vital, devastating piece of information being revealed? Surely one of them would have said something about an orphanage? During the evening, Jack asked if he could show us the documentary film. *It will explain a lot*, he said. So I popped the DVD into the player, and we arranged chairs and sofas and cushions around the television, and sat back to watch, a palpable sense of expectation in the room. I had a clear view of Olive's face from where I was seated, and I saw her tears flow as on the screen a younger Jack took us all to Millisle and the ruins of the orphanage that he and his siblings had spent years of their childhood in; four for him, five for Joan, seven for Kathleen, and eight for Ted. It was clear then that she had not known, and the revelation rocked her.

Not long after Jack's visit, I drove to Belfast to meet Ted and Noreen. I would soon meet Kathleen too, and eventually, once Covid and the lockdowns had been and gone, her eldest daughter Norma, and Ted's Gail, and Jack's youngest son, David. And in time, I would travel to Surrey and meet Joan's son Graham and his wife Karen. They have all become part of my life in a way I could not have begun to contemplate the day I first read those words in Aunt Brigie's letter: *she died and left four children after her. The husband decamped in the clouds of the night with the children and wasn't heard of since. It's supposed he's up North rearing them up good Protestants.*

"There's so much more to this story," I said to Ted and Noreen the first time they came to stay with us. "I don't want to pry if it makes you feel too uncomfortable, but if you're willing to talk, I'd love to hear it."

"Funny you should say that", said Ted, "our Julie always said there was a book in it."

Portrait of Ciss by her great-grandson, artist Karl Hagan (grandson of Ted Pakenham)

EPILOGUE

To grow outside ourselves,
To meet within each other's lives,
To lose our suffering,
To understand

~ Jack Pakenham

It is difficult to pinpoint the exact moment when the story of Ciss Beirne and Tommy Pakenham and their four children began. On the face of it we might assume the starting point to be the second that Ciss and TP met, whether that encounter was indeed in an office at Edison & Swan, or somewhere else entirely. Or was it when Ciss became pregnant with Joan, her conception laying a foundation for the chaos that would erupt eight years later. Perhaps we should mark their own births as the starting point, or the births of their four respective parents, or trace the story's roots back to the first names on my family tree. But I believe, wherever we begin, the story of Ciss and TP is entrenched in the history of Ireland; in its wars and battle wounds, in its divisions and discords, in its landscapes and folklore and songs and poetry, in its class structure, in poverty, and perhaps most of all, in its religious divide.

For generations, mixed faith marriages in Ireland were an uncommon occurrence, and Ciss and TP's union happened to come at a time of particular animosity between the Catholic and Protestant religions. There have of course been decades of pain and intolerance in the subsequent ninety-plus years, but the backdrop to their marriage was the War of Independence, the Civil War, and partition.

Protestants felt unwelcome in the South of Ireland, and Catholics in the North, while mixed-faith couples were shunned in both. Ciss and TP were victims of this intolerance, Ciss as we have seen, carrying the additional burden of being pregnant out of wedlock. But they overcame the obstacles that had been placed in their path and made a loving life together, building a family, creating a home, accepting each other's religious differences. If members of their own families and social circles were sceptical or unhappy about the union, they would have had to admit that despite their misgivings, the relationship worked, and worked well. But when life took that fateful turn, and death intervened, everything changed. To the Beirne family, TP was no longer just their daughter and sister's Protestant husband; he was her children's Protestant widower father, a threat to their Catholic upbringing, and that was an entirely different scenario to contend with. On the flip side, his own mother and siblings, who were less integrated into his young family's life than the Beirnes were, and his close circle of friends in Dublin, viewed Ciss's death as a chance to remove their friend, son, bother, cousin, from the grips of the Catholicism he had been living within for the best part of a decade, and turn his children into the Protestants they should have been in the first place. And TP was caught in the middle. Grief made him both paranoid and gullible, deeply mistrusting on the one hand, and much too trusting on the other. Grief also, inevitably, impacted on the Beirne family's actions and thinking; Kate's broken heart genuinely believing that the baby should stay with her, Pat and Bernie's deep commitment to the Catholic faith pushing them to fight, and fight hard, for the wishes of their beloved sister Ciss, and for her children's religious status. The same level of grief would not have extended to the Pakenham connection as Ciss was not their blood, and in spite of the eight years of marriage to TP, they did not know her well. They must have felt sad for him, and for the children, but their motivation was mostly religious. It seems there was no one person who truly had both TP and the children's best interests at heart, no one to act as a neutral negotiator, no one to put this reconfigured family unit first, to say, *let's set religion aside for a second, and look at the options here.* TP's breakdown was probably inevitable, the madness of his subsequent choices and actions perhaps understandable, to a degree.

We will never truly fathom why TP thought Charlie Pakenham's home in Lurgan was a suitable place of refuge for his three eldest children, why he moved Jack between so many foster homes, or why his own immediate family apparently provided such limited help. We will never fully understand why he put his children into an orphanage, nor why he left them there for so long. And we will never comprehend why he sent three of the children back to Dublin, to a private boarding school in the heart of the city he had smuggled them out of. But looking back to his own childhood, growing up in the grounds of a stately home that bore his name, witnessing the endless privilege that his friend and "cousin" Frank availed of, and immersing himself in the ways of an exclusive boarding school, it is no stretch to imagine that Thomas Pakenham had envisaged an entirely different life for himself, and was ill equipped for the one that he ended up living. Yes, he was happy with Ciss, yes, he loved her, and yes, he loved his children. He was fundamentally a good and honourable man, but he did not know how to make things right when they went so badly wrong, or how to be a father on his own. His upbringing and seemingly distant and unemotional relationships with his own parents and siblings no doubt played a part in this. TP's discovery of Methodism and the subsequent relationship he developed with God saved him, and quite possibly saved his children too. For if TP had not chosen those particular digs in South Parade, if he had not encountered the Methodist clergymen boarding there, he may well not have survived his breakdown, and what would have become of his four children then.

That they all survived is astonishing. That the five of them, TP, Joan, Kathleen, Ted and Jack, eventually became a proper family again is nothing short of a miracle. That the children all thrived, and carved out successful careers, and built their own loving families, and led happy, fulfilling lives is a testament to TP in part, but also to the love of their mother that they carried in their hearts, even when they didn't know it, and to their own remarkable resilience. Obviously, they did not come through unscathed. There was pain and there are scars. There was a lifetime spent without the love and support of grandparents and aunts and uncles and cousins and second cousins, a loss still sharply felt by the surviving siblings. There are memories still buried that will never be uncovered, and there are others that refused to be forgotten, horrors that lingered uncomfortably close to the surface for decade after decade, the eventual release of which were both devastating and cathartic. One of these memories belonged to Joan. Not long before her death, she told Kathleen on their weekly Sunday evening telephone call, that during the Childhaven years, the person we are calling Davy Barr had assaulted her. And while she never fully voiced what had happened in Lurgan, we are fairly certain her experience there was a similarly distressing one.

There are multiple "what ifs" in this story, but the "what if TP had stayed in Dublin with the children" is the most prominent imagining. The children would have grown up with their father, surrounded by family, and even if Jack had stayed on the farm for a time, he would probably have returned to Dublin at some point, as had happened with Bernie's son Brian when he was seven. They would have remained as

Catholics. They would not have been separated from their father, nor forced to live in an orphanage. And their stories and bloodline would carry on through different children made with different partners. Yet none of them would wish that for a second, not one. They bear what happened to them as children with grace and courage and humility, and any lingering frustration they may feel about their father does not diminish their love for him.

"I had a good life," says Jack. "I wouldn't change a thing."

In the light of all the knowledge they now have however, there is one thing that Kathleen, Ted and Jack would change if they could. Just one. They would ask their father to let Kate know that her grandchildren were safe.

We have been on quite a journey since I first held Aunt Brigie's letter in my hand and discovered my "good Protestant" second cousins "up North". Unravelling the story of their life has introduced me to some extraordinary individuals, both living, and deceased, people I would otherwise never have encountered. There is Kate, hounded by death and sorrow throughout her life, yet still she persevered, still she loved, still she hoped. A woman of great courage and compassion and faith, whose prayers for news about her grandchildren were sadly never answered. And Ciss, imbued with her mother's strength of character, who overcame first polio and then religious and social intolerance, and fought for the right to rear her family on her terms. A devoted mother and loving wife, her life was so tragically cut short, yet even facing death her spirit rose. On her deathbed Ciss's thoughts were for her "poor mother" Kate, about to lose a child for the third time, and for her own children too; her newborn baby son, ensuring he received a Catholic baptism, and his siblings, pleading with her husband to keep the family together. Then there is TP himself. We know so much more about him than his wife and mother-in-law, and yet he remains the greatest conundrum of this tale. A deeply complex character, a man who in the wake of tragedy made numerous questionable decisions. And yet, when Ciss told him she was pregnant he stood by her, and agreed to raise their children in her Catholic faith. This can't have been easy for a man of TP's strict protestant upbringing, but he embraced his new wife's family in Leitrim and Dublin, and their life was happy. It is clear he lost his way when Ciss died. Submerged by grief, he was derailed by opposing views on how he should move forward, and ultimately his children paid the price. However, as a committed Methodist with a social conscience, he undoubtedly carried out great work in his community, especially with underprivileged children, and in later years became a devoted and beloved grandfather; all of which adds to the enduring enigma of Thomas Pakenham.

Then there are the Pakenham children themselves. I never got to meet Joan, but we know that from the age of eight she carried a heavy load on her small shoulders. And though she went on to live a full and happy life in England, only allowing herself to do so once her siblings and father were all settled themselves, it was a weight she never fully shed. Katheen, in her ninetieth year now, still displays that feisty spirit that offered some protection to her siblings against the bullies at Childhaven. It was she and her own family who TP lived out the last sixteen years of his life with, and like her father, she has devoted much of her adulthood to helping those in need within her local community. Ted, though outwardly the sibling least affected by their turbulent childhood, to this day quietly mourns the mother he cannot remember but who he does know loved him dearly. That at least gives him comfort.

It is he perhaps who most vividly inherited the grit, determination, and strength of his mother and grandmother, pushing the multiple setbacks of his childhood aside to build a successful career and a happy, stable homelife. It is also, sadly, Ted who truly understands the particular pain that his grandmother suffered on losing a child, a grief that will bind the two of them through eternity with an invisible thread. Jack was the sibling most clearly impacted by the unremitting unpredictability of his early life, the constant moves between one "home" and another, the ever-revolving "parental" figures coming in and out of his life, none of whom were able to wholly parent him, for one reason or another. His memories of Childhaven and the suffering he and others endured there are the most vivid, the most disturbing. Yet he too has led a rewarding life, a creatively driven one full of travel and artistic fulfilment, and ultimately, of love. Each one of them is remarkable in their own particular way, and all have a trace of both their parents running through them. Joan, Kathleen and Ted became committed Christians with a strong social and community conscience, while Jack used his art and poetry to rail against intolerance and abuse.

I have enjoyed the pleasure of many hours in Kathleen, Ted and Jack's company since Aunt Brigie's letter set us off down this road of discovery. It has been a revelatory experience for all of us, and a cathartic and bonding one too for the three surviving Pakenham siblings, as for decades, while they remained close, they didn't discuss the traumas of their childhood years with each other, nor indeed their families. I am indebted to each of them, and to Joan's children Graham and Angela, for permitting me to tell their story, and for allowing the legacy of Kate and Ciss Beirne to live on.

THE END

Acknowledgements

If my grand-aunt Brigie had never written a letter to her brother James, telling him about the death of Ciss Beirne and the disappearance of her husband and their children, then the story that gave rise to this book may have lain silent forevermore. A special thank you to my cousin Mandy Conboy, a niece of Aunt Brigie, for giving me a copy of that letter, and ultimately starting me off on my search for those missing cousins.

I am indebted to Kathleen, Ted, and Jack, who so graciously agreed to help me with this project and allowed me into their lives even though we had only discovered each other so recently. Their openness, honesty, and patience with me throughout many hours of interviews and endless queries is a testament to each of them. There were numerous difficult questions and emotional moments, but they never shirked from revealing their memories and thoughts, all done without anger or rancour. There was much fun and laughter too along the way. To Ted's wife Noreen, a special thank you for the never-ending hospitality and to Kathleen's daughter Norma, for her warmth and assistance on my visits to her Mum.

I am forever grateful to Joan's children Graham and Angela for agreeing to the project, and for giving me access to some of the very personal letters their mum wrote to their dad before they married. Also to Graham's wife Karen, who Joan discussed some of what happened with, for sharing those details with me. Those letters provided invaluable details, especially for the period after Ciss died. I hope this book does justice to Joan's story.

To Ciss's cousin Olive, thank you for your time and patience with me over the past eighteen months. There have been many emotional moments and unanswered questions, but also much laughter along the way, with delicious lunches served at short notice. Heartfelt thanks too to Ciss's cousin John and his wife Lily, who live on the farm where Kate and Ciss grew up, and whose incredible memories and recall of all things past were invaluable in the piecing together of this story. And to Annette, Annie Kate's daughter, thank you for passing on the stories and memories from your mother who was such a close friend to Ciss.

Without the superb work done by genealogist Tony Hennessy, I would never have been able to uncover much of the important intricate details on many individuals in this book. Your endless patience to my never-ending questions, along with the countless interesting conversations we have had along the journey, have helped me more than I could have wished for. To Rosa Hick, who put her heart and soul into unearthing unsolved key information which helped me to fill in some missing gaps, Detective Morse would be proud of you! Thank you, Rosa. And to Aine, who worked her way through endless hours of interview tapes, with so many different accents and committed these precious accounts to paper, a very sincere thank you. To Helen Byrne, daughter of Jack's Godfather, a big thank you for sharing the memories that your Dad, Liam Keogh, passed on to you. He never forgot Jack even though he never saw him again after the day Jack was baptised.

When I was looking for someone to help and guide me on the writing of this book, Lesly Allen's name was suggested. On meeting her, I discovered to my great surprise that not only did she know the Pakenhams, but was a long-time family friend of Ted and Noreen, and lived in Donaghadee, close to Bangor where Ted and Kathleen live. It was as though this was meant to happen, and how lucky I was. Lesley, your efforts, guidance, professionalism, and, like others, endless patience, has gotten me to the end of the journey, and for this I am forever grateful. Thank you.

To Orla Kelly, the publisher, a special thank you for advise, guidance and hard work in getting the book published.

And finally, to my wife Mary, without whom this project would never have started, I am beyond grateful. Little did she know when she gave me a Christmas gift of a voucher to get started on my family tree, that the project would run and run for over six years. When I had many doubts about taking on the writing of this book, Mary was the one who gave me the encouragement to do it, and she never wavered in her support and belief that one day the book would get published. Along with keeping me well-nourished when I was locked away in my office, her thoughtful and incisive comments have played no small part in completing the book. Thank you does not do justice to your support and help over the past few years.

Thank you too to the countless other people who have helped with this project in numerous ways. I hope this book does justice to the story of Kate, Ciss, TP and their four children.

www.ingramcontent.com/pod-product-compliance
Lightning Source LLC
Chambersburg PA
CBHW061229070526
44584CB00030B/4043